SHINING LIGHT

How one woman read, baked, calculated, cooked, loved and wrote her way back to life after coercive control

Dr Helen Willmot

ISBN: 978-1-9163064-0-0

Posigivity Publishing

ABOUT THE AUTHOR

Helen Willmot studied Sociology and Social Policy at the University of Leeds. She went on to do a Sociology Ph.D. and then worked in academic research, publishing within the area of families and social exclusion. She set up and ran a cake business before training as an Independent Mental Health Advocate. She lives in Leeds with her two children. She Fights Like A Girl. She doesn't pair socks.

DEDICATION

For B and S, so that one day they know.
And for my parents, to whom I owe everything.

ACKNOWLEDGEMENTS

This book would not have been possible without a great many people, some of whom I know and love and some whose work has inspired and helped me to write.

Sarah Molloy at Behind Closed Doors in Leeds provided me with much needed emotional support and also essential reading homeworks which started me on my journey of both recovery and reading about and understanding the domestic abuse I had been living with.

As I read, the writers of personal accounts of domestic abuse moved me and inspired me to write my own account, this book. The books of Pat Craven, Evan Stark and Lundy Bancroft helped me to truly understand the nature of the domestic abuse I had experienced and wanted to write about, hence their insightful works are cited throughout this book. Clementine Ford's glorious book/manifesto/bible for girls - *Fight Like A Girl* - inspired my writing enormously and thus is also cited throughout this book. Lynn Jamieson, Claire Hennessy and Donna Garfoot provided me with much needed references and reading materials as I progressed the book.

Abbey Southall introduced me to the work of David McCandless which led to the idea of including diagrams. Vicky Casey then produced the finished diagrams. I do not have the words to adequately thank them both here, because the diagrams transformed my book into something I could never have envisaged or created alone (but there is more on this later). Vicky Casey also read and proofread and commented on the manuscript so helpfully, along with Olivia Davidson and Carrie Hill. Other friends and family members read early drafts and fed back words of encouragement. Rebecca Emin edited and formatted the manuscript for publication and as she did so gave me sage advice and more positive feedback. Maureen Vincent-Northam then proofread the final text. The cover was designed by Victoria Casey and created by Jonathan Temples. Becky Boyd introduced me to - and educated me on - social media, where I found the wonderful, supportive world of fellow writers on Twitter.

Finally, this book would not exist without three people. Firstly, my counsellor - Lesley Warriner - who told me that I was living with domestic abuse. Secondly, Liz Green, without whose writing advice I do not think I would ever have sat down and written my story, this book. And thirdly, Mr O. Without his presence in my life I could never have sat down and written this book (again, more on this later).

I am a good mother. I am sexy. I am loving. I am beautiful. I am generous. I can take criticism. I am not ill. I am not a skivvy. I am a shining light. This is the story of how I saved my own life and came to believe these things in the process. This is my story.

DISCLAIMER AND WHAT THIS BOOK IS (AND WHAT IT IS NOT)

This is a memoir. I have described events, incidents and conversations from my memories of them to the best of my recollection. Others may have memories of events written about here that differ from mine. At the request of some individuals written about, I have changed their names and other identifying features, in order for them to maintain their anonymity.

I am a sociologist and in this book I engage with various theories. However, I do not do so academically because this is not an academic book, it is a memoir. The books that I have read and the theories which I have devoured enabled me to understand what happened to me and thus to write this memoir about it.

Just in case this is not already clear then, this book is a memoir, it is about me. And it is deeply personal. I had wondered and worried and fretted and even stressed (a bit) about just how deeply personal this memoir is. Then I read the following point made by Neil Gaiman and that all melted away:

"The moment that you feel that, just possibly, you're walking down the street naked, exposing too much of your heart and your mind and what exists on the inside, showing too much of yourself, that's the moment you may be starting to get it right." (Gaiman, 2018, Make Good Art', pages not numbered)

INTRODUCTION TO POEM

My friend Olivia organised an amazing day out for the two of us - child free time so grown up and relaxing. We went to Salt's Mill and browsed the very, very middle class shops there. A book in the book shop caught my eye: *Ten Poems to Change Your Life* (Housden 2001). How cocky, I thought. I saw this as a challenge. We each took a copy off the shelf and opened it at a random page. Very quickly Olivia shrieked and shut the book. Then she told me which page to go to. I did so. Even more quickly I shrieked and shut the book. The supposedly life-changing poem was beyond pornographic (whatever that means, suffice it to say Olivia and I are 'nice' girls and were not ready – and probably never will be ready - to read, never mind have our life changed, by this poem). The page I opened my copy of the book on had the following poem. Again, not life-changing, but it could have been written about my life. Hence it is here, helping me to introduce my story.

The Journey by Mary Oliver

One day you finally knew
what you had to do, and began,
though the voices around you
kept shouting
their bad advice –
though the whole house
began to tremble
and you felt the old tug
at your ankles
"Mend my life!"
Each voice cried.
But you didn't stop.
You knew what you had to do,
though the wind pried
with its stiff fingers
at the very foundations,
though their melancholy was terrible.
It was already late
enough, and a wild night,
and the road full of fallen
branches and stones.
But little by little,
as you left their voices behind,
the stars began to burn
through the sheets of clouds,
and there was a new voice
which you slowly recognised as your own,
that kept you company
as you strode deeper and deeper
into the world,
determined to do
the only thing you could do –
determined to save
the only life that you could save.

Every difficulty in life presents us with an opportunity to turn inward and to invoke our own submerged resources. The trials we endure can and should introduce us to our strengths. Prudent people look beyond the incident itself and seek to form the habit of putting it to good use. (Epictetus, The Art of Living)

Were you born to resist or be abused?
Best of You, Foo Fighters

CONTENTS

PLEASE NOTE

This book was designed to be printed in colour. As this version is black and white, the following colour coded content will not be so clear: the opening table: *Stages of Domestic Abuse: Textbook and Mine* and the related chapter headings; *His and Hers Weeks Diagram* and *Timeline of My Abusive Relationship Diagram*. This black and white version has been produced to ensure there is a more affordable version of the book than the colour version. Because this book has been written and published with the aim of it reaching and helping people.

NOTES ON DIAGRAMS

A simplified drawing showing the appearance, structure, or workings of something; a schematic representation. (Definition of a diagram in the Cambridge English Dictionary)

Throughout this book there is a range of beautiful diagrams. These serve two purposes. Some are purely fun and cathartic, a diagrammatic form of me screaming at the top of my voice that, for example, I DO NOT PAIR SOCKS (this *will* make sense as you read on) and a £12 'debt' SHOULD NOT PROHIBIT A MORTGAGE (ditto). Others serve a more serious, learning purpose. In his introduction to *Information is Beautiful* (2009) David McCandless writes that:

"In a way, we're all visual now. Every day, every hour, maybe even every minute, we're seeing and absorbing information via the web. We're steeped in it. May even be lost in it. So perhaps what we need are well-designed, colourful and – hopefully – useful charts to help us navigate. A modern day map book." (McCandless 2009)

Having experienced the utter confusion of what I eventually, after over a decade, learnt was domestic abuse, I believe that what we need, what millions of people need, are well-designed, colourful and most definitely useful charts - or tables or diagrams - to help people to recognise and understand and navigate out of domestic abuse. I believe that this is what some of the tables and diagrams in this book are. For example, the *Stages of Domestic Abuse:*

Textbook and Mine table, the *His and Hers Weeks* diagram and the *Timeline of My Abusive Relationship* diagram.

My background - my education and training - is in sociology. And I am a *qualitative* sociologist. In his introduction to *Knowledge is Beautiful* (2014) David McCandless moves beyond information to knowledge and writes of two concepts absolutely key to any sociological research I ever designed and carried out: understanding and context:

"Understanding really is the key. When you understand something, you're able to perceive its structure: its connections, its relationships, its significance relative to everything else. How it fits. You see-feel-intuit the fit. You know it. You know? Context, I'm realising, is the field of these connections, the network we plug any new information into... The more you understand information in this way, the more connected and contextualised it becomes, the more it starts to morph and grow into knowledge."

I believe that the learning tables and diagrams in this book do just this: provide much needed understanding and context. This is perhaps best exemplified by *The Wake-up Post-its Diagram.* In doing so, they help to tell my story.
The first table in the book is colour coded (I *love* colour coding and even managed to colour code a chapter of my doctoral thesis, my proudest achievement, back then). This table shows both the known and my personal stages of an abusive relationship. This colour coding then runs

throughout the book to remind you, the reader, where you are at in my story, as it is not told chronologically.
One final and very important point about the diagrams in this book is that they would not exist without my equally beautiful friends Abbey and Vicky, as I explain in the chapter (most fittingly) entitled LOVE.

"Remember that a noble logical diagram, once recorded, will never die; long after we are gone, it will be a living thing, asserting itself with ever-growing insistency." (Willis Polk)

Here's hoping.

	TEXTBOOK STAGES OF DOMESTIC ABUSE	STAGES OF MY DOMESTIC ABUSE
0	**Love Bombing** (aka grooming for domestic abuse)	The Meet Cute
1	**The First Crisis of the Relationship** This is the start of the cycle of abuse, the complex tangle of love and abuse which leads to the traumatic bond attachment	The Question Mark: The laundry incident
2	**Distortion of reality** Anxiety. Fear. Second guessing. Stage managing. Placating. Walking on eggshells.	**The Shift:** From equal to skivvy
3	**Disclosure that the relationship is just 'not right'**	Coffee and Cakes
4	**Recognition of the relationship as abusive and thus re-evaluating whether you want to be in it**	Counselling
5	**Ending the relationship**	The Smear Test Catalyst
6	**The continuation of abuse post separation**	Moving out threats Buying out threats

HOLIDAY

You can turn this world around
And bring back all of those happy days
Put your troubles down
It's time to celebrate
Let love shine
And we will find
A way to come together
And make things better
We need a holiday
Holiday, Madonna

She looks at the clock by her bed. Woken early as usual. Why? Baby? Baby preparing her for when it is born? Mind racing. So much to do before they can leave. Try to have a decaf. tea before daughter wakes? She goes to the toilet. Baby again. Doesn't flush. But damn it. Failed. Daughter up. No stillness this morning. She puts the kettle on and sets the table for breakfast and eats with her daughter. Better wash up afterwards, she thinks. Can't use the dishwasher before they leave. This is on her list. She puts a film on for her daughter and sets about packing for her. An all weathers capsule but eclectic wardrobe. She wonders if capsule and eclectic is an oxymoron? All the other mums compliment her daughter on her knack of putting together an outfit. Little star. She turns her attention to packing her own bag. Nothing to decide. Capsule wardrobe by necessity. Maternity wear minimalism. Stretchy black and grey everything. Wearing thin, some items. Others have tiny holes appearing at the seams. She loves them all. No point packing the one nice maternity top she owns as she will never have the energy to go out once her daughter is in bed. Even if her mother in law offers, which she will, so she can go out with Him.

She glances at the scarves hanging up on her rail and at her jewellery box. All thrift store finds; birthday money treats; TK Maxx bargains; gifts. She opens the jewellery box and goes through her favourite things. The *Shpock* sourced Vivienne Westwood watch. Her late grandmother's wishbone ring. The tiny caged bird necklace. She thinks about the caged bird. She holds each piece. All so beautiful. All so treasured. She often spends a few moments just enjoying them in her hands before putting them back where they live. It flickers through her mind to put something in her bag but the thought is gone no sooner than it is formed. No point. Won't go anywhere. Can't go anywhere. It will just be nice not to have to cook tea for a few nights. But she knows she will help in the kitchen. She always likes to be a good, helpful houseguest.

She hears Him getting up on the top floor. She glances at the coffee pot. She remembered to make it the night before. One less thing to do this morning. She has a moment of feeling organised, efficient, clever. She asks herself, what's that Nigella Lawson book? *The Domestic Goddess*. She concludes that is a step too far. She tells herself she does not *feel* like a Domestic Goddess and she most certainly does not *look* like one. I am not a Domestic Goddess, she concludes. She gets into today's stretchy black and grey outfit.

He comes downstairs from the guestroom. She asks Him how He slept. She asks Him how His back is. He explains He will need to exercise, for His back, before He can get in the car. He says what time He wants to leave. She agrees it is okay to leave then. She asks her daughter to get dressed and does an inventory of the food in the fridge: what is okay to leave, what they can take to His mum's and what she needs to take over the road to the neighbours. She writes down the food to pack, adding to her holiday packing list. She crosses the fridge job off her holiday jobs list and takes the food over the road for her neighbours. So organised. This makes her quietly happy. She sits down for a few moments. The nausea went about a month earlier but the tiredness remains. Weary after being up less than two hours. But then she has got a lot done. She likes to get a lot done.

She reflects on her morning achievements, looks at her lists, quiet happiness again. She makes sure her daughter brushes her teeth properly and then packs her toothbrush. She needs to get petrol. She wants to take her daughter, doesn't want her getting bored and disturbing His exercising. She promises her a babyccino afterwards. Deal made. The café is busy and loud. At least she is sitting down. She looks at her lists. Ticks off petrol. Feels organised. No quiet happiness though. The anxiety starts.

It is a long drive. They agreed a time, His time, to leave. They agreed His chosen time to leave. Will He be ready? Will it happen? Should she remind Him before she loads the car? She thinks about it on the drive back to the house. She cannot hear the shower. He is still exercising. She goes upstairs. She does it. It goes okay. She enlists her daughter to help load the car. It must be in her mum-side genes because she loves to be helpful too. Afterwards, still nothing happening in the house. How long has it been since she reminded Him? She decides to wait a while. She puts the film back on and watches it with her daughter. None of it is getting through though. Too anxious. She wonders what is wrong with her, why she cannot stay calm, why the anxiety is building, perhaps the anxiety is feeding off her tiredness? She stares at the credits. Time to remind Him again as it won't happen otherwise, it cannot happen, time is running out, they will pass the window of (enough) energy for the two hour drive. She walks up the two flights of stairs again. She does it.

What happens next terrifies her. Fury like she has never seen before. He orders her to leave the room, to go downstairs. But He is soon downstairs with her. He is talking to her daughter, to their daughter, tears are rolling down her young face and she is pleading with her dad to not leave mummy at home. She cannot make out what He is saying, although He is loud enough. Something is stopping her from hearing Him, self-protection maybe, because stress is not good for the baby? Everything is blurring. Then He is talking to her. Telling her she is tired, unwell, needs a rest, a nice rest at home with no one to look after, she will have a lovely time and they will have an adventure. 'They'? Who is 'they'? Still His words are blurring. Her daughter cannot stop crying, she is gasping for air, she should not be, she has asthma, her inhalers are packed now though. Slowly the comprehension: this time she has angered Him so badly that she is not allowed on the family holiday. All her hard work. One foot wrong. A few badly chosen words. Badly *timed* words. All is undone.

She starts to think. He can't do it? Yes, He can. He can do it. She cannot stop Him. She cannot stop this happening. Who can stop it happening? Think. Who will He listen to? Who can she tell? How can she tell anyone? How can she explain leaving the house in this state? Need to calm down. Got to calm down. How to calm down? He goes back upstairs. He resumes exercising. She holds her daughter. If she can stop crying for anyone it is for her. Then her daughter might stop crying too. She cannot stop though. "Cheer up, Charlie," she says. A line from *Charlie and The Chocolate Factory*, a favourite film of her daughter's and a favourite line from it, said when her daughter is upset. She comes around. It worked. One down. One to go. She cannot say it to herself though. It doesn't work on her. Nothing does. Nothing will. But she tells herself if she is going to go over the road she will have to tidy herself up, have to stop crying first and wait for the aftermath to fade from her face. Then she can do it. So she has a goal. She has a reason to stop crying.

But she dare not go. She realises she hasn't packed the food from the fridge. So she has a job to do. She does it and then ticks this last job off her list and carefully puts both holiday lists in her handbag. She feels scared and dazed and shocked. She wonders if she is *in* shock, or whether that is too melodramatic? She tells herself she is being ridiculous, she *is* ridiculous. She wonders if it is really happening, if it is really going to happen. She will be separated from her daughter for *a week*. That cannot happen. The neighbours. She has to tell the neighbours. Now is her chance. She checks herself in the mirror. She looks presentable enough. But still she dare not go. Because if she does she will be telling them. So then someone will know. Someone else will know. Someone else will know how she is living. How He treats her. How unhappy she is. She is too ashamed of her life, of her existence, in the house, in her own home, what she calls her 'Best Nest'.

She rings His mum, she has to, she has to say they are going to be late, whoever 'they' are. The advice was as usual: He won't do it, He doesn't really mean it, He loves you, He *adores* you, He will calm down, don't worry, calm down. And think of the baby. Think. Of. The. Baby. Those four words. Again. Their meaning: you have not been thinking of the baby. That is what people mean when they say those four words, she thinks, she fumes. So mad. Mad at who? Mostly herself. What *is* she doing to the baby? She feels guilty: not a good enough mother. Again. Already.

She hears the shower. She tries to compose herself when He comes into the kitchen shortly afterwards. Bag packed. He talks as if she is going to His mum's. She deduces she is going. She is allowed to go. She is allowed to drive them to His mum's (He doesn't drive). So she is going on the family holiday. She is allowed to go on the family holiday. She is allowed to go. So it is over. So it is all okay again.

COUNSELLING

Don't be scared
You'll never change what's been and gone
May your smile
Shine on
Don't be scared
Your destiny may keep you warm
Stop Crying Your Heart Out, Oasis

My name is Helen Claire Willmot, I am forty three years old and, just to be clear, I have a first class honours degree and a Ph.D; I have been published; I have set up and run two businesses; I am a qualified Independent Mental Health Advocate; I bought my first house at twenty two; I have given birth to two beautiful children (one breech) with no interventions (I feel very lucky about this) and no epidurals (I feel ridiculously proud of this) I have breast fed both (ditto). However, by the age of forty two I was living with a very strict set of bizarre rules that I did not know to be bizarre. I did not even realise that they were rules. Because they were my normal. They were a huge part of my hugely unhappy life. So I did know that I was unhappy. Good God I knew that. It was in a desperate bid to get back to being happy that I sought counselling.

In her introductory chapter to *Fight Like A Girl* (2018), Clementine Ford writes of how she came to finally call herself a feminist. She explains: "And so I continued, stockpiling examples and experiences of injustice that would later prove too heavy to bear anymore in silence. I was a camel crossing the desert, and I was starting to feel the rumbling strains of thirst." (Ford 2018: 3) This is an accurate way to describe why I was unhappy, so immensely, core-deep unhappy, in the last few years of my relationship with Him, and thus how I came to be seeing a counsellor. As the examples and experiences of injustice piled up I had had to conclude that the relationship had become so unbearably unequal it was verging on the surreal.

I had one session with the counsellor, a straight talking counsellor. I was told that I was being abused. I was told that I was living with domestic abuse, specifically emotional abuse and coercive control. It was suggested by the counsellor that when I go home I do two things. Firstly, read up on these two forms of domestic abuse. Secondly, explore how I could survive financially as a single mother.

I saw these tasks as homework and thus did them promptly (I love homework; born geek). I am still unable to remember how, from reading about domestic abuse, it sank in that I was living with it, that it had become my life, my normal, my existence behind closed doors. But it did. Because this definition of emotional abuse summed up my relationship, my life, as though it had been written for me, as though it had been written *about* me:

"If your partner's behaviour makes you feel small, controlled, or as if unable to talk about what is wrong, it is abusive. If you feel like your partner is stopping you from being able to express yourself, it is abusive. If you feel you have to change your actions to accommodate your partner's behaviour, it is abusive." (Relate website).

Tick. Tick. Tick.

So I read more. I read up on coercive control. There is widespread inconsistency in the literature regarding how it is defined and measured. I found this to be immaterial. Because however coercive control is defined, it felt familiar to me, frighteningly so. Definitions include the entrapment of women in personal life; obtaining control through the deployment of credible threats; and the use of nonviolent tactics, including isolation and monitoring, to maintain dominance over a partner.

Tick. Tick. Tick.

"I realize that if I want to be rescued, I'll have to do it myself."
(Kandasamy M, 2017:201)

I knew, then, that I had to separate from the man I had loved with all of my heart for over twelve years (Note: the average length of time of domestic abuse for a victim is three years, so well done me, and thank God for my counsellor), the man with whom I had had my two beautiful children, the man who shared my sense of humour and my social conscience, the man who had said He could not believe He had landed me because I am beautiful and clever and kind.

To ensure that I left Him, I texted two people and told them what I was going to do. Firstly, my manager, secondly, my financial advisor. My manager had witnessed a number of episodes at work where I had been harassed and stressed and deeply affected by His behaviour towards me. I knew she would understand, and probably be glad that I was taking positive action. My financial advisor was due to come and see me for an annual review of the household finances. I asked him to come prepared to advise me on how I could move forward as a single mother.

I did not know when I would separate from Him. But it happened very quickly after I had sent those two texts. I went to collect my son from nursery the next day and a staff member asked how I was. I said I was okay. Then I said I was very not okay. Then I told her my story.

She said she had been waiting for this day. All at the nursery had. Because I had changed. I had lost weight, become a lot thinner over the last few months and begun to look unhappy. And downtrodden. That is a moment I will never forget, a word I will never forget. What woman wants to be told she looks downtrodden? Of all the words that could be used to describe a woman (and I do not count the misogynistic sexual ones for political/feminist reasons) that surely has to be one of the worst, one of the most negative, one of the most depressing. I will never forget that word, that description, as long as I live.

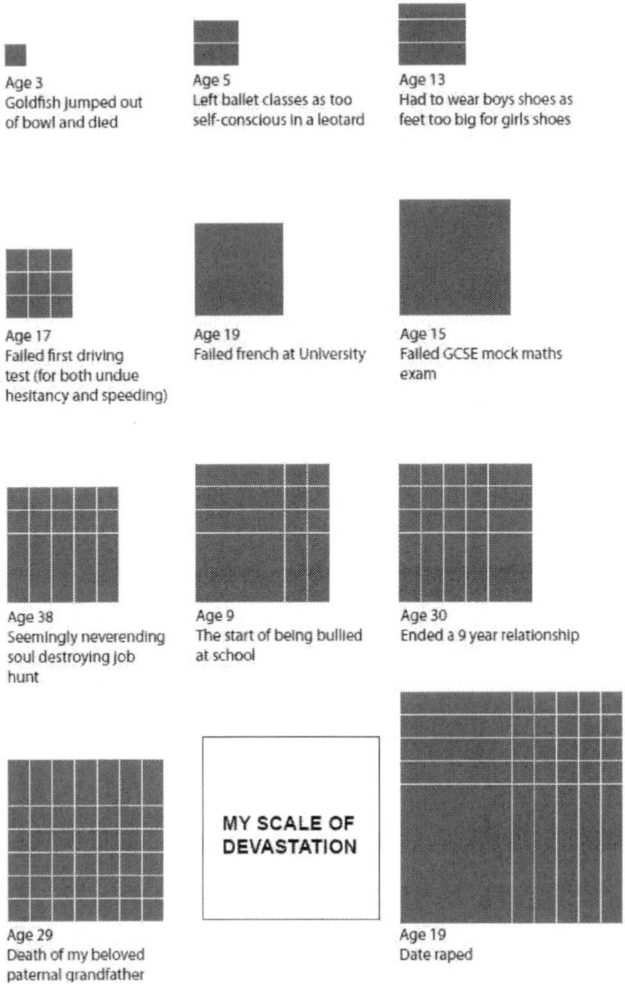
Age 3
Goldfish jumped out of bowl and died
Age 5
Left ballet classes as too self-conscious in a leotard
Age 13
Had to wear boys shoes as feet too big for girls shoes
Age 17
Failed first driving test (for both undue hesitancy and speeding)
Age 19
Failed french at University
Age 15
Failed GCSE mock maths exam
Age 38
Seemingly neverending soul destroying job hunt
Age 9
The start of being bullied at school
Age 30
Ended a 9 year relationship
Age 29
Death of my beloved paternal grandfather
MY SCALE OF DEVASTATION
Age 19
Date raped

Age 42
Told by a counsellor I was living with domestic abuse

That evening I did it. When He was unhappy with my unhappy, not-at-all smiley demeanour following His latest apology, following His latest bout of silent treatment, following my latest apparent transgression. He asked me how long I was going to be like that for. I said I did not know. At that point He asked if I wanted to separate from Him. My answer: "YES". His response: "Can I see other people?" Bullets have left guns slower. That was both a very hard question to hear and a very useful knee-jerk response to hear, after twelve and half years and two children together. How could I ever have a moment's doubt after hearing it? (Note: I have not.)

"[W]e might do well to turn to storytelling as a means of overcoming the pain, the shame, the loss, the grief, the anger, the sadness… [and] to tell the story may very well be the only ethical thing to do." (Poulos 2008: 60&64)

So what is the story I told to that nursery staff member? My name is Helen Claire Willmot and this is that story. This is my story.

MIND

Words like violence
Break the silence
Come crashing in
Into my little world
Painful to me
Pierce right through me
Enjoy the Silence, Depeche Mode

"Fuck Off"

"Fuck off, Helen." It is hard to put into words how I felt the first time He said this to me. But I sure as hell am going to try. It felt violent. It felt like violence. I felt like He had hit me. In just three words He unravelled years of my life. Everything was undone. Everything was changed. Everything would be different from that moment onwards. I now had a partner, a life partner, the father of my beautiful daughter, who had told me to "Fuck off".

At that point in my life, no one had ever said those two words to me before. As I write now, I can say that no one else has ever said those two words to me.

To this day, I cannot remember what led Him to say them to me. I can tell you what did *not* lead Him to say them to me. I had not hit Him. I had not told Him that I slept with His best friend (I hadn't), or anyone else (ditto). I had not told Him that I was in love with someone else (I wasn't). I had not told Him that He was bad in bed (despite His near constant, subtle alluding to the fact that *I* was, which in effect *did* make *Him* bad in bed). I had not told Him that He was not allowed to do something that He wanted to do (this I *never* did). It will have been some minor transgression on my part, which is why I cannot recall what it was. I can recall another incident, though, which occurred a few years later. I told Him that He needed to work on His time management, after He pulled me away from seeing a dear friend, whom I rarely saw due to our conflicting paid work schedules, to drive Him somewhere. Driving Him with those two words ringing in my ears was beyond demeaning. But by that point in the relationship, being demeaned was a regular occurrence; it was the relationship; it was my life.

"Has he ever been violent?"

"Many abused women define the psychological effects of domestic abuse as having a 'more profound' effect on their lives – even where there has been life-threatening or disabling physical violence. Despite this, there is almost always pressure to define domestic abuse in terms of actual, or threatened, physical violence." (Lisa Firth (ed.) Domestic and Relationship Abuse, *Issues*, Volume 224 (2012) Cambridge: Independence; p3)

I cannot tell you how many times I have been asked this question. Just about everyone to whom I have ever described His domestic abuse has asked me this question. The most professional, trained, enlightened, domestic abuse aware people have asked me this question. In fairness, many may well have asked me to find out if they can help me or if they can expedite any help that they may be able to offer to me. But still these five words have each time had a similar effect on me as His two words have. They have felt violent. They have felt like violence. They have felt like the slap in the face I eventually came to wish I would receive from Him. They have dialled down the abuse. They have unravelled the story of abuse that I was trying to tell. The above quote spoke to me when I read it. And the words of Stephanie Sweetnam in her article *Where Do You Think Domestic Abuse Hurts Most?* did the same:

"The superficial scars visible to the eye cannot be compared to the emotional and psychological scars that are *permanently etched in a victim's being*." (Sweetnam 2013: 136, emphasis added)

I mean no disrespect to Sweetnam or any other woman who has experienced both violent and non-violent domestic abuse when I say this, but I would rather He had hit me that day than ever uttered those two words to me. Because I would have left Him. I would have picked up our beautiful daughter and left Him. Because there would have been no way for Him to explain away what He had done to me. There would have been no seed of doubt that He could have planted in my mind that first time.

I remember telling Him, so calmly, that I could not hear those two words from Him, that I could not love someone who said those two words to me. I promised Him this (and I kept my promise; I always do). I remember Him telling me so flippantly that it was no big deal; that He tells His friends to "Fuck off", all of the time, as they do to Him; that His mum has said it to Him; that it did not mean anything. So I tried to work out why I was different to all of these other apparently normal people and whether I could be more like them; because I was the odd one out; so I must be wrong, flawed, not normal, difficult, demanding, in possession of far too high an opinion of myself. Yes, *He* told *me* to "Fuck off" and as a result *I* tried to work on *my*self; to improve *my*self; to change *my*self.

But no amount of self-analysis or desire to change myself ever altered the fact that those two words did mean something to me, they meant two things. Firstly, they meant that I had an entirely different life partner to the one I (thought I) had. Secondly, they meant that my mind became fogged with doubt as it became a part of my very DNA.

Former Me

What might be the opposite to doubt? Confidence? I cannot pretend to be a particularly confident person, skills wise. I have always (semi) joked that my big sister got my share of confidence as well as her own. I always used to be waiting for the confidence to arrive; to make me believe in my skills and abilities; to engulf me and make me whole and normal. When I was awarded my Ph.D. at the age of twenty six I thought it might appear. But it never did. I felt exactly the same as I always had. One of my Ph.D. supervisors said to me that confidence is incremental. It made me feel a bit better, but not much. I wanted to be different to how I was

STRAIGHT AWAY. I wanted to not feel that I was different to everybody else. I was happy studying but very anxious about leaving that cocoon and having to be in the real world, with a Ph.D. which makes people think you are confident, which I was not.

Around the age of thirty, however, I think I had become (incrementally) a bit more confident. I was living on my own. I was still researching but also building up my own business. And the business worked. It became a full time venture. I had done everything myself and I did feel quite confident. It was new. I liked it. At around the age of thirty, then, around the time that I had met Him, I was more confident than I had ever been in my life.

One thing I had always been confident about is my relationships with people. This stemmed from my belief that I was basically the good person that I strived to be. I have always believed myself to be a good friend. A good sister. A good daughter. A good granddaughter. A good neighbour. And a good partner too. However busy I have become, with study and/or work and/or child care, I have never neglected the people that I love and feel blessed to have in my life. I show them I care with baked goods. I share food. I share whatever I can. I remember birthdays. I put other people first. I put myself out. I care. I love. I give. I do. All of this applies to my children too, of course. I had always believed that I was a good mother. Not just a good *enough* mother, but a good mother: present, interested, enthusiastic, creative, loving and with a passion for providing home baked treats.

Disappearing Me

When I started writing about what had happened to me I looked out an old journal from 2014. I had forgotten I ever tried to keep it until I began calling to memory pivotal incidents and how I had tried to deal with them. I noticed that I did not keep it for very long. It came flooding back to me why not: I had been too unhappy writing down all of my unhappy thoughts (unsurprisingly), so I had very quickly stopped torturing myself with doing so. In an entry dated 190714 I instructed myself to seek counselling to work on becoming more assertive because He kept shouting at me. To be clear, then, again, *He* was shouting at *me* and I had concluded that *I* needed help? I had not realised how deeply, and for how long, I had absorbed His criticisms, come to believe that, if there was any problem in our relationship, it was *me*. Problematic, flawed, difficult, incapable, probably mentally unstable me. I had not realised how much I had already come to doubt myself back then – as Vivian Ward explains in *Pretty Woman*, "People put you down enough, you start to believe it."

It got worse.

Disappeared Me

A feeling of not being certain about something, especially how good or true it is. (Meaning of 'doubt' in the Cambridge English Dictionary)

"The idea of not being "enough" was the root of my self-doubt and self-hate. My abuser exacerbated my already fragile self-confidence by reminding me that I was unworthy and thus deserving of his abuse.... He made me doubt everything I did and blame myself for the abuse. He made me question the very person I was and slowly begin to hate myself." (Sweetnam 2013: 137)

He planted seeds of doubt within me. Seeds which grew through His constant nourishment of them. Leaving me doubting just about everything that I could – my ability to be a good partner, my ability to be a good mother, my being a good i.e. unselfish person - as I (very passionately) define such a thing, and ultimately the soundness of my mind. He obliterated my personality. He obliterated my personhood. He obliterated me.

Seed One: Bad partner

There were no arguments. This was something that long bothered me and told me that something was very wrong with the relationship. Towards the last year or so of it I confided in friends and family (and colleagues, and neighbours, and people I had just met and barely knew) about my desperate unhappiness and utter confusion. Oftentimes the person would say things like 'I hope you two can work it out' or 'I hope you two can start to get on better'. But we could not work anything out. And we didn't not get on. There were no arguments. Because I was not allowed to raise a counter point. Ever. If He said something and I raised a counter point it was over. He controlled arguments by not allowing them.

I was not even allowed to raise for discussion any aspect of the relationship that I was concerned about and ask Him to talk about it with me. Ever. Because doing so stressed Him out. He would literally order me to leave the room, calmly and firmly, with a long arm pointing at the door. (It is so obvious to me now that I was never going to be granted my wish of us attending couples counselling; something He refused to do for nine months, the last nine months of the relationship; more on this later.) I began to believe that I was a difficult, irritating, stress-inducing partner for wanting to talk about anything in the relationship that worried or upset me, never mind for trying to argue a counter point. I was someone so difficult and awkward and demanding and needy and greedy (and you name it basically) that I needed to be silenced. When I explained my lack of the right to talk to a girlfriend she was aghast; she said that being able to talk about something that is bothering you in a relationship is one of the cornerstones of a relationship.

Despite working very hard to meet His every need I also grew used to being blamed for anything and everything. Asking Him a simple question as He was leaving for work (already late) meant I got it in the neck for making Him late for work and putting His job in peril – a practice that I was eventually banned from doing (see The Rules I Had To Live By). But His time keeping was terrible. I never made Him late. This was a lie. I was an unsupportive, unhelpful, unkind, lazy partner because I refused to pair His (all black) socks. I was a greedy partner, for wanting more help with child care so that I could have a bit more me time. I was unsexy and bad in bed because I refused to wear (supposedly) sexy underwear and to cavort around for Him in it. I was blamed for becoming upset when He told me to "Fuck off" - apparently a sign of my pesky problem of being oversensitive – and I was blamed for becoming upset when He criticised me (see His Criticisms of Me) – it was my 'perfection complex' rearing its pain-in-the-ass head (so add minimising tactics to the list of abuses employed to paint me as a bad partner then). And to cap it all, I was deemed incapable of change (one of His reasons for refusing couples counselling). So I was a bad partner *and I always would be*.

And I did come to believe a lot of this. I did internalise a lot. I doubted myself as a partner. I talked endlessly to my girlfriends about the relationship in a desperate attempt to find out how other women conducted themselves in relationships, to ascertain whether or not I was all of the bad things that He said I was, or even some of these things, or even any of these things. Listing the ways in which I was apparently a bad partner shocks me even now, I am shocked to think I could have ever absorbed, internalised, believed any of it never mind all of it:

The ways in which I was a bad partner

- Difficult
- Irritating
- Stress-inducing
- Unsupportive

- Unhelpful
- Unkind
- Lazy
- Greedy
- Unsexy
- Bad in bed
- Oversensitive
- In possession of a 'perfection complex'
- Incapable of change

Seed Two: Bad mother

I am and always have been the primary caregiver of our two children. I only work in my paid job part time because I want to be more with my children than not with them. I do not mind what I earn. I do not worry about future earnings, future earning potential and pensions etc. Right now, as a mother of two small children, my priority is enough time with them. They are my priority. My life. My world. When I separated from Him I listed all of my work on and for and about my two beautiful children, so worried was I that I might lose them. What stands out from this list, at least for me, is the number of tasks that either one of us could have done or be doing (the first item on the list aside):

My Work On And For And About The Children

- Breast fed both babies on demand, day and night, for eleven months (my daughter) and nineteen months (my son)
- Bought and filled out First Year books, involving logging milestones and putting in

photographs

- Taken photographs of the children and got them printed out and filled albums (N=10 and counting...)
- Selected best photos and bought frames and displayed them around the house
- Sent best photos to relatives, on both sides of the family
- Monitored weight and height and logged in red books from health visitor
- Taken them for immunisations
- Registered them with a GP (mine)
- Registered them with a dentist (mine) and organised six monthly check ups
- Visited child minders and then found the nursery, looked around it, got on the waiting list, settled them in
- Applied to get our son into the same nursery
- Filed their key documents such as birth certificates and passports
- Filed favourite pieces of art work
- Decorated their bedrooms
- Furnished their bedrooms
- Baked and decorated all of their birthday cakes
- Regularly get their feet measured and ensure they have the right size shoes (which have always been paid for by my generous mother)
- Regularly applied (organic) preventative head lice treatment
- Looked around schools and applied for a

school place for our daughter

- Applied to get our son into the same school
- Oversee and sign off on our daughter's homework
- Regularly brought both children's red nursery books home to add in observations and photographs
- Bought and instigated a reward chart for our daughter
- Make packed lunches for our daughter to take to school each day
- Pack our daughter's school bag daily including with sports and swimming kits and library books and whatever other random and bizarre items she has to take into school on any given day
- Diarise and always ensure our daughter has her asthma and eczema medications
- Attend our daughter's parent teacher meetings
- Knitted and crocheted (quite ugly) blankets for both their beds (our son stuffed his finished blanket straight into a drawer the day that I gave it to him because he has such good taste)
- Provide predominantly home cooked and baked snacks and meals

I was born in 1975 and was thus mothered (and fathered) as a child in the 1970s and 1980s. It involved the following. Watching *Emmerdale Farm* and eating crackers and cheese with my mother;

going on endless amounts of endlessly long and boring (I thought) country walks with my mother and my father - so that my father could look at ferns (which reminds me, on just about every walk I would very excitedly tell my father that I had found him a fern, only to hear the heart breaking words, "No Spadge, that is just bracken," – a sodding plant that grows EVERYWHERE it seems, or at least EVERYWHERE WE EVER WENT. EVER); eating spam and Bean Feasts (not necessarily together, the human body can probably only withstand the two individually before they serve to function as an emetic); my mother being prescribed Valium at one point (she chose to never take the last one though); and me being given baby sedatives (yes, you have read that correctly). And I have turned out okay, I think, haven't I? I mean, I can read and write (e.g. right now I am writing this book) and I am not on Valium (although I do prescribe myself a G&T at times) and I have two children who are not on any sedatives (although, don't judge me but on the odd occasion I have wondered what I would do if they were available).

The landscape of mothering seems to have altered somewhat since I was growing up. In *Militant Lactivism? Attachment Parenting and Intensive Motherhood in the UK and France* Charlotte Faircloth argues that

"[T]he social role of mothering has expanded in recent years to encompass a range of tasks, beyond the straightforward rearing of children. Parents do much more than simply feed, clothe and shelter their children today." (Faircloth 2013: 2-3)

Faircloth calls this new climate in which mothers currently raise their children 'intensive mothering'. This new framework of mothering has two major characteristics. Firstly, in an age of increased concerns regarding health and safety there is an inflated sense of risk and thus the role encompasses risk management and necessitates paying attention to what experts say about the raising and protecting of children. Secondly, optimal childcare is presented as being child-centred, thus mothers are expected to be pseudo-teachers who turn every activity into an opportunity for maximising their child's learning and development and ultimately their intelligence. Thus

"Touching, talking and feeding are no longer ends in themselves, but tools mothers are required to perfect to ensure optimal development... playing with a child: no longer simply an enjoyable activity for adult and child, it has become an instrumental way of ensuring positive long-term outcomes. The everyday experience of mothering is re-written as a set of skills to be honed and perfected if one is to achieve optimum development (Rose 1999)." (Faircloth 2013: 22)

Wow.

There is more (yes, really). Whilst 'intensive mothering' is financially, physically and emotionally intensive, it is also something which Faircloth argues mothers are supposed to find emotionally absorbing and personally fulfilling. Given what the mothering of small children often entails, I often found myself wondering whether I was a good enough mother (I still do) because, despite all of the above listed parenting work that I do, that I *choose* to do, I am most certainly not very/always/ever emotionally absorbed by finger painting or personally fulfilled by watching *Peppa Pig* (over and over and over again). So sick have I got of children's TV shows, in fact, that I have let my children watch the bawdy comedy *Blades of Glory*, telling myself that this was totally fine. I thought it was, until my seven year old daughter asked what it meant to "get your jugs waxed". Oops. Furthermore, I have always found my children's pre-school 'gymnastics' classes to be mind-numbingly annoying and wonder whether the other parents who apparently enjoy doing the Hokey Cokey at ten on a Monday morning, require some form of therapy (when the Hokey Cokey disappeared from the songs section of the class only to return after only a term long hiatus and the class teacher explained that she had brought it back due to "popular demand" I would very much like to have strangled or at least slapped the parents responsible). Despite all of the parenting work that I do, with my errors of judgement and my feelings of bemused (in)difference alongside happy, fulfilled-seeming happily Hokey Cokeying parents at pre-school 'gymnastics' classes, I often found myself wondering what the hell kind of a parent or mother I am.

There is even more to 'intensive mothering'. Faircloth argues that "whichever way an 'informed' woman in the UK chooses to mother, she must now do so intensively." (Faircloth 2013: 21). Yes, there are different *ways* to mother now, and mothers are thus now expected to make informed choices, and be accountable for their choices, between the different ways or styles of child rearing. So it seems there is yet more to worry about as a mother today. It is no longer sufficient to simply worry about whether you are a good enough mother, you have to worry about what *kind* of a mother you are. Certainly, my thoughts and worries about being a mother have at times shifted to this question, because whilst I never read a book on any style of child rearing, I was aware from other (devout devotee) mothers, and popular culture (including American TV show *Sex And The City*), that different styles exist. So it is based on scraps of information from these two sources that I can sketch out here what kind of a mother I might be.

Types of Mother

- 'Tiger Mothers': no idea what these are, actually, but I am going to choose to take the name far too literally and then discount this type of mother on the grounds that I am definitely not a tiger, or any kind of cat.
- 'Gina Fordists': I know little about Gina Ford and what I do know I don't like, so I can more sensibly discount this one (unless I am a 'Gina Fordist' by accident, but this seems unlikely, given the fascist regime type mothering that, in my opinion, Gina Ford advocates and my general lack of belief in fascism).
- 'Attachment Parents': I never wore either of my

children so I am totally sure that I am not this one.

- 'Stroller Mum': I might have made this last one up, it was mentioned on an episode of *Sex And The City*, I know no more about it than this, but I own a stroller, so whether or not it exists, I will go with this one.

That was quite easy.

Actually, none of these child rearing styles matter, and neither does all of the parenting work listed above that I have carried out (and continue to carry out on a daily basis) for that matter, not with Him. Because He defined a whole new, bespoke parenting style for me: Bad Mother. Given the 'intensive parenting' landscape, this criticism from Him seems to me to be not only personal but also political. Given all of my parenting work then, and the fact that I do sometimes put age appropriate TV programmes on for my children, and the fact that I have taken both of my children to pre-school 'gymnastics' classes even though I detest it, in what way am I a Bad Mother? What is a 'Bad Mother' as defined by Him? Well, it is three things, apparently. Firstly, I am an unhealthy mother.

I feed my children on fast food and fizzy drinks three times a day then? No. I sit them in front of computer and TV screens all day? No. As I put in my list above, I provide the children with home cooked and baked snacks and meals, for almost every snack and meal. I even feed them my healthy-as-possible H-Bars, which masquerade as cake – made with no butter or sugar or flour or eggs; only vegetables, fruit, dried fruit, nuts, seeds, oats, peanut butter (the healthy variety) and honey, with a topping of a very small amount of chocolate to entice the children into eating them, not meaning to sound too dodgy (Note: if you like the sound of these, the recipe appears in the chapter entitled Food). How then am I an unhealthy mother?

I sometimes buy the wrong baked beans. Yes, I sometimes fail to buy the low salt and low sugar variety of baked beans - because it involves driving to a second supermarket just to buy them. I used to get so anxious about this 'transgression' that I would bury the empty 'bad' baked bean cans in the regular bin, where He would never see them, rather than wash them and put them in the lid-free recycling box where He would.

And I once bought Crunchy Nut Cornflakes. Yes, just once I bought a sugary breakfast cereal. I can only assume that they are infused with not only the very well-publicised and generally shouted about honey and nuts (the clue is in the name basically) but also the lesser publicised and shouted about crack, given His lecture on their addictive nature. Apparently *one* bowl and children are *hooked for life*.

And I have managed to "Fuck up" the children's regular (twice daily) brushing of their (to this day unfilled teeth) - something which I ensure they do every morning and every evening, with the age appropriate tooth brushes and tooth paste that I buy for them - by *letting them rinse their mouths out after they have brushed their teeth*. Apparently mouth rinsing post brushing is catastrophically dangerous for their teeth and gums. Interesting that I have never heard this advice from our dentist. That is, my dentist, who I registered the children with (He does not have a dentist to register them with), who I regularly take them to see, who they *enjoy* regularly going to see – perhaps my single proudest achievement as a mother.

Secondly, I am a failed disciplinarian, on two (contradictory) counts (so more confusion then). I do not give the children time outs at exactly the right points in their tantrums and hissy fits. Sometimes this is because they are so bloody entertaining, as any parent of a small child will tell you, so I am busy trying really, really hard not to laugh - think Violet Beauregarde in *Charlie And The Chocolate Factory* for my daughter and a badly behaved *Despicable Me* minion for my son; now try not to laugh. I also raise my voice too much to the children. I apparently can never see the funny side of their various high jinks and am a shouts-a-lot, angry miserable mother. Surely every parent has lost their cool at some point and raised their voice to their children? Shouting now and then is surely normal and human? But He would chastise me for this, in front of the child in question, before then comforting the child in front of me. I was painted as the villain. The bad cop. The bad mother. A subtle attempt to turn them against me.

Thirdly, I am an overly protective, worry wart, fuss budget, cloying, neurotic mother. On one occasion He declared He was taking our then very young daughter (age 4) to Alton Towers. I said she was too young. He, of course, planned to take her anyway (and only did not, thankfully, when He failed to activate His money off voucher in time). He lectured me about stifling our daughter.

All three facets of my bad mother mantel got to me. I would feel slighted by His criticisms of me, yet somehow I still found myself doubting my abilities as a mother, believing I was not a good enough mother, not a good mother, in the face of great logical counter-arguments. Should I make the effort to drive to a second supermarket to get low salt and low sugar baked beans even when the children's diet is generally very healthy and low in these two evils and I am busy and sleep deprived and exhausted? Am I harming the children's teeth by letting them rinse their mouths out after brushing, despite our dentist never telling me this is the case? Am I a cruel, shouts-a-lot monster? Do other, nice, lovely, perfect mothers never, ever shout at their children, *ever*? This is something I do not even intellectually believe to be possible. Yet it contributed to the myriad of niggling doubts I grew to have about myself as a mother. I questioned myself as a mother. I questioned my instincts. I questioned my sixth sense, which has always served me well as not only a mother but as a human being.

He believes me to be such a bad mother – three bad mothers rolled into one no less - that He has sent me on a course of parenting classes. Well, He has sent me on a *mythical* course of parenting classes, which is slightly different – just as effective in getting Him off my bad-mother-case (albeit temporarily) but a lot less time consuming. It was one of His many threats when I was trying to get

Him to move out of the family home (more on this later). So I said yes, of course. I said yes to everything. To this day, He believes I completed the HENRY parenting courses at our son's nursery (my friend Sam's words ring very strongly in my ears when I think of the longevity of my fake parenting course story: "The man's an idiot. But he is consistent, I will give him that."). How galling, you might think. Yes, it is. But there is more. He continues to tell me that the first course of parenting classes that I completed were *not enough* (I am still a bad mother, then) and so *I need to enrol on more parenting classes.*

"The robbed that smiles steals something from the thief." Othello 1:3

I am no longer upset by these remarks. I am no longer even bemused by them. I am simply entertained by them. So very entertained by them. I cannot look at Him (I don't want to anyway). Because I cannot keep a straight face. I am back in Roald Dahl territory. He has become a monstrous amalgamation of the many hideous parents portrayed in Dahl's books. With each bad parent illustrating a specific type of bad parent, He is a myriad of bad parents rolled into one hideous but hilarious caricature. Think of the competitive, track suit sporting mother of Violet Beauregarde in the second Charlie and The Chocolate Factory film: He does not give a rat's ass about our daughter's homework, as long as she is physical, good at sports, good at climbing, and leaping and jumping and throwing people about, these ‘skills’ are what matter, these ‘skills’ are what will get her through life, not reading books; so He is both of Matilda’s bad parents too then. Then there is the lazy dad of Veruca Salt who spoils her rotten. As I will explain later, He was solely responsible for the children just 2.5% of the time when He lived with us, during which time He would shower them with gifts and treats.

A very clever friend coined the term ‘speed parenting’ for these times, which I believe must surely be the polar opposite to the construction of ‘involved father’ that has emerged alongside the intensification of motherhood (which Faircloth does argue is no more than a *discursive* construction). I cannot not laugh at Him. When I used the term ‘speed parenting’ during a conversation with another incredibly intelligent friend she pointed out that when He was ‘speed parenting’ what I was doing was ‘speed living’. This would explain why these supposed rest times usually left me with an all too familiar sense of tiredness. I believe my insightful, Christian, softly spoken friend Karen summed up the issue of my parenting perfectly when she said to me “You’re not a bad mother, you’re a bad motherfucker” (Karen, 110818).

Seed Three: Selfish person

His sense of entitlement is huge. Bigger even than His ego. No. I take that back. Nothing is bigger than His ego. It is second only to His ego, which still means it is enormous. His sense of entitlement extended beyond my time – in the chapter entitled

Time I explain all that I was expected to do for Him – to my possessions, to all of my possessions. Apparently, my possessions were not my possessions at all. They were *our* possessions. This meant He could do whatever He wanted to do with them, whenever He liked. This usually meant His borrowing them without asking me and then losing them and never replacing them. He controlled my possessions. Therefore they were not my possessions at all, were they?

In the space of one month He took, lost and did not replace my one and only phone charger three times (i.e. three times I had to buy a new one). This made me angry as I use my mobile phone for everything important to me on a daily basis (nothing unusual in that, I do not think, in this day and age): I receive messages from our daughter's school; my mobile phone number is top of the contacts list for both our daughter's school and our son's nursery; I receive notifications from the chemist of our daughter's asthma and eczema medications being ready for collection; I arrange play dates for our son via text; I would message all of the friends I barely saw to keep in touch with them; I keep (useful) lists galore on it (I do love lists); I order birthday presents for loved ones from Amazon on it; I check both my home and work emails on it; I play music on it; and I make the odd phone call using it too. The phrase I had long been saying never felt more relevant. I had no voice. I could not speak my wishes and be listened to, be heard. My wishes were ignored. I was ignored. I had no voice. I was silenced, again.

Had I ever borrowed a vital piece of His sports equipment, just borrowed and diligently replaced it, never mind losing it and never replacing it. Had He needed the item and not been able to use it, do you think I would have got off lightly? Been forgiven? *Ever* been forgiven?

When I had the audacity to tell Him that I was angry about His repeated taking of and subsequently losing and not replacing my phone charger, because of how hard it made my life to be without my phone, He overlooked the point of my anger entirely and levied yet another criticism at me. He criticised me for being too into possessions and not sufficiently a 'people person' like He (the God like therapist) is. He criticised me for being *selfish*. The audacity. Beyond audacity. This is a man(ish) whose life revolves around Himself. He was unable to put any of the three people in His beautiful family before Himself, ever. He is selfish, self-absorbed, self-obsessed, self-serving and narcissistic. So this criticism from Him was hypocritical. Beyond hypocritical. Hyper-hypocritical? Uber hypocritical? Hyper-uber hypocritical? The more letters and syllables I can shoe horn in there the better basically, because He was, He *is, that* hypocritical.

As well as hypocritical, this criticism was not original, according to Clementine Ford:

"Why is everyone so pathologically terrified of selfish women? The word is thrown around like an insult, as if the worst thing a woman could possibly do (aside from being fat, having sex with whomever she pleases and whenever, swearing, having an abortion, drinking alcohol, standing up for herself and being a working mother) is to decide that her life matters." (Ford 2018: 120)

When I first read this argument I felt compelled to think about my heinous, unwomanly crimes. This is how I fared:

I have never been fat (which I believe is down to my genes i.e. I am just lucky on this one, given how fat women are so vilified); I *have* had sex with whomever I please (but this only constitutes three people so is probably a crime requiring only a Caution, to use police terminology); I fucking *love* swearing (see); I have had an abortion (after I was raped, does this let me off the hook?); I drink alcohol; I stood up for myself when I left Him and when I fought for the family home and when I decided to write this book; I am a part time working mother of two (does the *part time* working balance out the *two* children, in some kind of magical Women's Crimes Maths? Hard for me to say as I am not good at maths, magical Women's Crimes Maths or any other kind); and I did decide that my life matters, hence I saved it, and now He has to pair His own socks. JUST SHOOT ME.

I have to add 'cruel' to the list of ways to describe this particular criticism levied at me by Him. Calling me selfish is perhaps the cruellest criticism He, or anyone, could ever hurl at me, someone who has always been acutely aware of how privileged she is and as a result has always wanted to give, to share, to be generous, and has always defined what a good person is in these terms

I was left money as a child which I inherited at the age of twenty one. Not a fortune but it meant no worries about the cost of studying and no worries about getting on to the beloved English property ladder. I had the money to put a deposit down on a back to back terrace house in Leeds, so a very modest little property, but I still feel so damn privileged. I worked incredibly hard for my Ph.D. but remain embarrassed to have been able to afford to pursue this qualification. I was uncomfortable in academia, in its ivory tower, researching poverty and social exclusion with millionaire professors at the LSE (who are probably so rich that they actually own ivory towers). Clementine Ford argues that "[if] you're not routinely forcing yourself to interrogate the benefits you enjoy in society, it's all too easy to tell yourself that other people are inventing their disadvantage." (Ford 2018: 158) Oh yes, all those feckless layabouts without Ph.D.'s only don't have them because they could not be arsed to sit around reading books that they enjoy for four years whilst not having to engage in any paid employment to pay the bills, feed themselves and generally stave off starvation and it's natural (death)bedfellow: death.

My need to share my skills and knowledge, gathered through privilege, by being socially useful was not satisfied by the trickle-down effect of conducting social research and publishing findings which policy makers and practitioners supposedly read and use to enact socially helpful changes. I now work in the Third Sector. I trained as an Independent Mental Health Advocate (an IMHA) to be more directly, instantly, hands-on useful in society. I earn a lot less as an advocate than I did as a Research Fellow. I do not care about this. I have never been driven by earnings, by money, by wealth. I have only ever wanted to be comfortable (I do not want an ivory tower, for example).

What matters to me, and what I am trying to raise my children to believe too, is to be a good person, which I define, so very passionately, as a kind and generous, not-at-all selfish, people person. Alongside health, this is what I believe matters in life. Not credentials such as qualifications, salary, wealth, 'disposable income' (a term and concept I find abhorrent – how can any income, any money, be disposable, when there are people starving on the breadline?) and having a 'good job' (another term I find distasteful, given what people tend to mean when they use it: status and high salary; no thank you to the first and the second is not necessary if you do not want 'disposable income' - how ludicrous to want, and to chase, and to be desperate for, and to measure your own success in terms of having, something that apparently gives you so much of something that you do not need it all and can therefore dispose of it i.e. throw it away).

I seek to have enough in life and to share that enough. My children receive bags and bags of hand me downs from my family and friends and I share them whenever possible. I have already said that I bake for loved ones at every opportunity and I am also so purely happy when I am able to feed people. If I end up with two of something I always try to re-house one of them. It was only recently, when a very dear friend said to me that he would never, ever think of me as being overly into possessions that I began to believe it, to believe that I am the good person, as I define this, that I have always wanted to be. Because for so long it had been drummed into me that I am not this. That I am mean and selfish and greedy and materialistic. He had made me doubt myself in the cruellest way imaginable for me. He had made me believe that I am selfish and thus doubt that I am the good person, as I define it to be, and as I so dearly want to be.

Seed Four: Unstable person AKA HYSTERICAL woman

"[T]he root of the term *hysteria* – *hyster* – comes from the Greek word for 'womb'." (Wolf 2013: 173)
"[C]ontemporaneous medical texts on hysteria describe an affliction that shares many characteristics with what we know as psychosis or depression. Frightful dreams, drowsiness, nightmares, peevishness, wandering thoughts, impaired memory, groundless fears, and disturbances of the imagination were common manifestations. However, unlike psychosis or depression, victims were almost solely female." (Meek 2009: 108)

The word 'hysteria' was not removed from the DSM (Diagnostic and Statistical Manual) until 1980.

I had long had a nagging feeling about His being slightly different with me, to me, around me, about me, in front of friends and neighbours. He would put His arm around my shoulders and speak nicely to me and be generally very nice and normal. He has never, ever told me to "Fuck off" in front of anyone but our very young daughter (thankfully she never seemed to learn this new word). He would ask how neighbours and friends are and make polite, phatic conversation with them, despite having no interest in them, in spending time with them, in socialising with them, in being a part of the supportive network of parents that was essential to my life as a pseudo-single mother and remains to this day essential to my life as an actual single mother. His two such different faces or personas left me doubting myself for thinking He was cruel; doubting whether or not He was cruel; doubting my own mind.

I lived with almost daily declarations of love, which left me utterly confused, because none of His behaviours felt loving (see above, see below, see the whole of this book). This was a confusing reality that I lived with for a very long time. His constant declarations of love and its related foreverness existed alongside so many monstrous behaviours and treatments. As I have said already, I would talk to anyone and everyone about my relationship worries in a desperate attempt to find the answer that would end my confusion. I remember going on a work Away Day, not long before I managed to separate from Him, and pouring it all out to a colleague I barely knew (luckily we became and remain friends, so she cannot have thought me completely inappropriate or absolutely terrible Away Day company). I kept on asking myself why I felt so unloved when He continually told me that He loved me and would always be with me? (I now see the first part of His regular declaration as His attempt to get *me* to love *Him* more i.e. do more for Him i.e. be more fully devoted to Him. For example, "I love you" could be loosely translated into "I love you, so love me back and pair my (all black) socks". And I now see the second part of His regular declaration as a terrifying threat). I was left thinking I was not of sound mind; that I was going mad; that I was already there: that I had already gone mad.

It was not only His contradictory words and behaviours which made me doubt my own mind, doubt my sanity. He would twist everything into its opposite. For our son's first birthday we decided to have a family meal at a pizza place. There were two next to each other and I let our daughter pick which one we went to. She picked her favourite (she was five years old, why wouldn't she? And had she been older, and more able to think about picking the birthday boy's favourite, there was no such thing, he was one, he was a baby). This decision of mine, a kindness to our daughter, managed to pass Him by. When He found out on the day He was angry. Furious. He did not like the one that had been chosen. He sat fuming at the dinner table. He curtailed the meal. He ruined it. I was heartbroken. Luckily I don't think our daughter picked up on this (she was five years old, she was eating pizza and making her own ice-cream sundae at her favourite pizza place, she was in heaven). I was told that I had ruined the first birthday celebration. I *knew* deep down that *He* had. But somehow He managed to twist this reality into its opposite. And I did what I always did. I believed His (twisted) version of the reality. I had to. I had to believe *I* had ruined it, so I found a way to do so: I reasoned that *I* could have prevented it being ruined by Him. So it was therefore ultimately all my fault. If only I had not had the idea to let our daughter choose the restaurant. If only I had chosen the one I knew He liked. If only I could go back in time and undo my decision, my mistake. If only, if only, if only. How many times did I wish I could go back in time and change one tiny action or one brief sentence to make everything okay again?

Added to all of the (apparently madness inducing) confusion was His apologising after being abusive; making promises of change/improvements: this was a recurring theme over the course of the relationship, said with a laugh and a smile, as I was left waiting for Him, yet again, or left to clear up after Him, yet again. Then there were the gifts, the confusing gifts. Significantly, He spoilt me in an alarming fashion on my forty second birthday. My last birthday with Him. Whilst also, at this time, maintaining His steadfast refusal to discuss the relationship and why it was making me so damned unhappy, or to go to Relate to try to get our relationship back on track. So, so confusing. Nothing in the relationship, nothing in my life, made any sense. My mind was mush. I was mad. I had to be. I did not just doubt the soundness of my own mind, I ended up absolutely convinced that it was no longer sound.

All of these manipulative tactics that made me doubt my own mind laid the foundations for His explicit playing of the mad, hysterical woman card. The worse such time involving a family holiday. He told our daughter that I was not only tired but also *unwell* and so I needed a rest, a nice rest, with no one to look after. He pushed me to the edge of sanity by letting me do all of the family holiday work (whilst heavily pregnant – I was only half way through my pregnancy with our son but I was truly enormous by about nine weeks) and then flying into a rage when I asked Him a second time if He could get ready and pack and honour the schedule which He had dictated - a schedule based on His needs and not my needs as a pregnant woman who had been up since the crack of dawn and was exhausted by all the family work and child care she was doing alone pre-holiday - and then refusing to let me go on the family holiday that I had worked so hard to organise and facilitate. So yes, I did end up crying hysterically on this occasion. But I was not a mad, hysterical woman, I was a scared and devastated - and I now understand, thank God, abused, woman.

Later on I will explain that at the first (and only, because I would never let it happen again) opportunity He had to talk about me to a professional (someone at Relate) He labelled me as suffering from anxiety (the modern day abusive man's version of hysteria?) By the point of that utterly futile Relate session, however, I was aware and strong enough to know and to say that I was not suffering from anxiety, rather, the only thing that made me feel anxious was Him.

I have explained that the worst example of His explicit playing of the mad, hysterical woman card involved a family Holiday. I have also explained that His behaviour with my phone chargers made me "angry". I need to revisit both of these points. In reverse order. To say I was "angry" about my phone charger is something of an understatement. To put it mildly. It is just a big fat lie, actually. To say I was "angry" suggests I had some kind of politely acknowledged negative emotion going on. I did not. The family holiday *was* the worst example of His explicit playing of the mad, hysterical woman card. But this is because He did not see the aftermath of the culmination of His on-going phone charger behaviour. Had He seen it, I do not know where I would be today. To put it mildly, again, I played right into His hands, and He would surely have run with it, used it to finally convince me that I was actually totally unhinged and unsafe and just completely mad basically, had He seen me that evening.

I unleashed years and years and years (over a decade, to be specific) of rage at having my possessions and my requests and my wishes trashed and my voice silenced. I screamed and shouted about not being able to live like that anymore as I furiously searched the house over for the phone charger that I knew would not be in it, tossing and flinging items around as I did so, slamming doors in my wake. And I did not like what I was doing. I did not like what I had become, what I had been reduced to. I did know that I had been reduced to this state, this creature, by His actions, and this is all I can hold on to from that night. His mother witnessed it. I will never forget how she looked at me. And it was the next day that I went into work and sought the counselling that began my journey that has led to this book, because I knew I could never again morph into what I had morphed into the night before, because it was vile. I was vile. But I was vile because I was angry. I was not, and I am not, mentally unwell.

There is a long history of women being pathologised, medicalised and declared in some way mentally unsound, unstable and unwell, and often locked up as a result. Thus again, as with His bad mother criticism of me, which tapped into the very contemporary mothers and guilt issue, His accusation of me being mentally unsound or unstable, tapping this time into a worryingly long, persistent, historic women's issue, was not only personal but also political. Basically, if His domestic abuse lacked originality, then His labelling of me as mentally unwell was about a million times more unoriginal. In *Fight Like A Girl* Clementine Ford summarises the myriad of reasons which have been dreamt up to institutionalise 'mentally unstable' women:

"Over the centuries, women have been institutionalised and subjected to the most horrendous treatment for such 'crimes' as becoming pregnant outside of wedlock; having sex before marriage; having sex outside of marriage; enjoying sex; being depressed; wanting to live independently; being lesbians; being transgender; living in an era where no-fault divorce didn't exist but having husbands who automatically possessed power of attorney and wanted to marry someone else; being women's liberationists – the list goes on and on." (Ford 2018: 212-3)

In *The Female Malady Women, Madness and English Culture 1830-1980* Elaine Showalter goes far beyond arguing that throughout history women have been excessively labelled as mentally unwell. She argues that there exist – and vociferously critiques - dual images of madwomen. Firstly, madness as one of the wrongs of women and, secondly, madness as the essential feminine nature. She highlights another duality: psychiatry recognising an English malady associated with the intellectual nature of men, and a female malady associated with the sexuality and essential nature of women. What unites these two dualities is a fundamental alliance between 'women' and 'madness'; a cultural construction of female insanity; a cultural tradition that represents 'women' *as* madness. She links this to an imbalance of gender and power that has kept madness a female malady. This is most clearly illustrated by one mental illness: hysteria.

Hysteria is a condition which surely everyone reading this book will associate with women. Because it *is* a condition wholly associated with women. Isn't it what all of us women are, at some point and/or deep down at our very cores, apparently, 'hysterical'? 'Hysterical women'? What I do not imagine that anyone reading this book will have is any association between men and hysteria. 'Hysterical men' ring any bells? I doubt it. However, a European theorist of the condition, Jean-Martin Charcot, who began his work in 1870, developed a theory that hysteria had psychological origins and demonstrated that *men* also experienced the symptoms of the condition. Indeed, it was *men's* experience of hysteria, AKA the much more manly and macho and masculine sounding 'shell shock', during and after WWI, that was such a huge epidemic it changed the direction of English psychiatry, which had been built upon an ideology of absolute and natural differences between men and women, and ushered in what Showalter describes as the era of psychiatric modernism.

In *A History of Psychiatry From the Era of the Asylum to the Age of Prozac* Edward Shorter sums up just how enduring hysteria diagnoses in women were when he writes of "the effects of nineteenth-century neurologists to pathologise various internal sensations in women with the "hysteria" diagnosis and *make hysteria virtually coterminous with femininity*." (Shorter 1997: 292, emphasis added). Elaine Showalter makes a similar point when she argues that "[b]y the end of the [nineteenth] century, 'hysterical' had become almost interchangeable with 'feminine' in literature, where it stood for all extremes of emotionality... 'Hysteria' was linked with the essence of the 'feminine'." (Showalter 1985: 129)

I will try to give as brief as possible an account of the history of hysteria, or HYSTERIA as I will from now on refer to it to convey just how ridiculous a concept I believe it to be (and I am holding back from also putting the term in bold and underlining it too for good measure). The following potted history follows my reading a paper entitled *Women And Hysteria In The History Of Mental Health* (2012) written by Cecilia Tasca, Mariangela Rapetti, Mauro Giovannie Carta and Bianca Fadda.

HYSTERIA is apparently the first accurately defined mental disorder since the second millennium BC. Two defining characteristics of the condition were seizures and a sensation of choking caused by the feeling of something rising in the throat. This second characteristic led to the 'wandering' of the uterus or womb being considered the cause of HYSTERIA. Plato (yes, Plato) argued that the uterus is sad and unfortunate (and presumably this is why it wanders aimlessly about the body?) when it does not join with the male and does not give rise to new life. Aristotle and Hippocrates agreed. So a philosopher, with a supposedly great mind, owned by a man, i.e. someone who had never possessed a womb, 'wandering' or otherwise, came up with a theory which links women's mental illness to 'wandering' wombs, and two other philosophers, with supposedly equally great minds, and also no wombs of their own, jumped on board and agreed with the bonkers idea. Then wine and orgies were prescribed for the symptoms of HYSTERIA, along with acrid or fragrant fumigation of the face and genitals (of course they were, why on earth would they not have been?).

Similar sexual theories of HYSTERIA continued to emerge. A Greek physician came up with an opposing cure for it though: sexual abstinence and perpetual virginity. In the Middle Ages HYSTERIA was linked to unfulfilled sexual desire. Trotula, considered the first female doctor in Christian Europe, gave advice on how to placate sexual desire as she believed abstinence to be a cause of illness (not a cure for it). From thirteenth century onwards the struggle with heresy assumes a political connotation and HYSTERICAL women were subject to exorcism, i.e. punishment. HYSTERIA was confused with sorcery. With the Devil believed to be the cause, women were deprived of confession and forgiveness leading to suicides.

During the Renaissance the uterus remained the organ that allowed explanation of the vulnerable physiology and psychology of women. The concept of inferiority of women remained. HYSTERIA remained the symbol of femininity. The sixteenth century was a period of important medical developments. It saw the birth of modern medical science, combined with the 'philosophical revolution' which saw the emergence of the explanation that actions attributed to the soul are actually linked with organs of the body. Physician Thomas Willis (1621-75) introduced a new etiology of HYSTERIA, no longer attached to the central role of the uterus but rather related to the brain and to the nervous system. Thomas Sydenham (1624-89) published a treatise on HYSTERIA. He demonstrated that the uterus was not the primary cause of HYSTERIA, which he likened to hypochondria. In the eighteenth century, theories of women's reproductive organs persisted, but HYSTERIA did start to be gradually associated with the brain rather than the uterus.

In another paper, entitled *Of Wandering Wombs and Wrongs of Women: Evolving Conceptions of Hysteria in the Age of Reason*, Heather Meek (2009) puts forward an argument as to why this movement away from the bonkers initial 'wandering wombs' theory took place. Her paper explores a dialogue that crosses the borders of literature and medicine by looking at accounts of women who were themselves victims of HYSTERIA and by the doctors who studied and treated the disease. She argues that the women and the doctors influenced and informed each other's theories throughout the eighteenth century and a dialectically constructed version of HYSTERIA emerged as a result of this dialogue. Women's mental health problems ceased to be aligned with wandering wombs and inherently disordered female bodies and instead were aligned with the depressed social conditions of eighteenth century women – what Mary Wollstonecraft in 1798 termed the "wrongs of women". This perspective is not without its critics, for example, Elaine Showalter as I mentioned earlier, but it is a perspective which speaks to me and my story, as I will explain later.

Evidence of this transition to associating women's mental health problems with their social conditions is found in medical texts but most eloquently and comprehensively in the poetry, fiction and life writing of Anne Finch, Elizabeth

Freke, Lady Mary Wortley Montagu, Hester Thrale Piozzi and Mary Wollstonecraft, all of whom, Meek argues, seem to have suffered from HYSTERIA to some degree. They were educated and literary women and as a result they have left behind a rare and neglected portrait of the illness, via a unique body of writing which records an array of experiences of the ailment and theorizes HYSTERIA. Doctors tended to silence victims of HYSTERIA, women described as ignorant members of the lower classes or as frivolous ladies of fashion. These very articulate women writers, written about by Meek, drew upon and reworked the existing medical theories to reflect what they saw as a more accurate female experience of HYSTERIA. In doing so, they gave the silenced women a voice.

The institution of marriage was often looked to by physicians and female sufferers of HYSTERIA who tried to theorise the illness, to such an extent that marriage was given as a prescription for HYSTERIA. Montagu and Finch challenged this medical view, they contested the idea that marriage and domesticity freed women from HYSTERIA, and marriage became a cause of, rather than a cure for it. Montagu recognised in her private letters the isolation of domesticity as causes for mental troubles. She pointed to a need for a life that extends beyond the home. Piozzi, Freke and Montagu identified their isolation and their husband's mistreatment as causes of depression. Piozzi's influence led Samuel Johnson (seen as a representative of the medical community but not actually a practising physician) to include women as well as men in his innovative thinking on the subject of depression and to recognise that female isolation and inactivity led to depression. In correspondence and private writings, these women evoked the social causes of their mental distress. Mary Wollstonecraft was one of the first to do so in an overtly political fashion. She pointed to an aspect of the female condition that directly influenced mental health; she theorized the experiences of eighteenth century women, their daily lives of domestic sequestration and trauma. The experiences and traumas she wrote of include childbirth and motherhood and these were taken up by Bernard Mandeville in his 1711 medical treatise. He offered alternative diagnoses to the prevalent medical models that simplified or ignored female experience.

In the following lengthy extract Meek sums up the impassioned way in which these women writers sought to address their unhappiness, and in doing so successfully moved understandings of HYSTERIA away from the unhelpful theorising and related 'prescribing' which actually *fed into* their unhappiness, connecting it instead to the difficulties of domesticity and womanhood ('difficulties' which I prefer to refer to as the boredom and misery of supposed domestic 'bliss' with bad, at best, and cruel, at worst, husbands):

"As is obvious from Wollstonecraft's writings and, to a degree, from those of other eighteenth-century women, a lament for the condition of woman often moves beyond mere complaint and carries with it a searching impulse that seeks to discover explanations for unhappiness. The personal experiences of hysterics were eventually heard, and the "echoes of grief" of Finch, Freke, Montagu, Piozzi, Wollstonecraft, and others reverberated beyond the walls of their private chambers. Of course, views of this kind were only gradually embraced in the eighteenth century, but people began nevertheless to recognize the condition of woman as an underlying cause of the ailment. In the last decade of the century, Mary Wollstonecraft would vehemently make a case for the oppressiveness of women's social roles, and she would use this emerging idea to challenge perceptions of hysteria." (Meek 2009: 124-5)

The history of HYSTERIA resonates with me and my story. Firstly, His myriad of tactics that I believe were employed by Him with the purpose of making me doubt my own mind, along with His actual declarations that I was "not well" (told to our four year old daughter) and that I was suffering with "anxiety" (told to a Relate counsellor) fit within this historical discourse of women and (poor) mental health. Secondly, the connection between women's mental health problems and their social conditions, especially their relationships with men, *really* resonates with me and my story. The female writers of the eighteenth century wrote to shine a light on the social causes of HYSTERIA and thus wrench it away from all of the 'wandering' womb nonsense. The social causes in question concerned women's at best unfulfilled and at worst cruelty laden lives, and the lives they describe rang true for my life with Him. In the following extract, Meek contrasts the diagnostic criteria of HYSTERIA (all physical symptoms) with what women sufferers actually described experiencing (psychological symptoms):

> "[P]hysical symptoms – ranging from headaches, salivation, and trembling to paralysis, choking, and epileptic-like fits – were central diagnostic criteria. This somatic element is less prominent in women's accounts of hysteria. Rather they focus on a continuum of psychological states ranging from persistent sorrow, social isolation, and depression to paranoia and anxiety." (Meek 2009: 108-9)

Persistent sorrow, social isolation and depression (or at least low mood) reigned during my abusive relationship. So tick. Tick. Tick. Furthermore, I was also frequently paranoid and anxious about adequately meeting all of His needs and keeping to all of His rules. So tick. Tick.

From my undergraduate degree in sociology and social policy, which included elective modules in women's studies, I knew of this distressing history of 'HYSTERIA', of the social control (and at times eradication) of women via mental health diagnoses. However, I had pushed it to the back of my mind which was fogged with doubt. When He was cruel and then 'nice', when He gaslighted me, when He was subtly but most definitely different towards me in front of a neighbour, and I doubted my own mind, I could no more bring this knowledge into play in any useful way - to tell myself that I was not in any way a mentally unsound woman, but rather this common patriarchal tactic was at work - than I could have served Him a meal without two tubs of cottage cheese on the side (this will make sense once you read the chapter entitled Food). Doubt reigned. Returning to this area of scholarship once I had been enlightened about the domestic abuse I had been living with, in what I read, I saw in a heartbeat its significance for me.

He planted four seeds of doubt within me. I did everything I possibly could for Him but I was still left feeling that I was a Bad Partner. Doubt. I have always (and will always) put our two beautiful children first, but I was left feeling that I was a Bad Mother (or three bad mothers rolled into one, remember). Doubt. I always try to be kind and generous but I was left feeling I was a Selfish Person. Doubt. And I have never been diagnosed with a mental health condition but I was left feeling like a mentally unstable and possibly even HYSTERICAL woman. Doubt.

Doubt, The Trilogy of Protection and The Law

Not only was I left doubting myself but, despite living in a state of tear-soaked fear and unhappiness, I doubted I was being abused. I put this in large part down to three key aspects of His abuse. Firstly, His abuse was largely emotional and psychological. I was never hit, He never left visible marks on me, I have no visible scars. Secondly, His abuse was cyclical, peppered with 'nice' bits, leaving me in doubt about what He was like, whether or not He was cruel. And thirdly, His abuse was imperceptible, invisible, hidden from the outside world, behind the closed doors of our family home, outside of which He was a very different being. Lundy Bancroft explains this well in *Why Does He Do That? Inside The Minds of Angry and Controlling Men*:

"One of the obstacles to recognising chronic mistreatment in relationships is that most abusive men simply don't seem like abusers... An abuser's friends may think the world of him. He may have a successful work life and no problems with drugs or alcohol. He may simply not fit anyone's image of a cruel or intimidating person. So when a woman feels her relationship spinning out of control, it is unlikely to occur to her that her partner is an abuser." (Bancroft 2002: 8-9)

So there was no physical evidence of His abuse to show everyone else, to convince them of the real Him (had I dared to); He would sometimes be nice to me, so I myself doubted who the real Him was and I doubted the cruelty and the now *legally defined* abuse that was happening to me; and the abuse took place only behind closed doors so everyone else saw a different Him. These three things are surely what makes this kind of domestic abuse so hard to see whilst in it, and thus so very damaging. How could there not be doubt raging through my mind with this trilogy of protection for abusers, protecting them from being labelled as such by their victims. And if their victims do not see them for what they are, who will? Who *could*?

There has been progress with the issue of non-physical domestic abuse:

- In 2013 the government's definition of domestic abuse was revised to encompass alongside physical abuse: psychological, sexual, financial and emotional abuse, stalking, harassment, 'honour-based' crimes, female genital mutilation, forced marriages and coercive control.
- In 2015 The Serious Crime Act was amended to introduce a new Controlling or Coercive Behaviour Offence. The offence, specific to intimate family relationships, allowed for justice to be sought against perpetrators whose behaviour includes psychological and emotional abuse.
- In 2019 the government unveiled its most comprehensive package with which to tackle domestic abuse. The Draft Domestic Abuse Bill was published in January 2019 and encompasses nine measures that require primary legislation to implement. The first of these measures is the first ever *statutory* government definition of domestic abuse to specifically include controlling and coercive non-physical domestic abuse.

In the year ending March 2018, 9, 053 coercive control offences were recorded by the police and prosecutions for 960 such offences were commenced at magistrate's courts (statistics taken from *HM Government: Transforming the Response to Domestic Abuse: Consultation Response and Draft Bill, January 2019*).

But what was the conviction rate?
Statistics tell us that with domestic abuse generally the rate is low:

"[M]uch of the domestic abuse that takes place does not come to the attention of the police and there remains a gap between the level of abuse measured by the CSEW and the level of abuse recorded by the police. It is estimated that around one in six of domestic abuse victims report their abuse to the police (Office for National Statistics, 2018a). Much of the extent and impact of domestic abuse therefore remains hidden." (Home Office: The economic and social costs of domestic abuse; Research Report 107, Rhys Oliver, Barnaby Alexander, Stephen Roe and Miriam Wlasny, January 201: 7)

"Domestic abuse is often a hidden crime that is not reported to the police. Thus, the estimated number of victims is much higher than the number of incidents and crimes recorded by the police. There were 488, 049 domestic abuse-flagged crimes recorded and an additional 579, 971 domestic abuse incidents that were not subsequently recorded as crimes in 2016/17." (Home Office: The economic and social costs of domestic abuse; Research Report 107, Rhys Oliver, Barnaby Alexander, Stephen Roe and Miriam Wlasny, January 201: 35)

Perhaps more importantly when it comes to coercive control, what is the *recognition* rate, *amongst victims*?

I was left questioning whether or not I was the victim of domestic abuse even after a counsellor had told me that I was; even after Women's Aid and Behind Closed Doors told me that I was – and put me on the waiting list for an Emotional Support Worker because of the fact – and even when a myriad of other professionals categorically stated that I was; that I was the victim of domestic abuse. Due to a trilogy of protection for abusers, in the face of such overwhelming evidence I still struggled to believe it; I still struggled to believe that I was being abused.

I am not struggling with this anymore. This is in no small part due to the fact that I have dipped into the research and writing on domestic abuse. I have done so in no systematic or thorough way (and to be clear, this book is in no way, shape or form an academic tome on domestic abuse), however, I have found a truism for me and my experience of domestic abuse in everything that I have read - in every academic article, every book and every personal account. So everything that I have read has helped me to overcome my doubt.

In *Why Does He Do That? Inside The Minds of Angry and Controlling Men* Lundy Bancroft argues that the roots of verbal and physical abuse are the same and that the same thinking drives them both. He goes on to argue that, in his extensive experience, women who have been physically abused and women who have been psychologically abused describe the same distresses in their lives. And he goes one step further still and argues that:

"The scars from mental cruelty can be as deep and long-lasting as wounds from punches or slaps but are often not as obvious. In fact, even among women who have experienced violence from a partner, half or more report that *the man's emotional abuse is what is causing them the greatest harm*." (Bancroft 2002: 8, emphasis in original)

Furthermore, the Home Office's report into the economic and social costs of domestic abuse makes the following argument:

"Overall, in the year ending 31 March 2017, domestic abuse is estimated to have cost over £66 billion in England and Wales... The biggest component of the estimated cost is the physical and emotional harms incurred by victims (£47 billion), *particularly the emotional harms (the fear, anxiety and depression experienced by victims as a result of domestic abuse),* which account for the overwhelming majority of overall costs." (Home Office: The economic and social costs of domestic abuse; Research Report 107, Rhys Oliver, Barnaby Alexander, Stephen Roe and Miriam Wlasny, January 201: 5-6, emphasis added)

For anyone who is still struggling with the doubt that I was, for anyone who is struggling to conceptualise any non-violent form of domestic abuse as the domestic abuse that it is, read Stephanie Sweetnam's (2013) personal account 'Where Do You Think Domestic Abuse Hurts Most?' (in *Violence Against Women*, Volume 19, issue 1, pp.133-138, also cited earlier). I did not experience violence so am unable to compare violent and non-violent domestic abuse. However, I find Sweetnam's take on the impact of non-violent domestic abuse to be hauntingly apt:

"Although the majority of people are quick to assume that the physical aspect of domestic abuse may be what hurts most, it could not be further from the truth. Scars are skin deep. Scars heal relatively quickly over time and leave marks that can be covered up if one chooses to do so. It is the emotional and psychological scars that do not heal as quickly and are not as easy to cover up." (Sweetnam 2013: 136, emphasis added)

When I was in the process of trying to get Him to move out of the family home, and was experiencing on-going psychological abuse from Him over it, I told people time and time again that I wished He would just hit me. Because then I could virtually click my fingers (or rather, dial 999) and get Him removed. And anyone still not believing of the fact that I was systematically and cruelly abused by Him for over a decade might start to truly believe it (including me). But He never did hit me.

From the reading I have done on some of the research into domestic abuse, however, I have learnt that there is more of a connection or a continuum than I had ever thought there might be. I have read the findings from a number of research projects into domestic abuse and learnt of the following links between the non-violent types of domestic abuse that I experienced and violent domestic abuse:

Links between non-violent and violent types of domestic abuse

- Verbal aggression can escalate and often spirals into physical abuse.
- Mentally cruel and intimidating men tend to gradually drift into using physical intimidation as well.
- Controlling behaviours can be a risk marker for high frequency, injurious, escalating physical aggression, because abusive men can use violence when they believe the tactics of control are failing.
- Research indicates that the best behavioural predictor of which men will become violent to their partners is their level of verbal abuse.
- Emotional and psychological abuse and controlling behaviour may underpin all other forms of physical and sexual abusive behaviour.

The findings of one piece of research into domestic abuse which I read go a step further than arguing that non-violent forms of domestic abuse can lead to violence. These findings suggest that one form of non-violent domestic abuse – verbal aggression - can itself have the same sorts of negative *physiological* outcomes that violence does, for example, shaking, panic attacks and nausea. When I read this research it really got me thinking, it got me remembering and thinking. In my experience, non-violent domestic abuse – specifically, verbal, emotional and psychological domestic abuse - *did* have a negative physiological outcome. These non-violent forms of domestic abuse frequently led to the instant obliteration of my appetite. This could happen *mid meal*. I have far too many memories of scraping half or more of my evening meal into the bin because I was no longer able to eat it after a verbal run in with Him in which He criticised me or guilt tripped me or denied a threat He had made earlier (AKA gaslighting). In my experience and thus opinion, non-violent forms of domestic abuse are mental *and physical* abuse.

In *Coercive Control How Men Entrap Women in Personal Life* (2009) Evan Stark explores the precursors to the coercive control method of domestic abuse. In doing so he writes of the work of a man who goes a step further still regarding the classification of different types of domestic abuse:

"When he founded Emerge in Boston, one of the nation's first counselling programs for violent men, David Adams... defined any act as violent "that causes the victim to do something she does not want to do, prevents her from doing something she wants to do, or causes her to be afraid "regardless of whether assault was involved"." (Stark 2009: 201)

Clementine Ford makes a similar point in *Fight Like a Girl* when she argues that "[t]hreats transpire as more than just the use of physical force, and *violence can be felt as more than just physical pain*." (Ford 2018: 260, emphasis added). I like Adams' and Ford's definition of violence. I love them. Perhaps more than anything else I have read on domestic abuse, these have helped me to eradicate the nagging doubt I had about whether or not I can say I have lived with domestic abuse given the fact that I was never hit by Him. It means that from the moment I woke up (very, very early) until the moment I went to bed (very, very early, exhausted) I was experiencing domestic violence; I was experiencing a form of violence; I as experiencing violence. I performed act after act after act because I had to, because I was scared not to, and I frequently missed out on doing things that I wanted to do, for me, as a result. And I was certainly constantly second guessing what He wanted and 'needed' to be sure I did not miss anything that I was supposed to be, and trying to work out what He might find as acceptable reasons for any failings on my part regarding the tasks I was supposed to accomplish, and basically living on eggshells and yes, feeling scared, often scared by threats. To reiterate then, I was experiencing violence, domestic violence.

In *Why Does He Do That? Inside The Minds of Angry and Controlling Men*, Lundy Bancroft draws the conclusion that an abusive man wishes to be mysterious so as to get away with his behaviour and not have to address his problems. He has to convince everyone that his behaviour makes no sense so that he can conceal and protect his very real, understandable, solvable problems that he doesn't want anyone to figure out and call him on and make him address. As Bancroft puts it:

"The abuser creates confusion because he has to. He

can't control and intimidate you, he can't recruit people around him to take his side, he can't keep escaping the consequences of his actions, unless he can throw everyone off the track." (Bancroft 2002: 20)

Pat Craven similarly places confusion centre-stage in women's experience of domestic abuse:

"[T]here is a very common misapprehension that a woman who has been abused has some understanding of what has happened to her. This is simply not true. When a woman is being subjected to abuse, she feels that she is in the middle of a very confusing mess and that it must somehow be her fault." (Craven 2008: 6)

He created confusion which left me living with unending, core destroying doubt. I doubted just about everything I possibly could doubt about myself, just about anything *anyone* could possibly doubt about themselves: my abilities as a partner, a mother and a human being, and the soundness of my very mind. My personality, my very personhood was obliterated. I lived nervous, anxious, confused, riddled with self-doubt and, worse, self-loathing. In another extract from her personal account of domestic abuse Stephanie Sweetnam just perfectly sums up this state of existing (to be clear, existing rather than living):

"I could not appreciate any of my own qualities because he was constantly reminding me how worthless I was. Abuse infiltrates one's mind and body, and affects the core of one's soul." (Sweetnam 2013: 134)

In the next chapter I turn to the issue of time, or my time, or rather my lack of time. His control of my time left me exhausted and I believe this is why I was unable to think logically and rationally out of the fog of confusion and fight the doubt filling my mind.

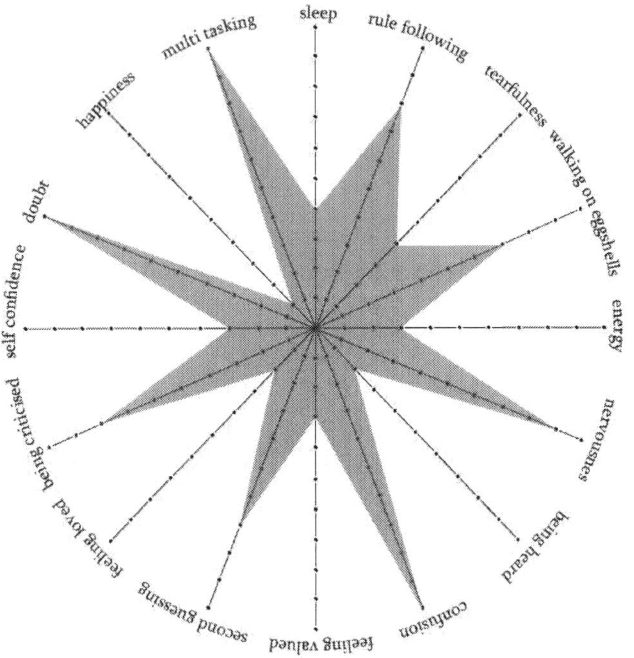

Radar Diagram of My Abusive Relationship

TIME

And it's hard to love, there's so much to hate
Hanging on to hope
When there is no hope to speak of
And the wounded skies above say it's much, much too late
Well, maybe we should all be praying for time
Praying for Time, George Michael

The Smear Test Catalyst

A cervical screening test (previously known as a smear test) is a method of detecting abnormal cells on the cervix. About 3,000 cases of cervical cancer are diagnosed each year in the UK. It's possible for women of all ages to develop cervical cancer, although the condition mainly affects sexually active women aged 30 to 45. Cervical screening is offered because it can detect abnormal cell changes in the cervix (the lower part of the womb) that could potentially develop into cervical cancer. If significant abnormalities are detected at an early stage, there's the option of having treatment to remove them before they have a chance to become cancerous. Since the screening programme was introduced in the 1980s, the number of cervical cancer cases has decreased by about 7% each year. It's estimated up to 5,000 cases of cervical cancer are prevented each year in the UK because of cervical screening. (www.nhs.uk/conditions/cervical-screening)

But I should not have gone for my last smear test. In doing so I had to break a rule. I broke a rule. There were a lot of rules. They were made to be followed. They were made by Him to be followed by me.

The Rules I Had To Live By

- Wake Him up every morning at the time stated on His post it note.
- Buy all of the foods He wanted every week, in the right quantities.
- Follow His method for teaching good behaviour to our two children, via giving Time Outs only for the bad behaviours that He gave them out for and giving them at exactly the right point in the tantrum or transgression in question.
- Do not ever ask Him a question when He is doing a task such as making His breakfast, because He finds this too stressful.
- Do not ever ask Him a question when He is getting ready to leave for work, because this would make Him late for work.
- Do not ever ask Him for help with the children when He comes in from work, because He finds this too stressful.
- Do not ever drink the last of the coffee in the pot and if I ever have the audacity to do so make a new pot of coffee in case He should want another cup.

"Each household governed by coercive control, each relationship, becomes *a patriarchy in miniature*, complete with its own web of rules or codes, rituals of deference, modes of enforcement, sanctions, and forbidden places, all devised with a particularity that is completely foreign to traditions of male dominance." (Stark 2009: 194, emphasis added)

When I read this description of the rules inherent within coercive control I had to laugh at the sheer irony. As children, my parents encouraged myself and my older sister to start collecting something (I guess this was so that wherever we went, we had a focus for our gift shop pillaging, which in my case was certainly my sole purpose for going anywhere ever as a child; and it pretty much still is). My sister chose to collect elephants. I chose to collect miniatures. Decades after I ceased and jettisoned my dusty and useless collection, then, I acquired a bespoke miniature, my very own miniature patriarchy.

My life, or miniature patriarchy, felt a bit like the movie *Fight Club*, in which The first rule of Fight Club is that you do not talk about Fight Club, and The second rule of Fight Club is that you do not talk about Fight Club, and The third rule... etc. I was kind of in a secret club too. Rules Club. More domestic. Less macho. Just as exhausting. And The first rule of Rules Club is that you do not talk about Rules Club, and The second rule of Rules Club is that you do not talk about Rules Club, and the Third rule... etc. Because if anyone ever enquired about, for example, the bizarre number of cottage cheese tubs in our fridge or the post it note system of waking Him up on a morning, and I started to explain these things, He would cut me off mid-sentence, smile, joke, put His arm around me, make like it was not a rule basically. But it was a rule. I know that now.

The first rule He was particularly strict about my following. I got it in the neck many times for waking Him up just ten minutes early. Just five minutes early actually. On the morning of my last smear test I woke Him up *twenty minutes* early. Cervical smear tests save lives – apparently maybe about five thousand a year. A cervical smear test could save my life. But His sleep was more important than this fact. More important than my health. More important than my life. Sleep (twenty minutes of) v your partner's life? I think this would be called a 'no brainer' to use current slang (which I feel suits Him quite well).

I had arranged a cervical smear test for 7.10am on one of my non paid work days, so that He could have the children and neither of us would need to take time off work to fit in this routine but important test. On the morning of the test His post it note said 7.20am. I realised He had forgotten about my test. I woke Him anyway at 7am. As I said, twenty minutes before His post it note dictated. He was furious. He said He needed seven hours sleep to run His clinic. He said I should have realised He had forgotten about the test and therefore must have gone to bed too late to get this required amount of sleep without sleeping until the wake up time given on His post it note (I was not awake enough to follow this ridiculous argument, and by this point I certainly did not care enough to). I dared to ask whether He would have missed going to the gym last night if He had remembered my test, to ensure He got enough sleep. He said no, but He would have not read for half an hour before turning His light out.

Needless to say, when I returned home I dared not tell Him that the nurse had been unable to carry out the procedure because of where I was at in my (wildly unpredictable, bleed-as-you-feel cycle – to borrow from a popular current concept) so I had to reschedule it. So I had woken Him up twenty minutes early for nothing.

He was still furious that lunchtime. I decided to do The Right Thing, as advised by relationship manuals everywhere, and apologised even though I knew I had done nothing wrong. This is supposed to make the other person equally apologetic, isn't it? It is supposed to move things on. Heal the rift. Fix things. Mend the relationship. Make everything okay. It did not. He calmly and coldly said He appreciated my apology and then told me I was to never, ever wake Him early again. He remained angry. I cried. He was unmoved by my tears (as always).

That evening He reiterated that I must never, ever, ever wake Him up early again (note that He added another 'ever', I had to know just how angry He was, just how bad my transgression was this time). I said I could not promise to never, ever, ever wake Him up early again (how could I? With two small children and the ever present possibility of one of them being upset or ill or just wanting their daddy?) This was the second time I had stood up to Him (having already refused to pair His socks, more on this later). He did not like it. I did. It felt new. And it felt good. It felt damn good.

Then came the forgiveness. The following morning He was happy and smiley and apologetic about being so angry the day before. So that was 24 hours of being sent to Coventry, a 24 hour long deafening silence, broken only once to respond coldly to my apology, and finally ended oh so beautifully, as His silences always were, with "Sorry babe".

But this was the occasion when "babe" did not put on her smiley face; when "babe" did not play His game. And that was all it took. It was game over. Relationship over. Twelve and a half years over. This was the moment when He asked if I wanted to separate from Him, which, as you already know, I said "YES" to.

I have to briefly explain here something that I learnt from Pat Craven's book *Living with the Dominator A book about the Freedom Programme.* She argues that one of the facets of the Dominator (the Headworker) is that he:

> "[D]oes not use our name. He calls us 'babe' or 'princess'... I am not saying that every man who does not use his partner's name is abusive, but I do know that every abusive man I have ever met does not call his partner by name." (Craven 2008: 48)

Can you guess what other name He lovingly gave me? Yes: Princess. Reading just how generic and DA 101 over a decade of my life has turned out to be was vile, just vile. I could hear His voice calling me these two names echoing in my head for a long time after I read Craven's book. Not easy to read and digest. Not at all. But I am still glad that I have done so. Because it has truly helped me to understand what I lived in/with/through.

The Wake-up Post-its Diagram

The Diary

"Women are the labouring sex. From the time girls are very small they learn that work is what time is for. Comparison of women's work-load with men's is difficult because a good deal of women's effort is not even recognized as work." (Greer 1999: 152)

None of mine was by Him.

During the last year of my relationship with Him, I grew so tired (no pun intended) of His attitude towards my life, His belief that I did not work hard, His laughter if I ever suggested (outwardly calmly but in a screaming voice inside) that *I worked very, very hard and did so seven days a week*. I grew so tired of this in fact that I decided to keep a diary for one week. I logged all of the tasks that I accomplished, the amount of time I was awake for and the amount of time I rested for. This hand scrawled (usually whilst very tired) data is compiled below in an easy to read table.

A Week In My Life: 121216 – 181216

	Mon	Tue	Wed	Thur	Fri	Sat	Sun	**Av.**
Hours Awake	18	17	17	16	16	17	17	**17**
Tasks Done	24	23	17	17	17	20	25	**20**
Paid Work			6 hrs.	6 hrs	6 hrs			
Rest Time	45 mins	35 min	45 mins	40 mins	30 mins	60 mins	120 mins	**54 mins**

What did I do with my collected data? Nothing. Of course. I did nothing with it except file it away (I do love filing). I dared not approach Him about what I had done, what I had learnt, what I had *proved* – i.e. that *I did work very, very hard and I did so seven days a week.*

Time Management 101

I think I have achieved quite a lot in my adult life so far. A degree. A Ph.D. Several paid research projects culminating in publications. Two businesses. I have volunteered. I have grown and delivered two healthy babies and then breast fed them both. I have trained to become an Independent Mental Health Advocate. I have also maintained and nurtured many friendships. And throughout all of this I have baked, at the drop of a hat, for all of my loved ones.

How has all of this been possible? How have I achieved all of this? It has been through skills that I have always prided myself in having: organisational skills, efficiency, the ability to multi-task and manage my time well. I love my diary. I love my lists (as you know). I plan. I do. I tick off. I get everything done that I need to every day. This is me. This is how and why I have achieved these things that I have aimed for, strived for. I am nothing if not a walking, talking example of good work ethic coupled with excellent time management. This is best illustrated by the times in my life when I worked six days a week – in academia and then in running a business – and still managed to get some rest, look after myself and stay well, and even to pursue my hobbies. But with Him I had virtually no down time, no me time; hobbies dried up; friendships were relegated to largely texts; and I was always tired, worn out, exhausted. This is I was not managing my own time, well or not. My time was completely controlled by Him. My time was His (because I was His).

Child Care

Listed in the facets or faces on The Dominator diagram, from Pat Craven's book *Living With The Dominator A book about the Freedom Programme* (2008), is 'The Bad Father', who persuades you to have his baby then refuses to look after it. On first reading this I took it far too literally and discounted it. Eventually, gradually, I realised this was exactly what had happened to me, what He had done to me. I did not sign up for single motherhood. I think it is more uncommon than common to do so. I think this is the case because I think it is really, really, bloody damn hard work. But this is what I got.

After I separated from Him, I wrote lists about who does what for the children, because I was so scared of losing them. This is the point when I calculated just how little He was actually *responsible* for the children, that is, *solely responsible* for them: approximately 4.5 hours a week, via doing the nursery and school runs on the three mornings of my paid work days. Percentage wise then, He was solely responsible for the children 2.5% of their lives. This was never going to change.

I have already explained many ways in which He

was manipulative. His changing moods, including sending me to Coventry (for up to 24 hours) and then switching to nice, apologetic, communicative; His pattern of threatening me and then denying the threats soon afterwards; His attempts to make me believe that I have made Him late for work; His blaming me for being upset after being criticised or told to "Fuck off" by pathologising me. Endless manipulations. His biggest manipulative move though, which I experienced several times, occurred when I had returned to work after our son was born and was exhausted and overwhelmed with all the work I had to do. Several times I turned to Him for support and each time I got the same response: another threat, wrapped in another criticism (He was nothing if not efficient with His abusing me, dare I go as far as to say that this is multi-tasking?) He would threaten to go to work that day (if He was due to go in) or the next day (if it was an evening) and reduce His hours to part time, so that He could be the primary caregiver of our children and I could work full time. Because, clearly, I could not cope with the children. I could not cope full stop.

He knew I have never wanted to, and will never want to, work full time whilst I have small children. So this manipulation, this tactic, shut down the conversation. And it ensured that He controlled the child care, specifically, He ensured that I did it all. The threat felt so real that on more than one occasion I contacted His mother, in a state of absolute panic, and explained my desperate fear that He was going to do it. Each time she reassured me she thought He would not do it. She was right.

He never did it - most likely because He does not want to be the primary caregiver of two small children - but He terrified me. That He could scare me so is, I believe, because of what His abuse did to my mind and my ability to think clearly. This is summed up brilliantly by Evan Stark in his book on coercive control, when he argues that "[t]he invasion and constriction of psychic as well as social space can paralyze independent judgement or thought." (Stark 2009: 210).

What a choice, then: admit I could not cope and face His cruel judgement and the pain of being away from my children, or give up asking Him for more help with His children. I chose the latter. Thus He controlled the child care.

His Time

To say that He had a sense of status and the entitlement that comes with it would be the biggest of understatements. He expected me to look after His every need, to meet all of His demands, on demand. It would be simpler to list the needs He did he *not* believe were more important than mine, the needs He did *not* believe that *I* should meet. However, as I love lists, that is not going to stop me. There was food - you will learn of The Food I Had To Buy For Him Every Week later, in the chapter entitled Food (just to be completely unimaginative); there was exercise, His hobby, His honing the body beautiful; there was sleep (remember the dictatorial post it notes?); there were His mountains of laundry that reduced me to living in a captive wardrobe (this is not a typo, as one proof reader thought, I do not mean *capsule* wardrobe, more on this later in the chapter entitled Love); there were the paired (all black) socks; and there was coffee.

You will enjoy (?) reading about the biggest coffee incident in, again, the chapter entitled Food. But coffee comes up more than once in this story. Shortly before I separated from Him I drank the last of the coffee, mid-morning. He emerged from working at home looking for a cup of coffee and found the pot empty. He was angry. He interrogated me: I only ever have two cups of coffee in the morning, why had I had a third and thus left the pot empty? I said I fancied a third (obviously). He told me to make another pot. At this point I was busy. I was supervising three small children (including two under threes) doing very messy crafts at the kitchen table and at the same time trying to prepare their lunches. So I said no. He said it was my fault there was no coffee left because I had had an extra cup so I had to make another pot. I reluctantly made another pot. This became one of The Rules I Had To Live By. He controlled coffee (before this, I did not think that coffee was something that *could* be controlled in a relationship).

Another facet of The Dominator is 'King Of The Castle'. Top of the list under this facet was that he treats you like a servant or slave. The word I had long been using was skivvy (no wonder I dressed so badly, so blandly, and looked 'downtrodden', I was a skivvy, not a role traditionally associated with sartorial elegance, think Baldrick in *Blackadder*, but clean(er)). A particularly nasty incident comes to mind that occurred the summer before I separated from Him. I had arranged for a friend to visit me, a friend I had not seen in a couple of months (traditionally, skivvies do not get much annual leave). I was really looking forward to seeing her. But His bike got a puncture as He set off for work and He returned home immediately and told me I had to drive Him to work. I said I could not. I explained why. He told me I had to. I drove Him to work. I told Him en route that He needed to work on His time management. This was one of the occasions, already mentioned, when He told me to "Fuck off". By this stage in the relationship, I was not doing things for Him out of love or a desire to help or any such positive reason. He controlled what I did for Him via the punishments, the abuse, if I did not comply (and I still got *verbal* abuse *whilst complying*).

(So called) Me Time

He controlled me time: the when and the what. Weekends were always organised, around Him, specifically His gym schedule. I would be told when He would do something fun with the children and I would have time to myself. His language said it all. He would talk about *giving* me time to myself. One day I pointed out this language and He asked whether I would prefer Him to talk about *letting me have* time to myself. Semantics, really? Talk about missing the point.

Whilst His life revolved around exercising, mine did not. Mine revolved around caring for two small children, and Him, running the family home, doing all of the wider 'family work' and holding down a paid job. Yet when He offered to watch the children and thus give me a half hour or so to myself He would always suggest "Why don't you do your exercises?" There has never been a more loaded question. He hated how little I exercised, but with maybe three half hours to myself in any week (*after* the time needed to wash; I have always washed (mostly), for the record), I needed to use this sparse and oh so special time to REST. It was terrifying explaining that I was not going to exercise, that I was going to take a quick unnecessary (because I had washed) but relaxing (because I was knackered) bath, that I was going to lie down and try to concentrate to read something. It was terrifying because I knew that it fuelled two of His negative beliefs about me. Firstly, that I am a slob – the entity which He probably hates most in the world. (For the record, I am five foot ten and have long had a stable weight of approximately 9 and a half stone, giving me a BMI of 19, which puts me at the low end of the healthy BMI range of 18.5-25, a place I occupy not through being a gym bunny but through running around after two small children, and a man(ish), holding down a paid job and basically rarely sitting down). Secondly, that I could not cope with all that I had on my plate (hence I needed a rest). So, more often than not, I would simply exercise. I would tell myself that it was not going to do me any harm after all, because it was exercise, it was good for me, how could it not be purely good for me? But it wasn't. It contributed to my exhaustion. So I had me time, in the house. But He controlled it. So it was not really me time at all, was it?

It did not just leave me exhausted. In his book on coercive control Evan Stark writes about 'safety zones', the spaces and times very much needed by women whose lives are micromanaged by controlling men, to reflect on their situation, think about their options, regain a fleeting sense of control or self-worth and recover pieces of their lost voice or subjectivity. At the time I could not see how vile it was that He even controlled the tiny slivers of 'me' time. I find Evan Stark's description of this aspect of coercive control chilling:

> "Because safety zones offer women an alternative to subordination, they rarely go unchallenged. If abusive relationships were filmed in slow motion, they would resemble a grotesque dance whereby victims create moments of autonomy and perpetrators "search and destroy" them". (Stark 2009: 217)

Another facet of The Dominator is 'The Jailor'. This was subtle but very real. He never actually said I could not leave the house, go out, see my friends, but with the way in which His schedule dictated mine, and with my time, my life, being dictated by both child care and His needs, it amounted to the same thing. I could no more say that I was going out somewhere or with someone and would be back at whatever o'clock than I could fly to the moon. He would have plans. And I would have too much work to do. Going anywhere was a major event. I had to pre-book, I had to organise weeks in advance of anything, I had to *ask*. I had to ask for *the right to go out*. I had to ask for *the right to go out of the house*. By default, I was in the house, the family home, with our two children, so He could (and did) do whatever He pleased whenever He pleased. Furthermore, He would so, so subtly make me feel guilty on the very, very rare occasions upon which I asked for me time that did not fit His schedule, that meant He had to miss doing something *for me*. He would be passive aggressive: quiet, moody, sulky, etc. (i.e. Passive Aggression 101). So I virtually gave up trying to have any kind of life outside of the home. Any me time thus took place in the family home. Another way in which He controlled my so called me time.

I was essentially trapped in domesticity; trapped in the family home. Exhausted and socially isolated, with a loss of any sense of identity outside of the home (beyond my paid work), a loss of any self-confidence I had previously had. There is something I find almost sinister about this: I found the house; I worked hard on making it a home; I love the home; I did, and I do, love being in my home; and yet it became a place of captivity; I was to all intents and purposes kept in the house. The Edwardian terraced house version of the cliché 'gilded cage'.

Us Time

We were a couple, partners, long-term partners, but we were not a team, we were not on each other's team. His never verbalised, never explicitly stated but omnipresent, inescapable *modus operandi* was 'My way or the highway'. This was never more obvious and never more wrong than when it came to the 'us time' part of our relationship. He controlled what together time we ever had. This was dictated by His schedule. His hobby. His gym going. His preoccupation with honing His body beautiful. I found it very hard to feel in any way special to Him when I was picked up and played with only when His soft play (the gym) was closed and when He had no other playmates (gym buddies) to play with. His passive aggression and emotional blackmailing was second to none when He wanted us to have us time and I was simply too tired and ready for bed, at about 8pm, having been up since about 4am with our robot baby son. (I must explain here that I am in no way criticising our beautiful son when I refer to him as a 'robot baby'. On the contrary, he was a dream baby, feeding and napping and going to bed and waking up so consistently and reliably. He just happened to consistently and reliably wake at 4am every day. For a very, very long time. I cherished our early mornings together, just the two of us in the stillness. And those early mornings required very early bedtimes).

On the rare as I could get away with occasions that we had 'date night' (a euphemism for sex), they were obviously fitted around His schedule, squeezed in between various different gym nights. So He controlled the when. He also controlled how it was done, to accommodate His 'bad back' and what He wanted to do 'for me' apparently (it wasn't for me; it was never for me). Worse yet He was obsessive about controlling how long it lasted. He insisted it had to last a certain length of time, despite the fact I would have been up for about 16 hours by this point, and would have sat down for approximately 15 minutes of them (if I was lucky), so time had a completely different meaning for me. If He thought I was going to have an orgasm He would abruptly stop what He was doing and say it had to last longer. So I was not even allowed to have an orgasm naturally, organically. Each time He did this it killed the whole encounter for me. It felt cruel. How, then, do you have an orgasm? How do you have an orgasm when you are upset, hurting, unhappy? When you are feeling these things on top of exhaustion? Surely it is impossible? It was for me. Surely there is an oxymoron quiz here: how many oxymorons can you make from the following words: cruel, upset, hurting, unhappy, exhaustion and orgasm?

So even sex, something that was supposed to be enjoyable and relaxing – was supposed to be the pinnacle of those things – was micro-controlled by Him. It added to my exhaustion by being passively aggressively secured by Him when I was already over tired and then dragged out by Him for far longer than I had the energy for (or the inclination, given the fact I was so angry). Too scared to stand up to Him over sex, to tell Him I was not enjoying it anymore, too frightened of the negative consequences of doing so, I let it happen. On one occasion I think I kind of dissociated during it (more on this later).

Thus He controlled child care (thus I did 97.5% of it). I met His every need. He controlled (so called) me time. And Us time necessitated sex and He controlled that too.

Women, Time and Inequality

"Women are still judged as more or less competent by how they perform their second shift. Nowhere is this more evident than in family court, where women's failures as homemakers are highlighted while men's neglect of domestic work is rarely considered a relevant factor in determining their fitness to parent." (Stark 2009: 211)

When I went to see my brilliant friend Sam one afternoon she summed up the continuing difference between women and men oh so perfectly when the first thing she said to me when I arrived, as she vacuumed the stairs, was "Hi, I am just doing jobs in between jobs." (Sam 170718)

On one rare occasion when I actually went out on a 'date night' with Him, because His mother was staying with us and offered to babysit, the difference between what that meant for us was laughable. Except that I did not laugh, I cried, with tiredness, by the time I got to bed. Upon returning home after the meal my domestic work had piled up and been exacerbated by an enthusiastic, mess-creating babysitting granny. There were dirty dishes everywhere, toys everywhere, the bathroom was in disarray, there was laundry to hang up and other laundry to put away to create the space needed to hang that laundry up, and there was still the coffee to be made for Him in the morning (remember how important coffee is to Him?) Whilst I did all of the above, He had a rest (the meal out must have exhausted Him) and then went to the gym (so a power rest then, which gave Him the energy to go back out *to exercise*).

Whilst my exhaustion was the result of my controlled existence, as I was effectively reduced to a skivvy, I was able to explain it away to myself by thinking about it politically and not personally, drawing on sociological and feminist debates learnt of whilst studying sociology, social policy and women's studies back in my twenties. I believe my knowledge of these debates, along with the doubt clouding my mind, facilitated my disastrous inability to see what was going on, to see what was being done to me. Through my studies, I was far too familiar with academic research on gender inequalities regarding time.

During my undergraduate degree, in the 1990s, I had learnt about the utterly doomed 'wages for housework' campaign of the 1970s. Whilst working on my Ph.D. in the same decade, I became familiar with the then current research into and debates about housework, family work, leisure and the whole issue of women's time - or lack thereof. I pulled two key books from this time off my shelves and reacquainted myself with their sad theories.

The time bind is a concept introduced by sociologist Arlie Russell Hochschild in 1997, in her book, *The Time Bind: When Work Becomes Home and Home Becomes Work*. This concept refers to the blurring distinction between work and home social environments. Hochschild found in her research that although most working parents, particularly mothers, said that family comes first, few of them considered adjusting their long working hours, even when their workplaces offered flexitime, maternity leave, telework, or other 'family friendly' policies. She concluded that the roles of home and work had reversed: work had become more attractive, offering a sense of belonging, while home had grown more stressful, becoming a dreaded place with too many demands.

This was true for me. Home had become very hard and my (paid) work remained an easier option, an easier place, probably the easiest 18 hours of my week. My paid work differed enormously from my unpaid work. I was considered an equal by my colleagues and my then manager, who did not tell me if and when I could take a break, but rather told me *to* take a break, to not work through, to *look after myself*. So at my paid work I felt both respected and cared for. I felt neither of these at home. My paid work was something of a haven. The time bind indeed.

In *The Second Shift: Working Parents And The Revolution At Home* (1989) Hochschild coins the term "second shift" to describe the labour performed at home by women in addition to the paid work performed in the formal sector (a concept/problem still observed and referred to twenty odd years later, for example by Evan Stark in his book on coercive control in 2009 – see the quote that opens this section). For the book, Hochschild and her research associates interviewed fifty couples very intensively and observed in a dozen homes, throughout the 1970s and 1980s, in an effort to explore the 'leisure gap' between men and women. Through the depictions of couples' day-to-day practices, Hochschild derived three constructs in regard to marital roles that she observed during her research: transitional, traditional, and egalitarian. The traditional woman wants to identify with her activities at home as a wife and mother. The egalitarian female partner wants to identify with the same spheres her husband does, and to have an equal amount of power in the marriage. The transitional woman falls in between, blending the traditional and egalitarian ideologies. The transitional woman is clearly today's middle class norm. Again, Hochschild's theorising matched my experience. As I tried to be a 'transitional woman', I was doing the 'second shift' and there was a definite 'leisure gap'. To put this in plain English rather than sociological jargon peppered English, I tried to have it all which for me simply meant *doing* it all (when does it not mean this?)

Germaine Greer published *The Female Eunuch* in 1970 and documented the sexual oppression and the many inequalities faced by women. She wrote in the introduction that she hoped that the book would quickly date and disappear. It did not. So in 1999, whilst I was enmeshed in my doctoral research, she published *The Whole Woman*. It documented the sexual oppression and the many inequalities faced by women. This is not a game of spot the difference but, rather, spot the similarity. The inequalities facing women in the 1970s may have altered by the 1990s, but the fact that inequalities remained is the point. Ditto between the late 1990s and today. I love and hate this quote from The Whole Woman in equal measure:

"Women don't allow themselves any spare time. Lots of women don't give themselves time for sufficient sleep. Women rushing to catch up with the day's complement of tasks are usually anxious and guilty, afraid that they are spreading themselves too thin, maybe skimping this or fudging that, not giving a child or husband or a project enough attention." (Greer 1999: 157)

I never gave Him enough attention, apparently. Consider the relevance today of some more points from *The Whole Woman*:

Much of women's work is not recognised and classified as such; much of women's work is as invisible to conventional data collection methods as the work of animals; any increase in the amount of housework and family work that male partners of women carry out is small and women continue to do the bulk of both; leisure is a masculine privilege; men regard weekends as time off whilst women use weekends to catch up with the tasks overhanging from an exhausting week; and once a woman becomes a mother she effectively loses any leisure time she ever had.

Recognise much? I do. I do not believe there has been any great change from the above. Many writers, researchers and theorists, writing today about many different things, are saying the same thing. For example, in *Living Dolls The Return of Sexism*, her follow up to *The New Feminism,*

Natasha Walter writes of the rhetoric of flexible working and of shared parental responsibility and the actual persisting pay gap between women and men. She argues that there does not exist equality between the sexes now but rather a stalled revolution, with women not progressing far within the corridors of power and men not progressing far into the (power free) domestic sphere. In *Militant Lactivism? Attachment Parenting and Intensive Motherhood in the UK and France*, Charlotte Faircloth addresses the interplay between 'intensive parenting' and gender equality. She argues that these are competing ideologies. In their book *Gender In World Perspective*, Connell and Pearse address gender and the overall gender arrangements, which they refer to as the 'gender order' of contemporary societies. They list the many continuing gender based inequalities and argue that it is men in general who benefit from the inequalities of this gender order. One gender inequality that they list is the (very time consuming) unpaid domestic and care work which is predominantly carried out by women. The point in brackets at the end of the following extract is why I simply *had* to quote it in this book:

"In all contemporary societies for which we have statistics, women do most of the cleaning, cooking and sewing, most of the work of looking after children, and almost all of the work of caring for babies. (If you don't think childcare is work, you haven't done it yet.)" (Connell and Pearse 2015: 3)

Amen to that.

In *Fight Like A Girl*, Clementine Ford argues why this is the case simply and I believe brilliantly, stating that "most girls are conditioned from birth to accept that unpaid domestic labour is our natural responsibility." (Ford 2018: 234)

These arguments concerning continuing gender inequalities are reflected in the findings of the British Social Attitudes Survey. The BSA 30th Report (2013) asks whether there has been a decline in support for a traditional gender division of roles in the home and workplace – i.e. has women's unpaid domestic work within the home declined - as their labour market participation has markedly increased over the past 30 years? That is, how far has a gender role revolution been evolving in Britain? It is concluded that whilst *attitudes* that there should be a clear gender divide have almost been eradicated (which is linked to generational replacement), *behaviours* have not. Thus it is reported that:

"When we combine self-reported involvement in household work and looking after family members, we find that men in 2012 report spending an average of 19 hours a week on these activities, compared to the 36 hours reported by women. A similar magnitude of difference is found when we consider the reported time spent by fathers and mothers specifically; while fathers report an average of 24 hours per week spent on household work and looking after family members, the comparable figure for mothers is 49 hours." (Park et al. 2013: 127)

And it is thus concluded that:

"[E]ven if dual-earner households are now the norm, it is wrong to think that the gender role revolution is anywhere near complete. Gender equality in terms of who does the bulk of the chores and who is primarily responsible for looking after the children has made very little progress in terms of what happens in people's homes. Men's uptake of unpaid domestic work is slow, and women continue to feel that they are doing more than their fair share." (Park et al. 2013: 134)

SHOCKING.

I know that there has been no 'gender role revolution' simply from observing my neighbours, my friends, my family, everyone I know basically. Women continue to carry the burden (for want of a better term) of child care and family work on top of the societal expectation - and for many financial necessity - of juggling paid work alongside these strands of demanding, relentless, often bloody difficult work. Women who do not have to work in paid employment or who choose not to are the minority today. Men who truly pull their weight domestically and child care wise remain not so much the minority today as the exception that proves the rule; beyond that even: the holy grail. I know two such exceptions: my friend Ginny's partner likes cleaning (a man who likes cleaning; he does exist; I am not making him up) and my sister's husband who was happy to work part time after becoming a parent, enabling my sister to return to work full time following both of her maternity leaves.

In her study of 'intensive mothering' which I wrote about in an earlier chapter, Faircloth argues that "women's entry into the market has taken place in parallel with an increasing emphasis on the importance of labour-intensive, emotionally absorbing mothering. The language of 'juggling' is – in the UK at least – now commonplace." (Faircloth 2013: 24) I talk to other mothers regularly and there definitely persists a discourse, about juggling and about trying to achieve a better balance between paid work and family work. Juggling is necessary and a balance is craved. So a balance is *not* being achieved then. Just recently one mother I know quit her PAYE paid work for home based self-employment – with all of the missing rights and perks that that entails - to accommodate her male partner's new paid job which precludes him carrying out much child care; another is talking about quitting her PAYE job for homeworking, simply to have more time at home with her children.

So my struggles balancing caring for a young family, running the family home, conducting all of the 'family work' and holding down a part time paid job – that is, my exhaustion - simply felt normal. I believed normal continuing gender inequalities were at play. I thought I was exhausted because of on-going, persisting, entrenched gender inequalities concerning time. I was aware that I had no me time, no down time, no damn time; I was aware that He did; I was aware that He had a hell of a lot of it; I was aware that this unbalanced, unequal, unfair state of play was not my choice, rather it was His choice; I just did not, *could* not see the underlying and yet overwhelming *control* at work ensuring this state of play.

I realise now that when I thought about, and dwelled on, and ruminated on, and worried about, and moaned incessantly to just about anyone I ever could about this state of play I never used the word 'control'. I would think and talk about Him being in charge, choosing, dictating, deciding, determining, ruling over, etc., time (and please feel free to whip out your thesaurus and add more words here) but I never thought the word 'control' and I never uttered it either. It was as though this word, this concept, had fallen out of my head, *whilst I was living utterly controlled*. (This strikes me as very, very odd now, and sinister, and surely to God somehow very significant?)

So I was aware, acutely and painfully aware, that I had no say in the timing of any aspect of my life, but I missed entirely the concept of *control*, and saw only the issue of *time*, which I could link to feminist and sociological research and theories concerning gender inequalities. Was this convenient? Was I *choosing* to believe this, to do what I was most comfortable with: going down the academic explanation route (I do love studying; the geek in me does), a route which offered a theory that told me the situation that I was in was sad and unfair but completely normal and that He was therefore not that bad? Never mind that we were a very 'middle class' family and therefore supposed to be slightly more progressive, slightly less traditional, not so old school, gender roles focused, etc. Was I glossing over this? Probably, I was glossing over a hell of a lot else at the time.

Women, Domestic Abuse and More Inequality

The gendered nature of domestic abuse is widely recognised and written about within legislation, academic research and more personal writing on the subject. For example, the Home Office Research Report into the economic and social costs of domestic abuse (published in 2019) provides up to date statistics on this:

"Evidence shows that domestic abuse is predominantly committed against women. According to the Crime Survey for England and Wales (CSEW) for the year ending 31 March 2018, 24.9% of women and 10% of men aged 16 to 59 have experienced partner abuse at least once since the age of 16, while 6.3% of women and 2.7% of men aged between 16 and 59 have experienced partner abuse once or more in the last year (Office for National Statistics, 2018a)." (Home Office: The economic and social costs of domestic abuse; Research Report 107, Rhys Oliver, Barnaby Alexander, Stephen Roe and Miriam Wlasny, January 201: 7)

And the Government Consultation Response and Draft Domestic Abuse Bill (also published in 2019) refers to a strategy aimed at women and girls: the Violence Against Women and Girls Strategy (2016-20) which sets out the government's ambition to protect women and girls from violence, support victims and provide leadership at a national and international level on ending abuse.

The following are some of the gendered domestic abuse facts and figures that I have come across through my not at all extensive - but very useful to me on my journey of understanding - reading around the subject, from within both academic and more personal writing on the subject:

Gendered domestic abuse facts and figures

- In the majority of cases, the perpetrators of domestic abuse are men and the majority of victims are women.
- 89% of those suffering four or more incidents of domestic abuse are women.
- One in four women will experience domestic abuse in their lifetime.
- Domestic abuse currently claims the lives of around two women per week
- The newly recognised form of domestic abuse - coercive control - is gendered, with the vast majority of victims being women.

In *Living Dolls The Return of Sexism,* Natasha Walter writes of an illusion of equality prevailing today. In the following extract she draws together many very different issues still faced by women, including violence and sexual violence and, in as far as arguing that they all add up to the continuing inequality faced by women, connects them:

"[I]f we look more clearly at the current situation, we can see how shaky this illusion of equality really is. To repeat some of the most basic facts: women still do not have the equal political power they have long sought, since only one in five MPs is a woman. They do not have economic equality, since the pay gap is still not only large but actually widening. They do not have the freedom from violence they have sought, and with the conviction rate in rape cases standing at just 6 per cent, they know that rapists enjoy an effective impunity in our society." (Walter 2010: 119)

There are many different ways in which gender inequalities and domestic abuse are connected in theories of domestic abuse. Again, the following are some such theories that I have come across through my reading around the subject, with some of my thoughts following them in brackets:

Gender based theories of domestic abuse

- Domestic abuse is abuse directed against women *because they are women. (beyond vague and thus seems utterly useless to me)*
- *Historic gendered roles* of men and women lead to domestic abuse. (better)
- *Gender inequality* leads to domestic abuse. (too vague)
- *Unequal gendered power relations* leads to domestic abuse. (better)
- *Economic inequalities* between men and women leads to domestic abuse. (better)
- A heterosexual paradigm that perpetuates a gender binary leads to domestic abuse. (too academic)
- Men become perpetrators of domestic

abuse having been *prepared for violence via how they are raised.* (better; very specific and thus helpful; and very, very alarming)

In *Fight Like A Girl*, Clementine Ford argues that since 2001 more women have been killed by their partners than by the politically or religiously motivated terrorists that western political agendas have been fixated on. She points out that such killers are *all individually labelled* 'lone wolves' (i.e. Ford is highlighting an oxymoron here) and argues that their crimes are actually "a symptom of social conditioning that breeds malcontented males". (Ford 2018: 14) This is a gender based theory of domestic abuse that I do not find to be too vague and thus utterly useless or just a bit better than that. It resonated with me (and it alarmed me, as the last point in the list above did). I was not sure exactly why, but it definitely did.

It was at this point that I read three key books on domestic abuse. These books offer extremely detailed gender based arguments for domestic abuse, involving unpicking and explaining gender roles/gender and power/gender and economics etc, with explanations and arguments grounded in actual aspects of daily life and wider culture and developments in society, all of which I recognised, thus they really resonated with me. So these three books are addressed individually in the remainder of this chapter.

In *Coercive Control How Men Entrap Women in Personal Life* (2009) Evan Stark argues that there does not exist a counterpart in men's lives to the entrapment of women by men that we are seeing in women's lives, a process which results from coercive control. He argues that this is because of what is at the root of coercive control: women's gains. That is, coercive control has been devised by men to offset the diminishing of sex-based inequalities in liberal democratic societies. He calls this 'sexism with a vengeance'.

I have to go off on a bit if a tangent here and have a small rant. When I read Stark's argument that men have *devised* coercive control; that perpetrators of coercive control have to go to some *effort* to achieve their malevolent ends - being inventive and experimental, employing trial and error, working alone as there is no guide book or explicit source of support for this endeavour, and applying *multiple technologies* of abuse simultaneously – I found myself smiling. Not because I do not get the serious and sinister nature of all that Stark writes about, I obviously do – hell, I have lived it – but because it almost makes me want to applaud Him for finally mastering the art of multi-tasking. As I have already mentioned, His ability to use more than one abusive tactic at once is the only evidence I have ever found of His having any ability in the multi-tasking arena. To put this in context, remember this is a man who apparently finds answering a question whilst packing His bag for work too stressful, so stressful that it was banned and thus became one of The Rules I Had To Live By.

Lundy Bancroft had worked with over 2000 perpetrators of domestic abuse, over fifteen years, when he wrote *Why Does He Do That? Inside The Minds of Angry and Controlling Men* (2002). His gender based explanation for domestic abuse focuses on power, specifically a power *imbalance*, as continues to exist between women and men. He argues that:

"[P]artner abuse has been found not to exist in societies where males and females have equal power. Thus the defining point of abuse is when the man starts to exercise power over the woman in a way that causes harm to her and creates privileged status for him." (Bancroft 2002: 123-4)

Bancroft goes on to argue that abusive men learn their manipulative and controlling behaviour, and gain their values about couple relationships, from a wide range of sources, including the family and neighbourhoods they grow up in; early training about sex roles and relationships; fairy tales; pornography; popular culture; religious beliefs and (most worryingly) laws and the legal system. He concludes that:

"In sum, an abuser can be thought of not as a man who is 'deviant', but rather as one who has learned society's lessons *too* well, swallowing them whole. He followed too carefully the signposts his culture put out for him marking the path to manhood – at least with respect to relationships with women." (Bancroft 2002: 330, emphasis in original)

In *Living with the Dominator A book about the Freedom Programme* (2008) Pat Craven argues that the Dominator – defined as one man who changes (very fast) into other characters to facilitate the use of different kinds of controlling behaviour – wants to control women due to the hundreds of beliefs which he holds, which stem from the society that he lives in. She thus makes an argument similar to Bancroft's, that the abusive man "is not a deviant but a product of his society". (Craven 2008: 14).

The abuse-enabling beliefs listed by Craven include (take a deep breath) that women are incompetent and cannot cope alone; that women are responsible for men's wellbeing and should mother them; that women are responsible for men's behaviour, including their violence towards them; that women are stupid and can be fooled into thinking that men cannot look after themselves; that women are chattels owned by men, to be used by men for sex and domestic work and child care – but they are incapable of disciplining children - and they need to be trained and kept in order and controlled by any means necessary; that women are inferior to men in every way possible and should be subservient; that women are not human beings; that bullying is normal, okay, not abusive and it works; that violence is permissible; that domestic work and child care are inferior endeavours and thus women's work and 'real men' do not do either; that men have (unending) rights and women and children have none; and that children are accessories which they can see whenever they feel like it, whilst at the same time taking no responsibility for them.

The societal roots of these abuse-enabling beliefs argued by Craven include (take an even deeper breath) parental and other relationships observed by men in childhood imbued with gender roles, inequality and in some cases abuse; men's experiences of being bullied in school; bullying condoned in the armed forces to 'break' soldiers; violent action films in which 'heroes' are violent and rewarded for it (with rewards often including 'getting laid'); the violent behaviour integral to contact sports such as boxing and wrestling; the football culture of victim blaming when one player attacks another; victim blaming and the argument that a woman should 'stand by her man', *whatever*, in popular music; MPs debates in the House of Commons incorporating jeering and interrupting which are known as giving the opponent a 'bloody nose', thus co-opting the language of violent contact sports; famous and very highly paid presenters on news and current affairs programmes browbeating interviewees; religious institutions promoting the idea of women being inferior to men via reluctance to ordain them; the persisting gender pay gap promoting the same; the courts granting access to even the most abusive of fathers; generations of media and political propaganda which stigmatises single mothers living on benefits and raising children whilst casting single fathers in the same situation as nothing short of heroic; political parties supporting traditional married two parent families and thus discounting the effects of male abuse on thousands of women and children; the abundance of derogatory terms for women (what *is* the equivalent of 'cunt'? I would *love* to know); the even more abundant jokes about women; the fact that men call other men 'girl' or 'woman' to *insult* them; popular terminology that suggests women are pieces of meat, such 'cattle market' for a club and 'mutton dressed as lamb' for a woman that a man believes is not dressed well/age appropriately; clubs that reinforce the idea of women not being full, equal members of society by refusing them entry; the media reinforcing the idea that women are subservient, second class citizens by using them to sell cleaning products far more often than using men (men do design and then advertise Manly Cleaning Machines though, of course, for example, vacuum cleaners, mentioning no names); the word 'housewife' implying that women should stay in the home; some religions reinforcing the message that women are sexual property, for example some Mormons have several wives; photographs of naked or scantily clad women being used to sell a wide range of items (that have nothing to do with women or even sex); historic social norms such as 'the rule of thumb' (archaic but who does not know what this supposedly means?); the traditional marriage ceremony in which women promised to 'love, honour and *obey*'; and in WWII women did *everything* that men did, then were forced back into the domestic sphere with the help of propaganda about how *awful* paid work is and how *destiny fulfilling* it is to look after a poor man who has the misfortune of having to do such work.

I felt that I had to recreate Craven's long lists of abuse enabling beliefs and their societal roots here because I believe it is the sheer quantity of both, especially of the root causes, that makes her argument, her book, so chilling and thus brilliantly useful for understanding the gendered nature of domestic abuse.

Significantly, the Draft Domestic Abuse Bill recognises and is intended to take action on these root causes of domestic abuse, as the following two extracts illustrate:

"We want to challenge the social attitudes that allow domestic abuse to occur. By making domestic abuse socially unacceptable in any form, we can start to prevent abuse before it happens, rather than repairing the damage once it has occurred." (HM Government: Transforming the Response to Domestic Abuse: Consultation Response and Draft Bill, January 2019, p14)

"We will work to tackle harmful gender norms, in recognition that all forms of violence against women and girls are both a cause and a consequence of wider gender inequality. Through the refreshed Violence Against Women and Girls Strategy, we are embarking on an ambitious programme to tackle restrictive and harmful gender norms, with a focus on working with the advertising industry on body image and through working with men and boys to challenge harmful attitudes." (HM Government: Transforming the Response to Domestic Abuse: Consultation Response and Draft Bill, January 2019, p15)

Craven's book included another argument, one which I initially struggled with. At the beginning of her Dominator book, Craven argues that women living in the same society as men are subject to the same conditioning as men and thus may hold many of the abuse enabling beliefs. She then goes on to explain that when she began to formulate her argument about the Dominator she came to the realisation that she had unintentionally colluded with every abusive man she had ever met. I found this startling and confusing when I first read it.

Further on in the book there is an illustration (by Jacky Fleming) of a man dropping a dirty sock on the floor. The caption reads "dirty laundry goes on the floor and eventually reappears clean in the cupboard. INCREDIBLE." (Craven 2008: 78) When I turned the page and saw this captioned illustration for the first time I felt incredibly sick and I can only assume that all of the colour drained from my face (I will never know, because I do not read and write in front of a mirror). Then I started to feel incredibly angry. Angry with the society I live in but mostly angry with myself. His father sent Him a birthday card with this 'joke' on it a few years ago, *and we both found it funny*. For me, right then in that nausea-inducing moment, I understood and one hundred per cent believed Craven's theory of the roots of the domestic abuse experienced by women being located in the society they live in, in its culture and history. And I was angry with myself because, like Craven, I recognised my complicity with the devastating process. This was pretty tough to take.

My believing (as I have already said, probably on some level by choice) that I was caught up in an age old gender inequality concerning time – the division of labour, domestic work, family work, leisure time, etc. . - began to seem a bit less dumb to me, when I read these three detailed theories about why gender and gender inequalities – encompassing all the old familiar issues of patriarchy, gender power imbalances, traditional gender roles and economic inequality - are intrinsic to domestic abuse, especially to one form of it - coercive control - that I had been living with. This is summed up brilliantly in these two extracts from Evan Stark's book on coercive control:

"Torture, kidnapping, and brainwashing are rare events that leave no doubt in a victim's mind about their risk. But the core tactics in coercive control build on practices that are governed by gender norms in relationships, such as ceding major financial decisions to men or quitting work to "make a home", or target devalued activities to which women are already consigned, like cooking, cleaning, and child care. When men extend these prerogatives in an abusive regimen… there is enormous ambiguity about where appropriate expectations end and risk begins, even if the woman feels unsafe." (Stark 2009: 210-11)

"Control often is literally hidden "behind closed doors."… it can also be difficult to detect because its means and effects merge with behaviours widely associated with women's devalued status in personal life – being deferential, thrifty, thin, and unnoticed. The tactics involved are easily confused with the range of sacrifices women are expected to make in their role as homemakers, parents, and sexual partners." (Stark 2009: 229-30)

So I began to seem a bit less dumb (at least to myself). Yes, I was abused for over a decade whilst all the time believing it was 'just' pesky old traditional gender inequality at play. However, it turns out that I am not quite as thick as I had begun to believe that I was, because this *is* intrinsic to my experience of domestic abuse (yay?).

I have further evidence of my not being quite as thick as I had begun to believe that I was.

Stuffocation, Minimalism and My Undergraduate Dissertation

As the writing of this book was drawing to a close and I began working on the diagrams for it, I began reading for pleasure. Unable to read novels i.e. stories, still – which I put down to two things: my being too absorbed in my own story and also my not being able to sufficiently relax to do it – I began to devour *non-fiction* books for pleasure. I spiralled off from the books that I read into various projects concerning my clothes, my finances, my cooking and my home, or rather my over-stuffed home. I read an astonishing book called *Stuffocation: Living More With Less* (2015) by James Wallman. This spurred me on to go further with my on-going project of clearing out from my home – and passing on – anything and everything that we do not need. It felt great. Clearing out every drawer, cupboard, room and floor of my home was beyond cathartic. So it was a sad day for me (probably because I am a bit sad, and not in the unhappy sense) when I realised that I had nothing left to clear out and pass on. The work was done. The family home was un-stuffed and as minimalist as it possibly could be (I own too many pairs of shoes to ever be able to declare myself an actual minimalist).

Then I remembered I owned vases! I owned four of the damn things and I do not even like receiving flowers – because they shed and then die so I find them pointless. More to the point, I have never received more than two bunches of flowers at any one time. So some maths I can do (there will be more): I passed on two of my vases. So I was definitely all finished at that point.

Then I spoke to my lovely colleague Sharon in work who told me she had managed to clear out boxes of Very Important and Special Paperwork and Things that she had been moving from house to house to house whilst never opening, ever. I felt a bit competitive (stupidly) and that weekend I unearthed the two huge boxes of Very Important and Special Paperwork and Things that I had been moving from house to house to house whilst never opening. Unsurprisingly, the two huge boxes were 90% full of absolute nonsense which I won't bore you (further) with. But one contained selected pieces of work from my undergraduate degree in sociology and social policy. These works included my long forgotten (HTF?) undergraduate dissertation on domestic violence. It was an illuminating find.

This is the snappy, memorable title of my undergraduate dissertation: *Domestic Violence Past and Present: What has changed? A comparison of women's demands and the state's response to domestic violence in the nineteenth and twentieth centuries via a comparison of the Matrimonial Causes Act of 1878 and the Domestic Proceedings and Magistrate's Courts Act of 1978*

And this is my concluding point (which is only marginally longer than the title):

"Domestic violence is not merely an economic issue, whereby giving women the right to occupy the marital home will alleviate it. Rather, *it is an issue of men's ideological power, beliefs, opinions, perceptions and explanations.* In comparing the nineteenth and twentieth centuries via a comparison of two pieces of legislation, I have attempted to demonstrate that *it is this that lies at the root of domestic violence.*" (Willmot H, 1997, The University of Leeds, emphasis added)

My own argument, from over twenty years ago, takes me right back to the abuse-enabling beliefs and the societal roots of these abuse-enabling beliefs listed (or rather very *long* listed) by Pat Craven, and cited above. So I already knew all of this, that is, I knew it *intellectually/academically*. What a shame it was of little use to me in the real world. Whilst I find the following extract from Pat Craven's book beyond depressing, I wanted to end this chapter with a more positive point than that last one:

"[I]n Britain a violent partner kills a woman every three

days. (London Home Office 2007). The depressing thing for me is that since I started the Freedom Programme in 1999 those statistics have not changed. Historically, most men who kill their female partners have been convicted of manslaughter instead of murder and consequently receive very short sentences.Abusive men have been reading the message that it is easier to kill your wife than to divorce her and you will probably get to keep the house." (Craven 2008: 21)

Lucky, lucky me (I do not mean this flippantly; I am serious): I am not dead *and* I have kept the house.

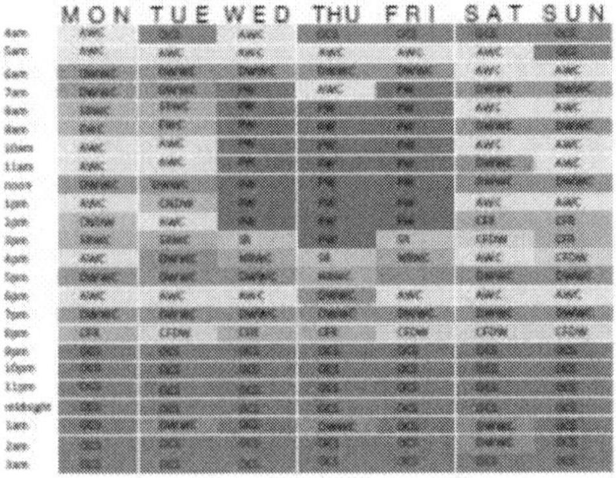

HELEN'S WEEK

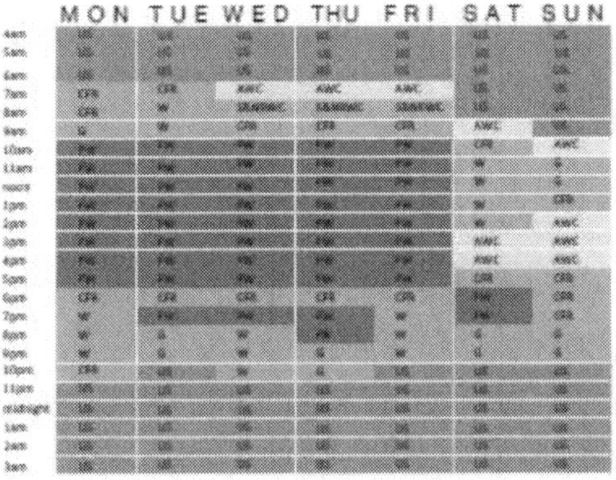

HIS WEEK

HIS
&
HERS
WEEKS

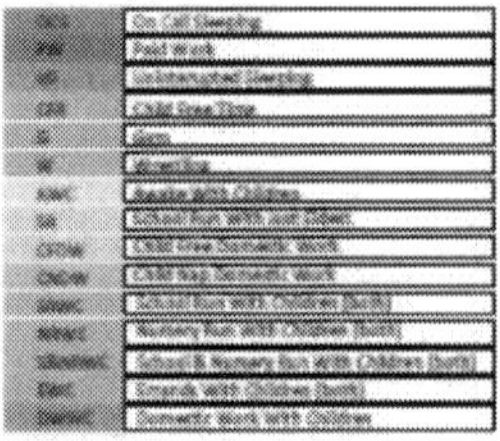

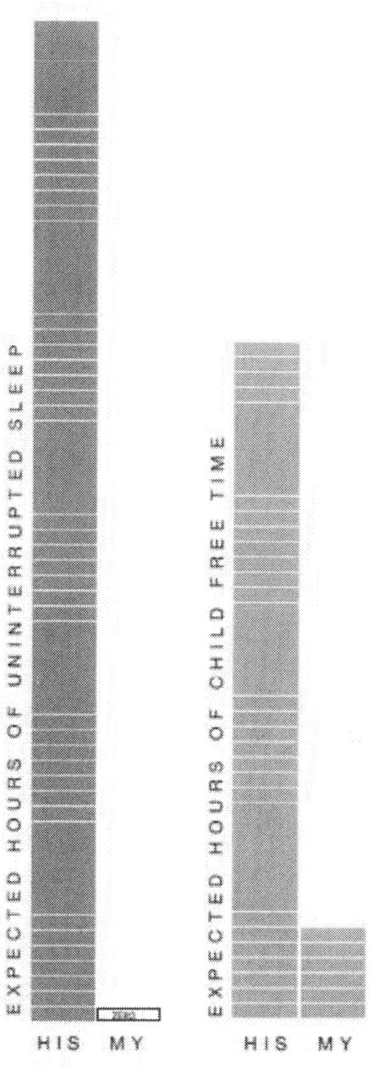
EXPECTED HOURS OF UNINTERRUPTED SLEEP
HIS
MY
EXPECTED HOURS OF CHILD FREE TIME
HIS
MY

FOOD

I want to be the girl with the most cake
I love him so much it just turns to hate
I fake it so real, I am beyond fake
And someday, you will ache like I ache
Doll Parts, Hole

Baking

"Not all feminists have regarded women's traditional skills with contempt; there are feminists who see the home as a creative opportunity, who bake bread and cakes, who knit and sew, who grow fruit and vegetables and make pickles and preserves in the forlorn hope that someone will value the work of their hands above the work of machines. These are the earth mother feminists, flat-footed, broad-hipped figures of fun. The reinvestment of women's traditional fields of expertise with prestige and value is one more feminist cause that is being lost." (Greer, 1999: 79)

He did not value the work of my hands.

Baking is how I express my love for people - my children, my wider family, my friends, my neighbours, my colleagues, basically everyone I know and love. It was a hobby born from love. My great, great love for my paternal grandad. I adored him. He was sweet, self-deprecating, funny, kind, clever, humble, interesting and interested in everything his grandchildren brought into his life. When one of us discovered a new band or record that we liked he would give us a blank cassette tape (yes, I am very old) and ask us to make him a copy so he could listen to it. Nine times out of ten he would hate the music. But he always, always wanted to listen, to see if he might like the new music that we grandchildren so adored. A quote from the American musician Frank Zappa captures him "A mind is like a parachute. It doesn't work if it is not open." I loved how his (great) mind worked. He once bought a Velvet Underground CD purely because it had a banana on the front of it, because he loved bananas, then was genuinely surprised and disappointed when it turned out not to be his cup of tea. He was adorable. I adored him. And he *got* me, no one else ever had. We were peas in a pod.

My grandad had a sweet tooth. A very sweet tooth. He used to say that he cleaned his teeth with a toffee every night (an interesting habit for a man whose eldest child was a dentist). My grandma would bake delicious cakes, pies and puddings which he devoured. As she became older and less able to do this for him I was entrenched in my doctoral research and was not able to visit them as regularly as I would have liked to have done. To show that I cared and was thinking of them I would bake and send what I had made to them. My grandad started to say I should start a cake business. He persisted. I brushed this idea off, for years. I was doing my Ph.D. I wanted to be a researcher, an academic, a Sociologist, I was never going to start a cake business, *obviously*.

However, eventually, inevitably, of course, shortly after my beloved grandad passed away, this is exactly what I did. I researched and developed and set up and ran a cake business. I started out with a stall at the fortnightly Leeds Farmers Market and built it up from there to a full time venture. The Helen Francis Cake Company was named after the two people at the heart of it - myself and my grandad – and it was a business with a big heart. It was a true labour of love. I worked very hard, six days a week, for over five years, and I loved doing so. But once I became a mother, I wanted a balance between work and home. I scaled the business back in preparation for motherhood. After our daughter was born, I never went back to baking for a living.

Baking thus reverted to being a much loved hobby, something I did purely for pleasure, which for me meant baking purely for loved ones. A good friend passed on an article by Julie R Thompson for The Huffington Post entitled '*Psychologists Explain The Benefits of Baking For Other People. It's not just about giving them something sweet*.' Thompson's opening point sums me and baking up perfectly:

"People who bake use any excuse to heat up their ovens. They bake a cake to crown someone's birthday, labor over cookies to celebrate a holiday, and whip up brownies because everyone loves chocolate." (Thompson J R)

I bake for any and all occasions and reasons: births, birthdays, weddings, anniversaries, bereavements, people leaving work, teachers leaving my daughter's school, the regular brunch with my neighbours, team meetings at my work, when I need to say thank you to someone, for Easter and for Christmas.

I also bake for me. In her article, Thompson goes on to argue that a host of psychological benefits accompany baking, especially when it is done for others. These include stress relief; mindfulness; and creative expression which is linked to overall wellbeing, with the selflessness and altruism of baking for others heightening such feelings of wellbeing. The saying 'there is no selfless good deed' springs to mind. I bake to express my love for people but *I* also feel very good when I bake for others, *I* get something wonderful out of it, it is a form of self-care, so when I bake I do it also for me.

Coffee and Cakes

I have never been particularly demanding, I don't think, not greedy for the finer things in life. I have never craved (or actively sought) a lifestyle involving meals in fancy restaurants, of which there are plenty in Leeds where I live. The only food cravings I have ever had have been during my two pregnancies. They can be summarised as cheddar cheese and carbohydrates with my daughter and cheddar cheese, carbohydrates and curry – not all together - with my son, alongside a complete aversion to anything resembling fresh food with both pregnancies. I did, however, during my relationship with Him, begin to fantasise about beans on toast. I fantasised, daydreamed, enthusiastically imagined, a life where I could put off food shopping if I had been very busy and was exhausted, a life where myself and my partner would declare ourselves too tired to cook and decide to *just have beans on toast for tea*. Bliss.

Heaven. Nirvana. The holy grail. A strange fantasy, to an outsider, maybe, but there was a reason for it.

He only eats certain foods. Every week I had to buy all the right foods for Him. This was my weekly shopping list for Him (another list, this one not beloved, just typing it I found chilling and I have not bought a tub of cottage cheese since I left Him, despite the fact that I do actually like it):

The Food I Had To Buy For Him Every Week

- 28 tubs of cottage cheese – plain or with chives, *not* with pineapple
- 5 jars of pesto – green *not* red
- 2 big bags of spinach
- 2 packets of tomatoes *on the vine*
- Gorgonzola cheese or goats cheese, *not* mild cheeses such as Brie or Camembert
- 10 packets of cashew nuts, *not* salted
- 5 packets of coffee, *not* decaffeinated (and I was often chastised for not buying Fair Trade, which I find interesting, to say the least: worried about people He does not know toiling in slave labour in far flung places but enjoying the many, many benefits of His very own skivvy AKA slave in His own home)
- 8 bottles of sugar free peach squash, *not* any other flavour
- 2 bags of porridge oats
- 4 packets of frozen berries, *not* summer fruits
- A selection of dried fruits

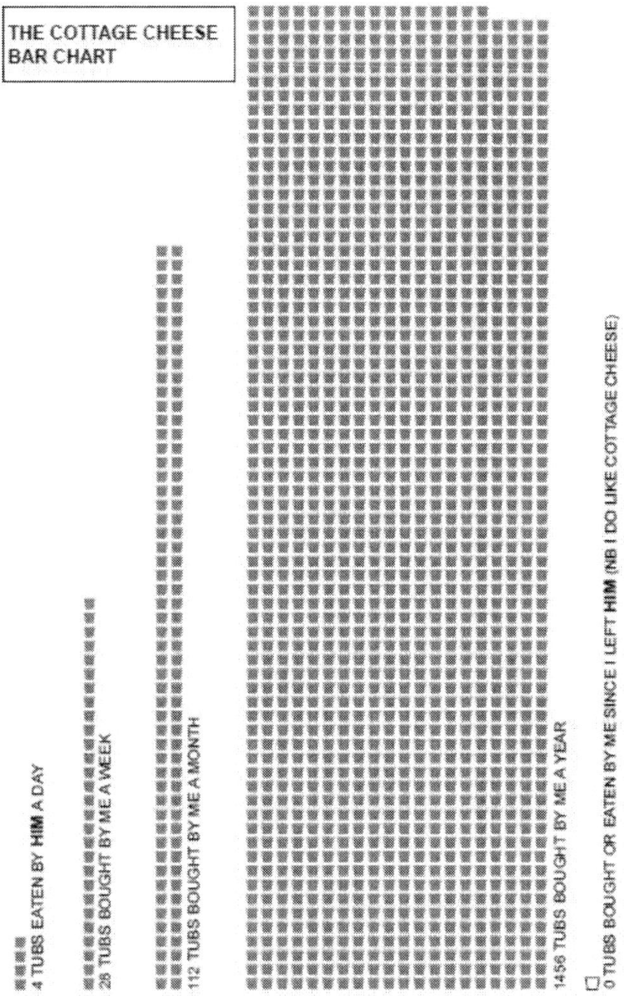
THE COTTAGE CHEESE BAR CHART
4 TUBS EATEN BY HIM A DAY
28 TUBS BOUGHT BY ME A WEEK
112 TUBS BOUGHT BY ME A MONTH
1456 TUBS BOUGHT BY ME A YEAR
0 TUBS BOUGHT OR EATEN BY ME SINCE I LEFT HIM (NB I DO LIKE COTTAGE CHEESE)

Unfitting my kitchen was a long held dream of mine. I defy anyone *not* to have had this dream had they moved into the house when we did. The onslaught of beige that was the kitchen was the opposite to sensory overload, whatever that is. I can say that wearing a blind fold and being sat in a very quiet room would have given my senses more to work with and enjoy than the kitchen did. I detest fitted kitchens, it is true, but this particular fitted kitchen was beyond detestable. How the designers managed to get so much beige into one kitchen, into one space, defies belief. The word bland is too vibrant and exciting to describe the room. Over several years, I collected eclectic, mismatched, vintage pieces with which to unfit the kitchen. Eventually, I found an incredible carpenter to do the work, who added to the mix a vintage, sky blue, Formica work top from an old school science lab. As I love things with a history, this work top ticked that box as well as making me feel like a dreamy 1950s housewife (which I know feminist-politically is a very bad, probably inaccurate and totally inappropriate thing to say, but it is the bizarre effect the work top has on me. Sorry. Given that it is from an old school science lab anyway this fantasy is a load of inaccurate old nonsense anyway).

"Creating a house and home provides most people with their greatest opportunity to express their tastes and preferences in a substantial and long-lasting way. Status, for some, will always be an issue, but building surroundings that have character and personality is ultimately more satisfying, rewarding and meaningful.

Homes are for living in." (Kiely 2012: 253)

Add to the end of this quote 'and feeding people in' and Orla Kiely could have written it about me. When hunting for a family home I had one key requirement of any house that we bought: the kitchen had to be the biggest room in the house. I am a home body. I don't want to go out in to the world. I want (representatives of) the world to come to my house, my home, my nest, my Best Nest, so I can feed them in it - especially with cake. For me, the unfitting of the kitchen enabled me to put my stamp on the heart of my home, the space where I spend the vast majority of my (awake) time in pursuit of the cooking and the baking with which I nurture all of my relationships by showing loved ones that they are exactly that: loved. For Him, the unfitting of the kitchen meant only one thing: the fitting in of a GIANT fridge in which to store His enormous weekly intake of foods – His quota of 28 tubs of cottage cheese per week alone took up one quarter of the space in the GIANT fridge.

Doggedly doing the weekly shop was not enough. If we ran out of anything He would become angry, ask me why we had run out, why did I not buy enough, was the shop low on stock, did I not try a second shop? Shopping with two small children is stressful and, given that I was granted very little time for myself, I was loathed to shop in it (I never dared to point this out to Him). I would do top up shops in a panic, to ensure that we did not run out of the things He wanted, when out with the children during the weekend or before or after a school run during the week.

The Christmas of 2016 was a 'His family Christmas' so I organised a pre-Christmas weekend celebration with my family. When I told Him of the plan, the dates, He asked if He could still go to the gym that weekend. I said yes (I never said no). Then He asked if He could go to His gym Christmas celebration that weekend. I said yes (like I said, I never said no). I cooked and baked and hosted the weekend. He interacted minimally with my family. He was out a lot (see above) and when He was home He got on with 'urgent' work.

I did one of my panic top up shops on the second day of the pre-Christmas weekend celebration with my family, dashing into the nearby M&S whilst out for a walk to buy spinach and cottage cheese and coffee. M&S prices meant that I grabbed coffee that was on offer that day, because it was affordable. It was Half And Half Coffee: half caffeinated and half decaffeinated. He commented how nice the coffee was. *To this day, I will never know how my life might have unfolded had I not said what I did.* I said "It is Half And Half coffee". He looked angry. Later that day I realised He was extremely angry, could barely look at me, was not speaking to me. I asked Him what was wrong. He said He could not talk about it. I insisted (very bravely I feel). He explained (and then some). He said I had rolled the red carpet out for my family and made five different cakes for them but bought coffee I *knew* that He would hate. I pointed out that He had commented how nice it was. He said that was not the point (WTF?). He said it was half decaffeinated and I *knew* He only drank caffeinated coffee.

I was devastated. I was heartbroken. I was confused (yet again). It was the most surreal moment of my life. I was shocked. No, I was beyond shocked. I was *in* shock. I truly believe I went into some kind of shock. I have Googled being 'in shock' and apparently I cannot argue that I went into shock in the *medical* sense. Damn it; I felt terrible. However, His behaviour, His definition of a transgression, His response to a situation, His treatment of me, were all so alien to me, to everything I had ever experienced and that I understood to be right and acceptable and 'normal', that I believe I must surely have experienced a form of *culture* shock that day. I looked it up. Its synonyms in the Cambridge English Dictionary ring very true for the state I found myself in that afternoon (another beloved list then):

'Culture shock' synonyms

- Addled
- At sea
- Confused
- Disorientated
- Dizzy
- Not knowing what has hit you (as I have already said, looking back, I wish He had actually hit me)
- Not knowing which way to turn
- Off balance

I took the kids to my friend's house where I sobbed

uncontrollably. She said I was already basically a single mother. She said I would be better off without Him. But I was not ready to hear this. I returned to the family home (obviously, where else was I going to go?).

"The injection of high levels of fear into the ordinary round of daily life and the difficulty in fixing its source are among the most remarkable features of coercive control." (Stark 2009: 211)

I discovered I was still being sent to Coventry. So I plonked the children in front of the TV and ran over to my neighbour and asked for a packet of caffeinated coffee - I needed to fix the source of this particular problem, I was definitely too scared to be at home with Him without having rectified my mistake: scared of more of His deafening silence followed by the inevitable two pronged interrogation about why I bought the coffee I did (i.e. why did I make yet another domestic mistake?) and when I would be going out and buying the correct coffee (i.e. when would I be rectifying my latest in a long line of domestic mistakes?) For the first time I said out loud what I had long been feeling, that I hated Him. His jealous fury at all of the baking I had done for the pre-Christmas weekend with my family was not just unkind, it attacked my very core, my essence, what makes me me. It felt like definitive proof that He did not get me, worse: He did not like me, and worse still: He did not love me. Because He *could* not love me. Because with His nasty, bitter, jealous, rant He trashed my love for my family and for myself and for me. He trashed me. But I also said to my neighbour that I could never, *would* never, break up my family, end of story (luckily it wasn't). My neighbour hugged me as I cried and told me that it would all be okay (luckily it is getting there, eventually). I dried my eyes and returned home with the caffeinated coffee. It went down quite well.

Porridge (AKA Oats: Latin Name: Avena sativa)

"Nothing in this world is at it seems. Except, possibly, porridge." (Stephen Fry)

Recipe One: Super Lonely Porridge For One

Ingredients

- One cup of porridge oats
- 2 cups of milk
- 2 tbsp ground flaxseed
- 2 tbsp wheatgerm
- 1 grated apple
- 1 mashed banana
- A handful of any dried fruits
- A sprinkling of any nuts and seeds

Method

- Stir the porridge oats and milk on the stove until the desired consistency.
- Add the fresh fruit.

- Add the dried fruit, nuts and seeds.
- Add the flaxseed and wheatgerm.
- Eat alone.

The beyond surreal experience that will forever be referred to as 'Coffeegate' was December 2016. I did not leave Him until October 2017. In those ten intervening months I lost my appetite, to put it mildly. My appetite had evaporated. I could not face eating. It just kept happening, or rather not happening. Food became unnecessary. Why? Because I could not enjoy it. Because I was numb. Because I was basically a zombie and so I could not see the point of food: why feed a zombie, it is already dead?

By the time I had left Him and moved Him out and bought Him out, I took up less space. I weighed less. Was it just that I felt like a zombie or was something more sinister taking place? I was so low, so riddled with low self-esteem and low self-worth, was I, on some level (a theory which assumes that I have more than one level, and I am not at all sure that I do) actively trying to take up less space, to shrink away, to disappear? Because if I disappeared I could no longer be abused, could I? (NB Clementine Ford writes of this practice in *Fight Like A Girl* and argues it is a form of self-harm).

The Zombie Theory and the Shrinking Myself Into Complete Disappearance Theory are both perhaps a trifle too dramatic (no food-pun intended). Clementine Ford sums up another theory which is perhaps more realistic for my story:

"Being thin is good. Being thin is healthy. Being thin is pretty. Being thin will make boys like you. Being thin will solve all your problems. **Being thin means you are in control**. And never underestimate how fiercely girls will grab onto the opportunity to feel in control of *something* in their lives." (Ford 2018: 45, italics in original; over the top bold and underlining combination my doing)

In his work on kindness, David Hamilton explores the *science* of kindness and this involves quite a lot of biology. Much of it relates to oxytocin, AKA the 'love hormone' which is released and floods our bodies when we are in love and also, Hamilton argues, when we perform acts of kindness. He also argues that it aids digestion:

"[T]he whole food-processing system needs oxytocin. And so our relationships with each other, which maintain oxytocin levels in the brain and body, actually play a role in how the body processes food. A kind attitude and healthy relationships equate to a healthy gut." (Hamilton 2010: 88)

I do think I shrank myself most likely in a bid to be able to make some choices in my micro-managed, uber-controlled existence, to be in control of something, anything, just one damn thing. And I can also say, hand on heart, that my appetite *does* go, leave me, evaporate, disappear, get the hell out of the equation, when I start to feel emotional pain. Maybe it does so because my body ceases to be *able to* deal with food?

However relevant these two theories actually are for me, I did not actually disappear (obviously).This is because of porridge. I could face eating porridge. Maybe because Stephen Fry is right, so it helped me when I was living so damn confused. It made sense to me. Porridge became my involuntary diet. It was like one of those milkshake diets: I simply replaced two meals with a nutritious bowl of porridge and then ate a 'normal' meal for my third meal (this 'normal' meal was porridge too, by the way). I cooked a wide variety of foods for my children and would cook and bake for just about everyone I could, at the drop of a hat, but all I really wanted to feed myself was porridge. I was elated when a Polish café opened in the town where I work. It sold the most delicious porridge full of fresh and dried fruits and nuts and seeds. Exquisite too: miniature bowl based works of art. Delicious and exquisite, what was not to like?

I even read up on the history of oats. I learnt that oats probably originate from a wild oat that grew in the Fertile crescent of the Middle East and that the oldest known oat grains are probably those found in Egypt and date from around 2000 BC. The earliest cultivation was probably during the Bronze Age, in caves in Switzerland. Cultivation spread but oats were often considered weeds, fit only for animals to consume. Scotland, however, appreciated the oat and, starting from medieval times, it became a diet staple there. Oats were introduced to North America by the Pilgrim Fathers in the early 1600s and were a commercial hit when the Quaker Mill Company, based in Ohio, began mass marketing them in the late 19th century. Fascinating, I thought. Delicious and exquisite and with a history – I do so love things with a history, this is why I buy everything that I possibly can pre-loved – even better.

Eventually, when shrinking and worried, I read up on the health benefits of oats. There were so many big words in the following account in *SuperFoods. Fourteen foods that will change your life*, most of which I cannot pronounce, that I was instantly believing of the theory:

"It's time for a renewal of interest in the power of oats. New discoveries, combined with what's been known about oats for years, have shown that their health-promoting powers are truly impressive. Oats are low in calories, high in fibre and protein. They're a rich source of magnesium, potassium, zinc, copper, manganese, selenium, thiamine and pantothenic acid. They also contain phytonutrients such as polyphenols, phytoestrogens, lignins, protease inhibitors and vitamin E (they're an excellent source of tocotrienels and multiple tocopherols – important members of the vitamin E family). The synergy of the nutrients in oats makes them an outstanding and formidable SuperFood. Indeed, the degree of protection against disease offered by oats and other whole grains is greater than that of any of their ingredients taken in isolation. In addition to their power to reduce disease and extend your health span, oats are a flagship SuperFood for practical reasons: they're inexpensive, readily available and incredibly easy to incorporate into your life... if you only remember to eat a bowl of oats regularly, you'll be on your way to better health." (Pratt S and Matthews K 2004:98)

Yay! I was on my way to better health then. Funny that I did not feel particularly healthy.

Oats can do truly marvellous things: they sustain energy (via low GI, slow-release complex carbohydrates); reduce heart disease and some forms of cancer (via phytonutrients); lower cholesterol (via the soluble fibre beta glucan); and the same soluble fibre that lowers cholesterol (so huge it needed re-stating) seems to benefit those who suffer from type II diabetes.

OK then, definitely some long-term health benefits at least.

Delicious and exquisite and with a cool history and mind bogglingly good for you too. Even better: my staple diet was a Super Food. More than this, actually, according to Pratt and Matthews, oats appear to be a Super Hero complete with not one but *two* Side Kicks (think Danger Mouse with *two* Penfolds; or if you are not middle aged like I am, please insert a more recent Super Hero and Side Kick example):

"An unusual feature of oats is that they have two 'Super Sidekicks': ground flaxseed and wheat germ. The Super Sidekicks really belong in a very special category because they're so nutrient-dense. Both offer super benefits in very small amounts. If you add just 2 tablespoons each of ground flaxseed and wheat germ each day to your cereal [in my case porridge, obviously] you will be on your way to better health." (Pratt S and Matthews K 2004:101)

Wow, I thought. I went out and bought ground flaxseed and wheat germ from my local health food store and became nutrient-dense, or dense for short. Because living on porridge was not really a good idea, was it? It constitutes disordered eating, doesn't it? Actually, I think it constituted *comfort* eating.

'The type of food that people eat when they are sad or worried, often sweet food or food that people ate as children.' (Definition of 'comfort food' in the Cambridge English Dictionary)

This definition of comfort food summed up why I was eating porridge, or rather existing on it. I put sweet things (rather than the alternative salt) on my porridge, but I did not eat it as a child, I was not harking back to a happier time (besides, a memoir about my school years would illustrate that my childhood was simply not a happier time). It is the reasons given for eating it within this definition which resonate with me: I felt sad and I felt worried, and I felt both of these things most of the time, amongst many other equally distressing emotions. Comfort food is often written about by those who produce recipe books. None more sensually and evocatively than Nigella Lawson:

"If I'm being honest, for me all food is comfort food, but there are times when you need a bowlful of something hot or a slice of something sweet just to make you feel that the world is a safer place. We all get tired, stressed, sad or lonely, and this is the food that soothes." (Lawson 2001: 31)

The world did *not* feel like a safe place for a long time, even the world inside my home did not feel like a safe place for a long time. And I was tired, stressed, sad *and* lonely. And bowls of something hot – porridge - did sooth me. They still do. Just not quite so often.

Super Healthy Bars AKA H Bars

I adapted a recipe I found in one of my recipe books one day. It became a staple in my house. This is because it was a way to move beyond my (too much) porridge eating and consume more fruits and vegetables. It remains a staple in my house to this day. This is because it not only helps me but is also a way to get my children to consume more fruits and vegetables – topping them with chocolate aids this goal no end. Marketing them to children as Healthy Bars is a dumb idea, friends have pointed out, hence they became known as H Bars.

Recipe Two: H Bars

Ingredients

- 50g/2oz butter
- 2 tbsp crunchy peanut butter
- 3 tbsp honey or maple syrup
- 2 mashed ripe bananas
- 1 grated apple
- 250g/9oz porridge oats
- 185g/7oz blended dried fruits
- 85g/3oz any nuts and seeds
- 100g/4oz milk chocolate

Method

- Preheat the oven to 160C/140C/gas 3.
- Grease and line a 20cm-square baking tin with baking parchment.
- Heat the butter, peanut butter and honey or maple syrup over a low heat, stirring continuously, until melted.
- Add the mashed banana and grated apple*.
- Add 100ml/3.5fl oz boiling water.
- Add the porridge oats, blended dried fruits and nuts and seeds.
- Spoon the mixture into the greased and lined baking tin and press down firmly.
- Bake for 55 minutes.
- During the final 15 minutes of baking, melt the chocolate in a bowl over a pan of water.
- When the H Bars are fully baked, pour the melted chocolate over it and smooth to the edges.
- Leave to cool fully and then cut into bars, the size of your choice.
- Keep in an airtight box in the fridge.
- Serve to anyone and everyone who comes to see you.
- *Substitute with grated carrot, grated courgette or grated pear, whatever your preference, or whatever vegetable or fruit you wish to sneakily get your children to eat via baking it and covering it in chocolate.

Sociable Salad

I stopped buying salad leaves because I went off them and got sick of all of the necessary washing and drying of the damn things and I hated the way that, left over in the fridge, they curl up and die (further) and become (more) unappetising (in my opinion) if not wholly inedible (ditto). Plus I had given my beautiful vintage, patent pending, 1970s salad spinner to Him when I moved Him out, because He needed it more than I did, eating enormous quantities of spinach (in-keeping with my do unto others... etc... motto - a lot more on this later). One day I decided to grate a courgette to form the basis of my salad instead. Grated courgette salad has become a new favourite – and healthier - comfort food and has had a ripple effect amongst my neighbours and friends and family.

I have (without seeking to and thus without trying to) converted just about everyone I know to my grated courgette salad. My friend David's mother has been converted and not only loves it but it became part of the health kick she wanted to pursue. When David asked if he could bring his father round to meet me he requested I make the salad for him to try. I have been asked for the 'recipe' many, many times by friends and family. This seems to be an odd question to me, given that you can see all of the ingredients quite clearly in the salad bowl. A salad is not a cake which involves the mysterious alchemy of the transformation of butter, sugar, eggs and flour into far, far more than the sum of those four disappeared parts. I would always write out the 'recipe' when asked to, of course.

I renamed my grated courgette salad 'Sociable Salad' because this is what it will forever be associated with in my mind: starting life as a single mother and being as sociable as possible as often as possible; filling my house whenever possible with people to feed, always with a box of this salad ready in the fridge, to ward off the evils of loneliness. I love Tom Hodgkinson's advice in *How To Be Free* on how to banish loneliness:

"Life is easier when shared with others. Guests are wonderful things; they entertain us, they bring wine and cheese; they bring their children so our children can play. We talk together about our problems; the women complain together about the men; and the men complain together about the women. Burdens are eased by being shared." (Hodgkinson 2006: 179)

Earlier in this chapter I gave my recipe for porridge for one, my solitary, quite lonely, actually very lonely, comfort food. I finish it with another recipe for another comfort food - because it seems to comfort those I share it with - a *sociable* one, so the polar opposite to lonely, then. Hence the name.

Recipe Three: Sociable Salad

Ingredients

- 2 grated courgettes
- Chopped cucumber
- Chopped celery
- 1 can of chick peas
- 1 jar of black olives

- I jar of sundried tomatoes

Method

- Serve with any salad dressing and roasted broccoli.
- Serve to as many people as you can fit around your table, as often as you can.

MATHS

Mathematics is a difficult thing
I never understood what was the missing link
And by the time I calculated the correct solution
The question had escaped me and so did the conclusion
So tell me everything must always equal two
Or nothing else is true
And I'll believe you
Cos your X is equal to my Y
But equations pass me by
Mathematics, Little Boots

The Meet Cute

In film and television, a meet cute is a scene in which a future romantic couple meets for the first time. (Wikipedia)

This story starts when I was 29 years old. I met a man on a counselling skills course. The only young man on the course of predominantly older women – He was 25 and must have lowered the average age of the course participants by at least a decade. He walked in late to the first class and the word 'wow' popped into my head. Actually, it was more like '**<u>WOW!!!</u>**'. To put this in context, I am not a woman who goes around thinking '**<u>WOW!!!</u>**' or even 'wow' when I clap eyes on men I find attractive. This was a totally new experience to me. It turned out that He was a health support worker. He had studied psychology. He was ditzy and disorganised (hence the whole being late for the first class). He was funny, cynical and clever. And He seemed really sweet. And did I mention that He was the only man on a counselling course? A counselling course seemingly designed to attract just about every demographic bar His, especially middle aged women, elderly women and gay women.

I fell in love with Him over the year long course, across the giant classroom, in which we all sat in a giant circle gawping at each other. By the penultimate class I knew I could not never see Him again and feared He would avoid like the plague the final class which was to be a bring-and-share fuddle. So I confided in another woman on the course. From my behaviour she had no idea how I felt about this man. But she was sure He was besotted with me. She played cupid. He attended the fuddle. We arranged to go to the celebratory end of course night out together. Later that evening, we ended up wordlessly getting together. This is not a euphemism, for anything. We simply wordlessly morphed into a couple whilst sat on His tiny sofa talking. Then He walked me home. It was, at that point in my life, the most intensely beautiful experience I had ever had.

So we were in love. We had fallen in love with each other across the room of a counselling course, each believing the other would never feel the same in a million years. He was besotted with me, as the course mate had deduced. He adored me. He was impressed by my intellect. He thought I was beautiful. He thought I was kind when I would buy and cook His favourite foods when He came to my house (yes, I get the sick irony here). And so it began. Two years of seeing each other. Of His arriving unannounced at my house many times because He just could not wait until the next time we had arranged to see each other. He gradually introduced me to His friends, who let slip that He had said I was "the one".

We joined a gym and exercised together. We used to joke that 'the couple who exercises together stays together'. We shared a sense of humour and would get stoned together watching the likes of *Peep Show*, *The Mighty Boosh* and *Flight of The Conchords*. His friends loved me. His family adored me – and said they worried about Him less now He had someone to look after Him. I don't think my friends had ever seen me so happy. It was after we had completed the counselling course that we had met on that I began researching and developing my first business. He was impressed with my skills, my attention to detail, my commitment and my passion. After two years I agreed that He could move in with me. Life carried on much the same. I was happy. I felt loved. No, I felt *adored*.

The Question Mark

The first incident occurred whilst we were living together in my house. I had slipped into the habit of doing His laundry along with mine. For so many reasons: it was my house, my domestic sphere, my washing machine; I am a very domestic creature; I am a nurturer (and an idiot). I say I did His laundry along with mine, but I did a lot more than this. I washed His endless gym kits. Not just daily. Very often, there was more than one kits load in a day. It was not just a case of my doing His laundry if and when I was working on my own laundry and shared laundry such as bedding, the issue was it became my sole *responsibility* to ensure that His vast array of gym kits were washed and dried and ready whenever He needed them. It became unstated. It became background work. It became something I found myself second guessing and panicking about. The gym, His fitness, His body, all so important to Him, and it was up to me and only me to ensure that He was always gym-ready.

He became incredibly angry one evening that I had hung up His gym kits in the kitchen on the ceiling drying rack and then begun cooking onions. It was so much more than anger, actually, He was enraged. He tore the laundry down. He made me vow that I would never make that mistake again. It shocked me. I was stunned. Stunned and confused (yes, again). And embarrassed. This first incident took place in front of a friend of mine. I was more than embarrassed, I was ashamed. But it was an isolated incident. A one off. Offset by over two years of plain sailing. How unreasonable would it be, would *I* be, to end a relationship because of one such incident? This was my reasoning on that evening. It seemed sound then. It continued to do so as many happy, incident free months then passed.

Then came the second isolated incident (not an oxymoron, it was many months after the first incident and thus seemed somehow protected by time, by plain sailing, from being linked to it; the two incidents seemed to exist as two individual one offs. Is this, if not an oxymoron, then at the very least terrible maths?) This occurred when I said I could not drive Him to the gym one evening. Because I was busy. I had a meeting with someone about growing my business. It was important to me. The business was doing well, better than I had expected, and I was considering the next step. A business customer – a coffee shop owner - came to see me to talk it all through with me. I was grateful for his time. We both worked six days a week. It was generous of him to give up some of the rare down time that he had. It was a big deal to me. Furthermore, I was always driving Him about (as I have already explained, He does not drive). It was exactly the same situation as with His laundry. The work involved was huge – at least one lift a day but usually more – and it was not the workload that was the real issue, it was, again, the *responsibility* for it. The responsibility for getting Him wherever He needed to be, when He needed to be there, had shifted from Him to me. It had become my job. I was solely responsible for this work.

As I write about the laundry and the lifts, the work load, the shift in responsibility, the pressure, I wonder how I ever let it all happen. I have to explain at this point, if only to remind myself, that He used to be nice to me. The times I have said this to people now. I will say it again, one more time, I may as well. He used to be nice to me. I think it needs further emphasis: *He used to be nice to me*. Alongside the domestic work and the responsibility there was something positive. (So perhaps I am not an idiot then?)

Back to the second incident. For once, then, I said no to driving Him to the gym. He sat in the lounge throughout my meeting, looking edgy and angry and waiting for it to end (NB as I write, I realise this is how He looked for the last year or so of the relationship) so I could drive Him to the class, so that He could catch the end of it. He was not happy. I found His unhappiness disproportionate to the situation. He was missing one session at the gym. Yet again then, I was confused.

He was not quite the same with me after this evening. Something was wrong. More disproportion at play. He seemed upset about this missed session, mad at me about it, for far longer than He should have been. Shortly after this evening I ended up getting angry with Him about the constant lifts. I lost it with Him, basically, I raised my voice at Him (big mistake). I said I could not drive Him wherever He wanted me to, whenever He wanted me to. His reaction was to declare that He would move out. I was heartbroken. I cannot remember what happened next. It is a blur. But He did not leave me. And a lot of me driving Him about continued.

The Commitment

After about five years together, the incidents were still rare, months apart, separated by long stretches of niceness. So I was still happy and I still felt more loved than anything negative. At this point, as I approached the age of 35 (hurtling towards it like a cliché) we decided to buy a house together and try to start a family. I had become what I vowed I would never be: a woman in her mid-thirties who because she was in her mid-thirties worked out whether or not she wanted children because it was her last chance to do so. I do not know why I thought I could fight nature, biology, evolution, etc. Unsurprisingly, it turned out that these things are all far greater than I am. I was quickly desperate for a baby. I scaled back my business and secured a PAYE job so that I could be pregnant, sick and paid and then sleep deprived and relatedly brain addled and paid (AKA on maternity leave). I also began searching for a family nest. Needless to say, I did all of the work involved in finding and securing said nest. I house hunted, I put my house on the market, I secured a joint mortgage and, when the time came, I arranging and oversaw moving day.

Four days after we had moved in to our new family nest, after I had unpacked and organised the house, I conked out. I hadn't overdone it, as I assumed, it turned out I was pregnant. We were elated. I began living on cheddar cheese. He continued as normal. I did wonder whether His gym going would abate at all after the baby was born. It did not. But He did seem to love our daughter. As a three we moved towards the traditional gender roles that I was born for with my domestic, nurturing tendencies. Post breast feeding, post maternity leave, I continued to be the primary caregiver of our daughter. I worked in paid work part time only (and my earnings nose dived accordingly). He continued to work in paid work on a full time basis and pursued a more highly paid and responsible post and then, following a gruelling year-long postgraduate course, a Very Responsible, Stressful and Demanding Job, a job I heard described as thus A LOT, and so you will, from this point onwards.

The Shift

"Nothing so clearly symbolizes the constricted world imposed through coercive control than the selection of the daily round of household responsibilities that are already devalued in a woman's eyes as well as in the eyes of others as the critical battlefield on which she must defend her dignity and autonomy." (Stark 2009: 212)

I gave birth to our son when our daughter was four and a half years old. I had almost a year of maternity leave, as I had had with our daughter. I ran the family home. I did the school runs. I breast fed another baby, day and night. I was a purely domestic creature. Over the course of this year there occurred a subtle, almost imperceptible change in the relationship. I could not put my finger on it, but I definitely began to believe that He did not think of me as His equal. Far from it. He clearly believed that I was not working in any way as hard as He was in His Very Responsible, Stressful and Demanding Job which required a certain amount of sleep to do. I was only feeding people, cleaning, cooking and not sleeping (due to night feeds and our robot baby son getting up for the day at 4am every day). It was around this time that I had to so, so sadly and shockingly finally admit to myself that I had no voice; that nothing I said had any effect on Him and His actions and His treatment of me.

Everything domestic had always been my responsibility since we became a family but this time was different. Now any additional task could be demanded of me, at any time, and nothing I said counted for anything. The most alarming task was something I have mentioned several times already but will fully explain now: I was supposed to pair His socks after I had washed and dried them, which are all black, but had, apparently, in their pairs – because they were always washed in their pairs - all faded to slightly different shades of grey (His initial lecture on this task has to be the most unsexy monologue on the topic of fifty shades of grey ever uttered). As for the task, it was like *Mission Impossible* – scrutinising piles of faded black socks to find the pairs of socks faded the exact same amount – and I found myself wishing that the sodding socks would just spontaneously self-destruct – along with their owner – each time I was assigned the mission. Apparently His service users had written comments about His 'mismatched socks' on their feedback sheets and His line manager was not happy. I had to use my unheard voice. I had to. I dared to suggest a reason why I could not do it - I was busy and tired. I dared to suggest the problem was the bizarre organisation He worked for who worried about their therapists' socks. I dared to point out that *they are basically all black.* I was shot down and sternly told off. Of course I was.

Conversely, nothing could ever be asked of Him

because He had more than enough on His plate with His Very Responsible, Stressful and Demanding Job, which involved working five days a week, that is, working approximately 37 hours a week. Whenever I pointed out that I worked more than full time, that I worked seven days a week, that I worked every single day of the week, the month, the year, with each working day starting at 4am due to our robot baby son, He laughed at me (you can see why I did not share my Week Diary with Him, can't you?) He similarly laughed at me for going to bed at around 8pm, whilst choosing to stay up late each night and sleep in the guest room. The following point from Lundy Bancroft's *Why Does He Do That? Inside The Minds of Angry and Controlling Men* rings very true:

"He never reaches the point where he is satisfied, where he has been given enough. Rather, he gets used to the luxurious treatment he is receiving and soon escalates demands." (Bancroft 2002: 43)

I did stand up to Him over the socks though. It was the first time I had. I was so tired. I was exhausted. I had to draw the line at pairing His socks, which, in case I have not mentioned, *are all black*. I was an autonomous being in that moment. I had held onto a modicum of dignity. I had found and used my voice. I am happy that I did. He was not happy that I did.

A neighbour passed on what I believe to be a great saying about the bizarre maths of parenting: one child is a pet, two is a zoo. I found this to be true, so very true – don't all parents of two children plus? I found life exhausting with *two* children, a paid job and a house to run. So after being back at work for a couple of months I attempted to get Him to help more with the children, the domestic sphere. I asked Him to take responsibility for meals for one of the weekend days. It did not work. It was more work than simply being responsible for this parenting work myself. He did not know what to feed the children so would ask me and then need help because He did not know how to cook the items in question (apparently you *do* need a Ph.D. to cook fish fingers, who knew?!) His gym schedule would often clash with the children's early lunch time (linked to their early waking times) so I would end up preparing a lunch despite His having said He would do so when He got in – this then gave Him license to feel that He was 'off the hook'. And He would take the children out in the afternoon and not factor in the time required to prepare their dinner when deciding what time to come home, so I would end up preparing tea during my tiny slice of (so called) me time, so that when they returned bang on tea time there was a tea ready. So it did not work. And I gave up. I conceded defeat. I carried on. I carried on exhausted.

The Pair The Socks Diagram

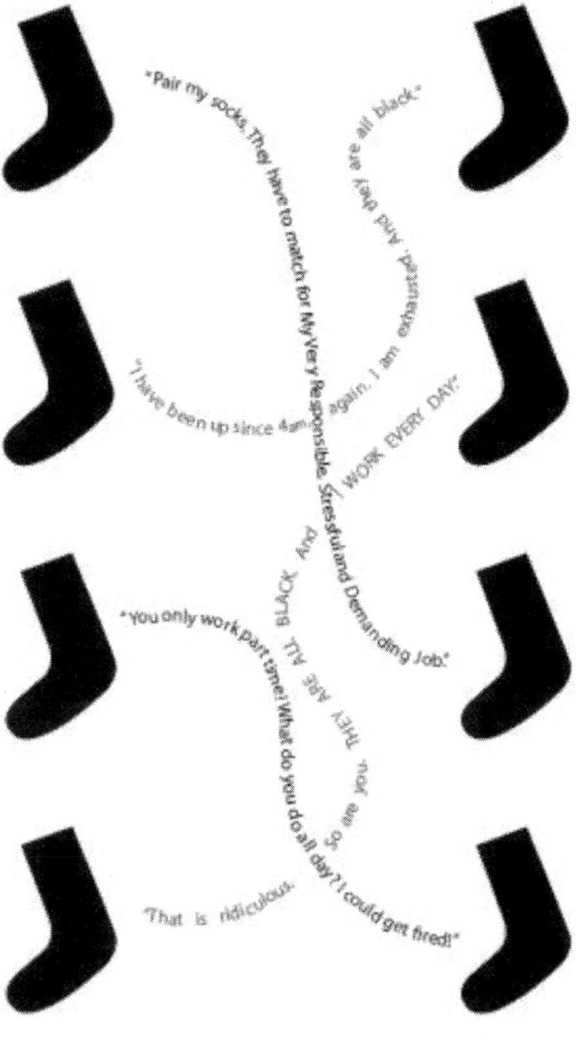

Traumatic Bond Attachment AKA Why I Stayed So Long

Even the most confusing or hurtful aspects of life can be made more tolerable by clear seeing. (Epictetus, The Art of Living)

When I read about emotional abuse and coercive control, following my session with a counsellor, both forms of domestic abuse spoke to me. I recognised them. I recognised in both of them my relationship, my life, my lost self. But there was still a lot that I did not know, and probably more that I did not know that I did not know, about the domestic abuse I had experienced, about my relationship, about over twelve years of my life. After a five month wait (during which time I received regular support over the phone from Behind Closed Doors) I started my face to face sessions with an Emotional Support Worker from the organisation. I was so relieved to be seeing someone who could help to fix me. We were in a noisy café for our first face to face meeting, as He had yet to be moved out. There was a lot to take in. I had with me my notepad and pen so I felt prepared (ever the geek). I was intrigued too. I had never had a support worker before. I work with people who have support workers. I provide advocacy for people struggling with their support workers. It was a new experience for me. I was so eager beaver. My support worker has since described me at that first session as more like the proverbial rabbit in the headlights.

My emotional support worker explained that we would work together through three stages. Firstly, understanding what domestic abuse is and the dynamics inherent within it. Secondly, exploring the impact on me of the domestic abuse I had experienced. And thirdly, recovery. I barely heard the first two stages. I heard 'recovery' and I thought 'Great! I am going to recover from this!' I did not realise that to do so I would firstly have to re-write history, re-write over twelve years of my life. But this is exactly what I had to do. *And the sweet man I met on a counselling course all those years ago slowly evaporated in front of my eyes.*

My Emotional Support Worker gave me work sheets to work through and I also had one from a friend who thought it was relevant (it was) and so thought it would be useful (it really was). These explored domestic abuse from different angles. Ever the student, I diligently went through them and I wrote pages and pages of notes on their relevance to my relationship, my experience, my life, my story. I wrote about all of the known facets or faces of abusers. I wrote about the different types of domestic abuse. I wrote about all of the classic tactics employed by abusers. I wrote and I wrote and I wrote (I like to write, which you had probably realised).

It didn't help me though. Because it didn't answer the one question that underpinned any other question or thought or vague feeling I had in connection to what had happened to me: why me? This question eventually became: why did it happen to me? Then: how did it happen to me? Then: how did I end up living with domestic abuse, on a daily basis, *for over twelve years*? Then: how can I ensure it never happens to me again?

What my Emotional Support Worker explained to me is that the question I needed to answer is not 'why me?' or any of the other questions that followed it. The question I needed to ask was *why did I stay so long?* More work sheets helped me to answer this question. They introduced me to the very clever - and equally cruel - traumatic bond attachment. This enabled me to start to contextualise my abusive relationship.

Love bombing

Traumatic bond attachment starts with something subtly but devastatingly different from the normal start of a relationship: love bombing. A form of conditioning or grooming, love bombing is hard to distinguish from the normal 'honeymoon' period of a new relationship when you are living it. In *Why Does He Do That? Inside The Minds of Angry and Controlling Men* Lundy Bancroft describes this beginning phase of a relationship with an abuser as The Garden of Eden and the following extract from his book which addresses its purpose helps me to not feel (too) stupid (for which I am so very thankful to him):

"The idyllic opening is part of almost every abusive relationship. How else would an abuser ever have a partner? Women aren't stupid. If you go out to a restaurant on a giddy first date and over dessert the man calls you a "selfish bitch" and sends your water glass flying across the room, you don't say: "Hey, are you free again next weekend?" There has to be a hook. Very few women hate themselves so thoroughly that they will get involved with a man who is rotten from the very start – although they may feel terrible about themselves *later*, once the abuser has had time to destroy their self-image step by step." (Bancroft 2002: 110, emphasis in original)

To understand love bombing was to understand that *I fell in love with an abuser.* It is love bombing, followed by the cycle of abuse, which together cause a traumatic bond attachment, a complex tangle of love and abuse. My Emotional Support Worker used a baking analogy (which I obviously liked a lot): she explained that the love and abuse are mixed together much like the ingredients in a cake, so that you can see neither, just as you cannot see the ingredients that go into a cake, all you see is the finished product – the (abusive) relationship.

His behaviour towards me at the start of the relationship I now see so clearly for what it was: the very calculated act of love bombing. He was incredibly complimentary, about my looks, my figure, my intellect and my kindness. His public displays of affection were second to none. He very early on – within weeks - talked of wanting to get a kitten with me, saying that it could "be our baby". He had told His friends I was 'the one'. He had wanted to move into my house after one year. He seemed to not only adore me – mind and body – but also to completely *get* me, as my beloved grandad had before (who, significantly, died not long before I began going out with Him, but whom I talked about with Him a lot).

The clearest evidence I see of love bombing now is His turning up at my house unannounced because He "just could not wait to see me!" It felt so romantic. I felt so desired and so loved. He could not keep away from me. This was not normal behaviour, I realised that at the time, but I very positively put it down to His enormous passion and love for me, not down to what I now know to be His purely negative and menacing need to be the centre of my world, at all times.

In a nutshell, He did not meet me and fall in love with me and become besotted with me (as I wrote earlier). He saw me coming. He saw me as perfect for grooming for His control - because I am a homebody, I am a domestic creature, I am a nurturer, I like looking after people and I like to be busy and useful and productive and kind. So He love bombed me. He love bombed me in preparation for the next stage.

The cycle of abuse

It was two years into the relationship, when He moved in with me, when He started to become furious with me (with very widely spaced bouts of fury to begin with) for caring about anything other than Him - my burgeoning business, my friends, my family, my *self*. He clearly thought I was selfish for loving anything other than Him. He could not comprehend that I could have, or want to have, anything in my life other than Him. The first incident, already described, was His rage at my hanging His laundry up in the kitchen and then cooking onions. Then, after a sizeable gap, came the second incident, also already described, His fury at my not giving Him a lift. So the love bombing had ended. The relationship had moved towards the next stage – the cycle of abuse – wherein everything that I did, and did not do, was a desperate attempt to bring back the sweet, wonderful, adoring man I had had in my life, in my home. And when His fury abated and He seemed happy and nice again it felt like I had succeeded, every time. But, of course, this man never existed, so all my efforts could only be utterly futile, couldn't they?

On-going cycles of abuse involve intermittent punishments and rewards which create two things. Firstly, powerful emotional bonds resistant to change. This is because when a person has experienced cruel treatment over an extended length of time it is natural for them to feel a flood of gratitude and love when someone brings an end to the cruelty. In domestic abuse situations, the perpetrator of the cruelty and the person who brings an end to it are, unfortunately, one and the same. Secondly, on-going cycles of abuse engender a climate of fear, which leaves the victim constantly second guessing. So many times I would think ahead to what He might say or do if He noticed something was not quite right or was missing and then try to fix the problem, so to avoid any kind of psychological punishment – such as silent treatment, guilt trips, emotional blackmail or playing the victim – or verbal abuse such as being told to "Fuck off" or more general bouts of explosive anger. Such second guessing happened a lot with cottage cheese. I would check the number of tubs of cottage cheese in the fridge mid-week and, if we were running low, I would work out, firstly, an explanation as to why this was happening – the supermarket was low on stock when I did the big weekly shop – and, secondly, a way to solve the problem – work out when I could fit in an emergency, panic, top up shop (as I already explained I did on the second day of the pre-Christmas weekend celebration with my family, in the chapter entitled Food).

Also integral to the cycle of abuse are attempts made by the abuser to normalise, legitimise, rationalise, deny or minimise the abuse, or to blame the victim for it. Remember He argued that I was unable to take criticism (itself a criticism, see His Criticisms of Me in the later chapter entitled Words) and that I had a 'perfection complex' (a made up mental health condition which I believe is on a par with HYSTERIA).

One form of abuse that was popular within the cycles He put me through was the sinister mind game of 'gaslighting'. This is a form of persistent manipulation and mind control that causes the victim to doubt themself, and lose their own sense of perception/reality and ultimately identity and self-worth. The term originates in the film *Gaslight* (1944), in which a husband uses gaslights to cause his wife to question herself and her reality and eventually conclude that she is going mad. At best (if such a word can be used in conjunction with this cruel tactic) gaslighting creates a subtly unequal power dynamic within a relationship, with the gaslightee subjected to the gaslighter's unreasonable, personalised, bespoke and ad hoc scrutiny, judgment, or micro-aggression. At worst (a much more fitting word to use in conjunction with this cruel tactic) gaslighting constitutes a severe form of psychological abuse that can be classed as mind-control. He would deny threats after He had made them and accuse me of starting arguments when I had absolutely no idea of what on earth I had said or done to trigger such an accusation. I did doubt my memory, my perception and, over time, my mental wellbeing. In *Why Does He Do That? Inside the Minds of Angry and Controlling Men* Lundy Bancroft sums up the devastatingly cruel nature of traumatic bond attachment:

"One of the great tragedies of all forms of abuse is that the abused person can become emotionally dependent on the perpetrator through a process called *traumatic bonding*. The assaults that an abuser makes on the woman's self-opinion, his undermining of her progress in life, the wedges he drives between her and other people, the psychological effects left on her when he turns scary – all can combine to cause her to need him more and more. This is a bitter psychological irony." (Bancroft 2002: 220, emphasis in original)

He has made many sly comments since I separated from Him. On one comedic occasion He came to see the children to read books to and with them at bedtime and our son (age 2 at the time) chose a *Thomas The Tank Engine* book for Him to read to him but said he wanted mummy to stay for bedtime books too. He read the book and I could barely keep a straight face, actually I did not keep a straight face at all. In the story the train with the same name as Him got into trouble for poor time keeping and was bought an alarm clock at the end of the book, with which to better manage his time. I could not resist pointing out the irony given His poor time management when He lived in the family home (which I now realise was a control tool). He proceeded to explain *to our two year old son* that daddy did not have a problem with time management, rather, "mummy did not love him enough".

Thanks to this work that I did with Behind Closed Doors, I now know that I could never have loved Him enough. I could never have loved Him enough to make Him stop abusing me. Nothing I could ever have done would have stopped His abusive behaviour. Because He did not want me to do anything to stop it. Because He wanted to abuse me. Because *He wanted the cycle of abuse,* with its necessary calms, *with which to control me* - getting what He wanted in the process: enough sleep, the right food, coffee on demand, paired (all black) socks, lifts, sex, etc. So win win for Him. And, depending on the numbers of His demands and His abusive tactics and behaviours, lose lose lose lose lose lose etc..... for me.

TIMELINE OF MY ABUSIVE RELATIONSHIP

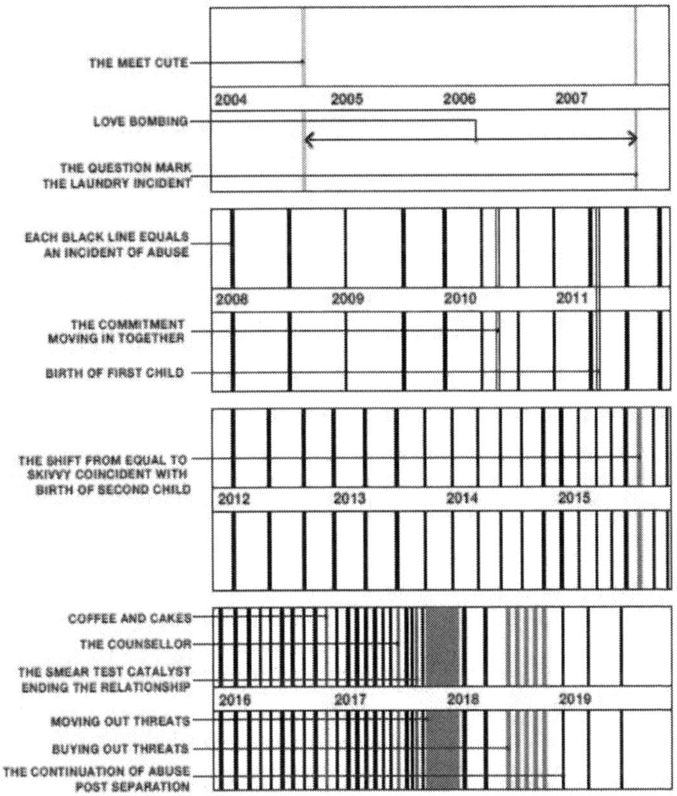

Maths I Cannot Do

The cycle of abuse can be summed up as involving four phases:

1. Tension Builds: tension increases, breakdown of communication, victim becomes fearful and feels the need to placate the abuser.
2. The Incident: Verbal, emotional, psychological abuse – anger, blaming, raging, threats, intimidation.
3. Reconciliation: Abuser apologises, gives excuses, blames the victim, denies the abuse occurred or says it wasn't as bad as the victim claims it was.
4. The Calm: The incident is 'forgotten' – no abuse takes place during a 'honeymoon phase'. In The Calm, the victim focuses on Reconciliation, takes responsibility and forgets The Incident.

As the years went by, the Phase 4's, The Calms, got shorter. It is this pattern which determined the length of the relationship, the length of time that I stayed with Him for. Because eventually the incidents were so close together that the gaps between them – The Calms – were so brief that they were useless to me, I was always reeling from the last incident and incredibly tense and anxious about when the next one would occur. So I hit a wall. And I got help (counselling). This gave me the knowledge and the understanding that told me I had to leave Him. And so I left Him.

There is probably a mathematical formula for this pattern and the timing of the wall hitting, an algorithm, whatever an algorithm is. I know they are common, popular even. If only I had done a maths Ph.D. then I could write one. But I struggled with GCSE maths so this would never have been possible, would it?

Maths I can do

"So numerous and varied are the tactics men use in coercive control that any attempts to categorize them are bound to seem arbitrary. Lists of such tactics are many pages long." (Stark 2009: 232)

"At the end of the day, we can endure much more than we think we can." (Frieda Kahlo)

So I understood the bigger picture, the whole relationship, the whole abusive relationship. I had slotted over twelve years of my life so very neatly into a textbook friendly format. It was both devastating and liberating. Now I understood the bigger picture, I wanted to fill in the details. So I went back to all of my pages (and pages and pages, as per Stark's quote) of notes on the different types of domestic abuse that I had experienced. My relationship had been reduced to a neat table. Next I reduced it to a neat list. My list. My own bespoke, lived domestic abuse check list (because I do love lists). As I worked with my Behind Closed Doors Emotional Support Worker and I learnt more and my understanding developed, I would revisit the work sheets, tick off more forms of abuse and add more to my list.

The final list encompassed every facet of 'The Dominator' from Pat Craven's book *Living With The Dominator A book about the Freedom Programme* (2008) – The Sexual Controller; The Bully; The Jailor; The Persuader; The Liar; The Headworker; The Badfather; and King of The Castle. It also included all ten realities from Lundy Bancroft's *Why Does He Do That? Inside the Minds of Angry and Controlling Men* – he is controlling; he feels entitled; he twists things into the opposite; he disrespects his partner and considers himself superior and objectifies her; he confuses love and abuse; he is manipulative; he strives to have a good public image; he feels justified; he denies and minimizes his abuse; and he is possessive. And it contained a large proportion of the abuses listed on the domestic abuse check list that was given to me by my Behind Closed Doors Emotional Support Worker. I had expected to be ticking off types of abuse listed under the headings of emotional, psychological and verbal abuse, but I also eventually found myself ticking off forms of abuse listed under three other headings - physical, financial and sexual abuse (more on this last one later). In the end, my very own bespoke, lived domestic abuse list included 66 forms of domestic abuse. This was maths that I *could* do:

66 forms of domestic abuse
Experienced over c12 years
That is 5.5 forms of abuse for every year that I was with Him

It was all about the numbers now.

My Abusive Relationship in Numbers

- £31,580 to secure financial separation (He abused hard for more and more)
- 14,472 tubs of cottage cheese bought for Him (28 per week, not an estimate)
- 4,380 declarations of love (a daily occurrence so, again, not an estimate)
- 3,120 loads of His washing done (5 per week, a conservative estimate)
- 66 forms of domestic abuse experienced
- 52 'date nights' in the final, terrible two years (one a fortnight)
- 40 pounds cost of F.L.A.G. tattoo
- 27 months He slept in the guest room
- 15 professionals seen between separation and moving Him out
- 13 minutes it took to get inked for the first time (more on this later)
- 11 criticisms He (repeatedly) made of me
- 10 threats He made between separation and moving Him out
- 9 months of asking Him to attend couples' counselling with me
- 8 weeks between separation and moving Him out
- 7 Rules I Had To Live By
- 7 face to face sessions with an Emotional Support Worker from Behind Closed Doors
- 7 days off work in total due to anxiety/stress

building up to move out and buy out

- 5 months of phone support from Behind Closed Doors prior to the face to face support
- 4 trips to my GP with anxiety/stress
- 3 trips to the Family Court (each time too scared to take any action)
- 2 years before the first major incident of domestic abuse
- 1.5 stone lost in weight through stress related appetite loss
- 1 session with a counsellor to learn that I was living with domestic abuse
- 0 seconds of regret since I separated from Him on 041017

My Abusive Relationship in Unknown Numbers

- Times I told friends and family He was working when He was avoiding them
- Times I called His mother in a blind panic after He had threatened me
- Times I lied and said "Yes" when He asked me if I loved Him
- Times I cried on the bathroom floor after He had abused me and then gone out
- Times I asked myself 'What is wrong with me?'
- Times He told me to "Fuck off"
- Times I have been told that I am 'brave'
- The time it will take for me to truly believe this
- The time that will pass before He does this

to another woman

- The time it will take the next woman to leave Him
- The number of women He will do it to
- The years before my children will understand why I left Him

Shame

"We can view the word 'shame' as being made up of two parts: sh (= 'shhh', to keep quiet/be silent) + ame (= *ame*, the French for 'soul'). Thus shame may be regarded as the silencing of the soul." (Fisher 2005: 176)

My voice had been silenced by Him; along with my soul it seems.

"Toxic shame is a rupture within the self, like internal bleeding. When we experience toxic shame, we will guard against the excruciating pain of exposing the core of who we are to others, because we believe that in our core we have failed." (Fisher 2005: 177)

I believed I had failed. Failed at choosing a life partner. Failed at building a family. Failed at the only things that ever really mattered to me.

In his book on coercive control, Evan Stark (2009) puts forward two arguments as to why it provokes such great feelings of shame. Firstly, because it occurs in liberal societies where officially female equality and independence are celebrated. Secondly, because of the nature of the crime, specifically "the familiarity of the setting where their abuse occurred, the widespread assumption they have freely chosen their lot, and because there is much less clarity than in other capture crimes about the duress under which they enact humiliating rituals."(Stark 2009: 204-5)

It was only after I had read Stark's book that I realised I was not addressing my shame, in my book or anywhere. I often find myself repeating my desperate explanation for how I got into the mess that I did (He used to be nice to me, remember?) I realise that underlying this plea, to not be considered a complete idiot by anyone and everyone, is a deep sense of shame concerning how and why I managed to end up living with domestic abuse and thus requiring the services of a much needed and woefully underfunded charity.

My shame goes beyond this issue of utilising the services of such an organisation. I think of all I have got: two beautiful children, a beautiful home (my Best Nest), many wonderful friends, a supportive family, a job I love and which affords me the opportunity to continue to study (this is very important to a born geek), and as if all of this is not enough, *I have my health too*. The shame. The audacity. Greedy, greedy, demanding, despicable me. How *dare* I feel sad, low, aggrieved, hard done by, unlucky, or anything else vaguely negative that this thing happened to me, and is still happening to me. Shame on me. Shame.

Learning about the cycle of abuse, and specifically the deceptively delicious/deliciously deceptive love bombing which characterises its start, has gone a long way towards enabling me to let go of this shame. I do still trot out my explanation for how I got into the mess that I did – He used to be nice to me – but look, the word 'explanation' is no longer preceded by the word 'desperate' there. Progress, surely?

NEST

And it feels like home
Like A Prayer, Madonna

The Best Nest

Once I had separated from Him I knew He had to go. I knew this unequivocally. My smear test had proved to be the catalyst, the straw that broke the (downtrodden looking) middle aged woman's back and I had separated from Him. We were no longer (pretending to be) a couple. As the primary caregiver of two young children (which I unequivocally was, given all the work I had always done - and always will do - on and for and about the children, oh, and the fact I have always looked after them 97.5% of the time) I knew that the children should stay with me, and would stay with me, regardless of the actions of their father. And I was ready for single motherhood, given the fact that since becoming a mother I had pretty much always been a faux single mother, one who resided in the family home with a faux partner who had morphed into a completely inappropriate lodger – expecting hot meals, guilt tripping me into cold sex and shouting at me whenever He felt like it.

I also knew that the three of us had to stay put in the family home. I could never leave the family home. The home I had found and furnished and organised. The home I ran, decorated and maintained. I knew this was the right thing to do for my children – for their stability and security and familiarity; their school and nursery; their neighbourhood friends – and I also felt strongly that it should be my right as the primary caregiver. Whether or not this was right or my right, or both, given all of the work I had always done and always would do on and for the family home, the home our children had lived in since their births, I would have fought tooth and nail to stay in it. And I did.

A sweet song sung by a bird in one of my son's favourite books makes me smile because it is how I feel about my house, my home:

"I love my house. I love my nest. In all the world My nest is best!"
(P.D. Eastman, 1968, The Best Nest)

My nest *is* best. It is my Best Nest. I once described my house as my 'dream house' to someone who had never been to it. They asked if it is detached. I explained it was a terraced house. They asked if it had two bathrooms. I said no. They asked if it had a garden. I explained it had only a yard. Silence. Tumbleweeds. I can only deduce my nest is not the best in their eyes. But like I said, it is in mine. Hence my not just desperation to stay put in it but my dogged determination. I made the following list (another beloved list then):

My work on and for the family home

- House hunted (in my spare time whilst He went to the gym in His)
- Found a financial advisor who organised the joint mortgage
- Researched and chose a moving company

- Packed up my house (in my spare time…)
- Unpacked the new house (in my spare time…)
- Furnished the house – involving wrestling with IKEA flat packs and driving all over Leeds to pick up Shpock and Preloved bargains and Freecycle freebies
- Decorated the house (my bulging Home Journal is evidence of this hobby/passion)
- Project manage all house maintenance and repairs
- Found a handyman (for the jobs I could not manage alongside my workload; the jobs that He literally laughed at the concept of turning His hands to)
- Found a window cleaner (for the windows I cannot reach)
- Found a plumber
- Found an electrician
- Found a repair man
- Found a cleaner
- Spring clean the house annually (obviously)
- Researched and chose a new boiler and a company to fit it
- Diarise and ensure it is serviced annually (to maintain the warranty and avoid it blowing up too I suppose)

The Move Out

He refused to move out. He said He was staying until the children were "older", whatever on earth that vague nonsense meant. So I knew I had to move beyond such listing and find out my actual legal rights. As Socrates said: wisest is she who knows she does not know. And I knew I knew zip. So I began hitting up as many solicitors as I could for their free half hours of legal advice; arming myself each time with my questions; searching for definitive answers. These proved to be quite elusive. Not least because His domestic abuse was emotional abuse and coercive control, newly recognised within British law and, new or not, hard to prove. Furthermore, I dared not tell Him that I knew He was abusive, for fear of His reaction. A sick catch 22. I did not even know if He knew He was abusive. As a therapist He works with abused people, He surely must know what domestic abuse is? But He *joked* about it, *to me, in front of friends and family*. He laughed about me "getting away from the abuse".

I remain unsure as to whether or not He knows He is an abuser. But one thing surely suggests He knows: He has never asked me why I wanted to separate from Him. Not once. I must have been so relieved to have done it (well, I was) that it took weeks for the penny to drop. One day it hit me out of the blue, it stopped me in my tracks, I realised He had never asked me to explain my desire to leave Him, after over twelve years together. To this day, He never has. He knows why. He has to.

One definitive answer I did get, from all of the various solicitors that I saw, was that, yes, there was no way I would ever have to leave the family home. The primary caregiver should stay put in it with their charges. I also learnt about the court orders with which I could have Him legally removed from the family home: an Occupation Order and a Non-molestation Order. I filled out an Occupation Order but learnt that it was largely useless without the Non-molestation Order box on it being ticked, i.e. a declaration of His abuse, which I dared not declare to Him. I learnt that the two orders would be served to Him *whilst He was living in the family home* and that, so He could put His side across, we would then have to attend the Family Court *together*. Back and forth I went to court, umming and ahhing. But I think I always knew that I could never take any legal action, not only because I was quite simply too scared to do so (remember how angry He can get over socks and coffee?) but also because of what I knew He would say faced with a professional. I had experienced this already.

The first condition He put on His ever moving out was that we go and speak to someone at Relate about separating. He made it all too clear that He would never leave if I did not attend a Relate session with Him (given that I had asked Him to attend couples counselling with me for the best part of a year, the delicious irony of this was not wasted on me, I dared not point it out to Him though). Thus this was as much a threat as it was a condition. I knew exactly what He would say in the enforced Relate session. I could have scripted His opening remarks myself. At this point I was proud of myself for standing up to Him over His sodding socks and proud of myself for separating from Him. But how I handled this session was my proudest moment up to this point. Firstly, He opened with a statement about me being not abusive but controlling (i.e. abusive). Secondly, He followed it with a diagnosis of a mental health condition: Generalised Anxiety Disorder (back to the 'HYSTERIA' issue then; I knew He would pathologise me, therapise me, thus abusing – there's that word again – His profession/knowledge/supposed standing within the world of mental health). Thirdly, He finished with a critique of my parenting skills: I shout at the children (I have been through this already, has not *every* parent, at *some* point, shouted at their child/children?). A perfect trilogy of criticism then (He does love to criticise me, see the above list). I tick, tick, ticked them off the list in my head. The following passage from Lundy Bancroft's book *Why Does He Do That? Inside The Minds of Angry and Controlling Men* sums up this Relate session experience for me so, so perfectly:

"There can be no positive communication when one person doesn't respect the other and strives to avoid equality. You can't take the leaps of vulnerability involved in working through early emotional injuries while you are constantly feeling emotionally unsafe – because you *are* emotionally unsafe." (Bancroft 2002: 351-2, emphasis in original)

I most definitely *was* emotionally unsafe in that Relate session, but I tried to stay as safe as possible with my response to His trilogy of criticisms, which was that we were not there to criticise one another but rather to discuss how we can best move forward as a separated couple parenting two small children (well, as I have already explained, I established that He was parenting them a mere 2.5% of the time, but I was not there to criticise Him, so I omitted to mention this point; although during my obligatory two minutes alone with the Relate staff member I did explain that I was not able to talk freely in front of Him; and I explained why; and if disclosing someone's domestic abuse can be defined as criticising them then I did so, vehemently).

Needless to say, the session was pointless, fruitless and utterly useless. I believe my calmness both unnerved and angered Him. The second we were out of the room and in the reception of Relate, He launched into another condition or threat: a demand for the money I 'owed' Him from when I was on maternity leave with our son and my earnings dipped too low to pay my usual half of the mortgage and bills. For eight months I paid less than Him (I should mention here that, despite ending up earning one third of what He did, partly because I worked part time to be the primary caregiver of our two children, we had continued to split all bills equally up until this point). Despite obviously knowing what He was by this point (an abuser) and forewarned is forearmed, and thus that I should know to expect such abusive, monstrous behaviour, especially when He does not get what He wants, as He didn't in the Relate session, I became upset and I cried. I said I was looking after *our* beautiful (robot) baby son for this period of time. He was unmoved. Of course He was. He left me crying. His usual M.O. Later the same day He denied making this threat (ditto).

Over the next couple of weeks He conceded that He would move out. But then came the next condition of His doing so, the next threat: this is when He told me that I had to take parenting classes. Because the children are not sufficiently well behaved for me. Because I lack basic parenting skills. I said yes (as I have already explained, I never said no to Him). I often think about when He thinks I actually *took* the classes, in my sleep perhaps? Over the course of the two months it took for Him to move out, I logged ten threats He made about never doing so (another less than beloved list then):

Diary of His moving related threats

- 061017: He threatened not to move out unless I went to Relate with Him.
- 071017: He threatened not to move out unless I enrolled on parenting classes. He added He would take me to court to get His family to testify that I am a bad mother who shouts at the children.
- 121017: He threatened not to move out unless He could still have breakfast with the children (I pointed out that whilst living in the same house as them He never ate breakfast with them, because He is never up in time to do so).
- 141017: He said He would move out in about a year's time. I said He needs to go as soon as possible. I said I can no longer live with Him because He keeps threatening me. He said He had never threatened me. I said

two days ago He threatened to take me to court and get His parents to testify I am a bad mother. He denied this threat.

- 191017: He threatened not to move out unless I paid back the money I owed Him from when I was on maternity leave with our son.
- 201017: When I asked about the local room for rent He had mentioned the day before He threatened to never move out if I asked about this issue "several times a day". He added I was not allowed to ever again raise the issue of His moving out (rules I had to follow were a big thing for Him, remember the list?).
- 041117: He threatened not to move out unless we sort out the house finances. (This was an impossible demand to meet as our mortgage provider had already explained to me, and I had explained to Him, that they needed to see 3 months proof of separation – physical and financial, including Child Maintenance payments, before they could consider me for the solo mortgage that would enable us to sort out the house finances).
- 181117: He threatened not to move out until we sort out who can have which of our shared possessions, including the Tupperware boxes (I said He could have whatever He wanted, including the Tupperware boxes).

- 201117: He threatened not to move out unless He is allowed to keep His key to the house.
- 251117: He threatened not to move out until we address our son's behaviour (a threat triggered by his not wanting to go to soft play with his dad). He congratulated me on making our son clingy and added that I had "fucked him up" (anyone who knows our son will tell you that he is the least clingy child you could meet, happy to be with anyone, so completely and beautifully secure and confident and sociable).

His threats extended beyond the issue of His moving out. On 301117, the day before the first Child Maintenance payment was due, He threatened not to pay it the next morning (and it is very hard for me to accept that I am writing what I am about to write) unless I made sure He had a cup of coffee in the morning (back to coffee, then). I dared to say to Him that that was ridiculous, that Child Maintenance is more important than morning coffee, to which He replied that coffee in the morning is as important to Him as receiving Child Maintenance is for me. He then let out a very long laugh as I stood and cried in front of Him. I found this to be the most cruel, menacing, chilling and heart breaking experience of my life. It wasn't so for long.

Unhappy with our daughter's behaviour shortly before moving day, He announced there was no *actual plan* to move out. There was a vague goal, but there had never been an *actual plan*. By this point I was buying boxing and packing for Him. I was counting down the days to moving day. I had just started beginning to feel a bit happy (or rather a bit happier, to further water down the point). I was devastated. I fell to the floor and cried. He stepped over me and went out for dinner with His 'is he/is he not' to be new flat mate. The following morning, the first time He spoke to me that day was to request that I go shopping for Him to buy the essential items He needed for the new flat. I said yes. Obviously. So it was more gaslighting then i.e. more abuse.

Over this unending seeming two month long period between separating from Him and getting Him out of the family home I spoke to or saw just about every professional that I possibly could, in my quest for assistance in getting Him to move out and leave me the hell alone. So, yet another less than beloved list:

Timeline of professional advice and help sought prior to moving Him out

- 041017 Children's Centre
- 091017 Women's Aid
- 091017 Solicitor
- 091017 GP Surgery
- 111017 Health Visitor
- 121017 Solicitor
- 131017 Women's Aid
- 131017 Paralegal
- 131017 Personal Support Unit at Combined

Courts
- 171017 Personal Support Unit at Combined Courts
- 181017 City Centre CAB
- 191017 Police Safeguarding Unit
- 031117 Behind Closed Doors
- 071117 Personal Support Unit at Combined Courts

Moving day

Moving Day was a big day that required a lot of organisation. Needless to say, this was left to me. I had arranged three friends to assist me on moving day: one to look after our son (our daughter was to be at school), one to help me actually move Him out and one to be with me back at the house afterwards (I assumed I would feel happy and relieved but other, more negative things too).

Moving day, the last day of sharing a house with Him, was the same as any other. We had agreed a time for something, His time, in this case for His moving out, linked to the availability of my friend providing child care and my friend helping with the actual moving. However, before that time came He declared He had urgent work that He had to do for His Very Responsible, Stressful and Demanding Job, and so would move later that morning. For years, over a decade, I had accepted that His time management issue is part of the Dyslexia that He has a diagnosis of:

"Contrary to popular belief, dyslexia is not only about literacy, although weaknesses in literacy are often the most visible sign. Dyslexia affects the way information is processed, stored and retrieved, with problems of memory, speed of processing, *time perception, organisation and sequencing.*" (British Dyslexia Association website, emphasis added)

I had similarly accepted His sudden and urgent need to complete work as a necessary part of His Very Responsible, Stressful and Demanding Job. By this point, though, I had come to understand that it is also likely to be as much a part of the coercive control so central to His personality and thus my relationship with Him. So I was one step ahead. I had arranged the moving friend but not informed Him of my doing so. When the doorbell rang He dropped His (clearly no longer urgent) work (or was never urgent work more likely) and got straight in the shower and was ready to be moved at the agreed time, no doubt so as to look like the good person He always pretended to be in front of my friends (oh how blissfully unaware He was that that ship had so long since sailed).

It was done in under one hour. The ending of twelve and a half years of togetherness, seven and a half of which had taken place in the family home we had just moved Him out of. I was happy. I was also sad. And I was dazed (so my prediction about my feelings was correct).

Best Nesting

After moving day it gradually sank in that I had

reclaimed the family home, my Best Nest, and I soon set about making it mine and my children's. I ripped out the huge fitted wardrobe on the first floor landing of the house, no longer needed to house all of the clothes that He never wore but refused to ever let go of. I charity shopped superfluous chests of drawers which had housed His hundreds of T-Shirts – some of which remained in the cellar for months, unmissed, not needed, never needed, that I now know was simply more house-fill that enabled Him to stake a claim to far much more of the space in the house than He clearly ever actually needed.

I reacquainted myself with my floor – no longer hidden under a sea of clothes that were not clean enough to be hung back up or put back into one of the many chests of drawers that housed them but were categorically *not* ready for the laundry basket. I had been caught out many, many times when I had scooped a pile of clothes up and washed them (the audacity) only for Him to go berserk when He discovered that the *one* T-Shirt (out of literally *hundreds*) that He simply *had* to wear that day was in the washing machine or hanging up drying, and *not* left screwed up on the floor where it was obviously waiting to be picked up and worn again.

I said hello again to many surfaces within the house, formerly covered in His vintage and *highly confidential* notes that could *only ever be shredded* or He may lose His Very Responsible, Stressful and Demanding Job. I put all of my beautiful toiletries out in the bathrooms. I had never been able to before because He would always help Himself to them despite how special and fancy they were - the beautiful Clarins sets my mother bought me after the births of my two even more beautiful children; the uber expensive Neal's Yard treats that my sister sends me; the overpriced hair products I needed for my dried out bleached hair (bleached for Him); everything. As I have already explained, nothing of mine was mine. What was mine was His. Because I was His.

Then there was the new fridge. The new GIANT fridge. It was now full of the foods that I fancied buying and cooking for me and my children, rather than The Food I Had To Buy For Him Every Week. And with the cottage cheese gone which formerly took up one quarter of the monstrous appliance there was space for whatever I fancied buying and cooking and eating for myself and the children. Bliss. Domestic bliss.

The Light Bulb Moment

"Never discourage anyone... who continually makes progress, no matter how slow." (Plato)

I had achieved solo occupation (along with my children). Next I needed solo ownership. Whilst I was still working through all of the Behind Closed Doors recovery projects/aids, my Emotional Support Worker came to see me for one of our sessions and said, quite simply, that I had changed. She said Behind Closed Doors call this the Light Bulb Moment. I was intrigued. I was definitely happy but her comment, her observation surprised me. I tried to work out what might have brought me to this point. I think it might have been my previous mortgage lender.

I never married Him so the only legal connection to Him was a jointly owned house, or rather, a joint mortgage. I wanted to buy Him out of it, the family home, my Best Nest, which, as I have explained, I had stayed in with our two children. He was happy about this plan because it meant He would receive a nice lump sum (c30k). That this was all He would be getting is down to a very good, and very wise friend of mine: Carrie. Having told her that I was buying a house with Him and that I had a much larger deposit than He did (60k whilst His was 15k) she advised me to have a Deed of Trust drawn up by a solicitor. I did. This legal document meant that upon the sale of the house, or upon the occasion where one partner buys out the other, each person gets back their deposit plus half of any equity in the property. I did pray (hard) for negative equity (an unusual prayer, I am aware of that) but, sadly, three valuations all said much the same thing: c30k equity in the property. Hence He was due a total of c 30k. He would gleefully remind me that I would have no money left after I had bought Him out of the house. I would (inwardly gleefully) say that I would cope.

Ready to go with my three months proof of income and child care costs I applied for a solo mortgage with the existing mortgage lender. All was fine. They said they just needed to do a credit check before they could process the application and do the related Transfer of Equity, i.e. the sale of the house from us to me, i.e. the buy out. A formality, I thought, as I have always been nothing if not responsible with money. I happily waited for the current mortgage lender to ring and say I had of course passed the credit check with flying colours etc. and that they would process my solo mortgage application and the Transfer of Equity ASAP. I was wrong. This is not what happened.

The current mortgage lender called to say that I had *failed the credit check*. I wondered what on earth they could be talking about. I thought about my financial history: a mortgage since I was 22 years old and a credit card since I was 18 (I was 43 at this point). I had never missed a mortgage payment and I paid my credit card bills in a timely fashion. What could they possibly have found? What could they possibly be talking about? The current mortgage lender explained: my credit report showed that I had missed a £12 payment to 'a communications company'. They said this was all they could say. It was a sick cryptic puzzle. Luckily it was not a hard sick cryptic puzzle to solve (so it wasn't actually cryptic then, although I am sure the current mortgage lender *wanted* it to be so, which I take as further proof of their idiocy). My contract for my mobile phone (a means of communication) was £12 a month. So I ordered a copy of my credit report and set about trying to decipher whether it indeed was a mobile phone company 'debt'. It was spectacularly unclear, at least to me, and then to my father (that is, to two Ph.D.'s). It took my very smart neighbour (Simon) to decipher it and conclude that, yes, my 'debt' was to my last mobile phone provider. I had missed the last £12 payment to my former mobile phone provider when I switched providers four months earlier, and rather than them ringing me and telling me this - *on the mobile phone number which they had issued me with* – they had reported this heinous financial misdemeanour to a credit company. It then rolled over every month after it was reported. To the financial world my credit report thus read: not paid; still not paid; **still not paid; still not paid; STILL. NOT. PAID**.

So twenty-one years of diligent, on-time mortgage paying was on my credit report but had been wiped out by one missed mobile phone company payment of £12. As I have already said, maths has never been my forte, but this was more maths that I simply had to attempt. And it turned out to be more maths that I can do.

The amount of money I once mistakenly failed to pay to a communications company

£12

What you can buy with £12

- A CD (I recently bought a CD; I still buy and play CDs.)
- Five hot drinks in an overpriced coffee shop
- Four summer beverages in an overpriced coffee shop
- A minimum of four items in my local everything-is £3-or less CRUK shop
- Twelve one pound lottery tickets

The (very roughly) estimated total amount of money I have spent on timely mortgage payments

21 years
12 payments a year
Each payment approximately £400
= £100, 800

What you can buy with approximately £100, 000

- 42, 000 hot drinks in an overpriced coffee shop
- 33, 600 summer drinks in an overpriced coffee shop
- 8,400 CDs
- A minimum of 33, 600 items in my local CRUK shop
- 100, 800 £1 lottery tickets
- A boat
- A very fancy car
- A house (ironically)

I straight away rang the mobile phone company and paid the 'debt' there and then over the phone. I requested a letter from them to the current mortgage lender explaining that the 'debt' had been paid. I informed the current mortgage lender of all of this, thinking I had sorted out my credit report 'problem'. Again, I was wrong. I had not done this in any way, shape or form. The current mortgage lender thanked me for the letter and then informed me that the point was not that I had now paid the 'debt', rather that *I had ever incurred a 'debt' in the first place*. So no solo mortgage for financially feckless me! I said "Really?!" The current mortgage lender employee reply "Yes." I said "REALLY?!" Again, reply "Yes." I said **"REALLY?!"** Again, reply "Yes." I tried to take the capitalisation and bold out of my voice and calmly pointed out that I had had a mortgage since I was 22... etc... a credit card since I was 18... etc. I even mentioned my marvellous maths. Reply: silence. So I said it one more time and this time went the other way and underscored it too: **"<u>REALLY?!</u>"** Yet again, reply "Yes." (of course). So I asked what the exit fee would be to leave the current mortgage lender.

I had waited three months to start work on the necessary financial separation from Him, necessary not least because it meant I could legally change the locks (all of the solicitors that I had hit up for free legal advice had said the same virtually useless thing, that denying a key to someone whose name is on the Deeds to the property is a legal 'grey area'; that's legal 'advice' I am glad I did not pay for). I had diligently gathered all of the documents required to prove what I already knew - that I could afford a solo mortgage if I paid a chunk of the mortgage off first to reduce it, which I also knew that I could afford to do. But it had all been in vain.

I did not feel down, or deflated, or despondent, or defeated. I felt strangely elated. Almost high. I was simply determined to find a new answer to my solo mortgage problem. I felt stronger at this point than I had at any other point in my story so far. Because the situation, the financial world, indeed the world, was so ridiculous, actually so far *beyond* ridiculous, that it had to be fought. And I had to win. I would have paid just about any amount to exit the mortgage I was tied into with the, what I believe to be, ludicrous financial institution that is the current mortgage lender. However, very luckily for me, my genius financial advisor – Super Roger - found a clever way to reduce this fee, so it was less exorbitant than it could have been. Already I was winning. He also found a solo mortgage deal with another lender that was a much better deal than what the current mortgage lender were ever going to let me have, as a feckless single mother of two on Tax Credits with a historic 'debt' problem. So I did fight. And I did win.

The Incredible Mortgage Maths Diagram

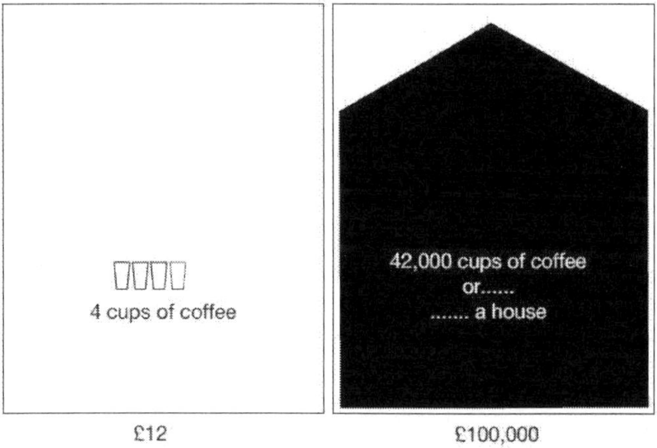

The Buy Out

My Emotional Support Worker from Behind Closed Doors had taught me that domestic abuse will continue post separation and that it will escalate as milestones approach. As I have shown, His threats and psychological abuse definitely escalated as moving day approached. It was the same, sadly, as the Transfer of Equity approached. It was the same pattern of conditions and threats and the pulling out of the rug from under my feet.

I had been able to start the process of applying for a solo mortgage with our existing mortgage lender in the February of 2018 and by the May He was hopping mad that He did not yet have His agreed 30k. He rang me demanding I "Hand it over now!" I explained that there was a process, involving a lot of financial and legal work being done, and that He could only have His money at the end of the process. I explained that this process had been slowed down by our current mortgage lender. That did not help. He demanded that I give Him the money before all of that is finished. WTF?! (I truly had no voice as far as He was concerned.) He concluded that He would use our existing mortgage as leverage to secure a second mortgage. Again, WTF?! He put the phone down and left me in a blind panic, worrying that He was going to do something to scupper the Transfer of Equity. I rang Super Roger. He said that he had no idea what He was talking about. Quickly he added that he was sure that He did not either. It turns out He didn't. A pointless, meaningless threat with which to instil panic (tick) and fear (tick) in me. At least I knew He was serious about the buy out, that He essentially wanted what I wanted – and needed, to be able to change the locks (thanks to that ludicrous legal 'grey area'). Furthermore, I knew He wanted it. Fast.

How stupid can I be? What followed after this angry phone call was weeks and weeks and weeks of procrastination and stalling via bizarre conditions or threats. He wanted half the contents of the family home or the value thereof. This is completely unreasonable, in family law terms, but I feigned agreement. Then He wanted us to go to mediation. I pointed out that we had no need for such a thing given that we had agreed on a sum for the buy out and I had also agreed to give Him half the contents of the family home or the value thereof. He conceded defeat and withdrew that ridiculous threat. Then He simply did nothing for a while, before coming up with the most inappropriate and cruel threat: I had to cancel a play date that I had arranged for our daughter so He could take her out, or He would not do the paperwork. I can take His cruelty, just about, I was used to it, but with this threat He was hurting our daughter. I am ashamed to say that I cancelled the play date. I also comforted our daughter when she cried (and rescheduled the play date for the following week, I am not that bad a mother, despite His opinion on the matter).

The following weekend He informed me that He had completed the first part of the paperwork and would complete the second, i.e. the last part on the following Monday. I was elated. It had worked. I had met His final (I thought) stupid and cruel demand and it had worked. I texted everyone who was following this latest sad and sick soap opera storyline, to tell them the good news.

Seriously, how stupid can I be? The next day He decided that He had witnessed poor parenting on my part – I was not a sufficiently strict disciplinarian – and concluded that when He had tried to talk to me about it I had been a poor communicator. He thus declared He would 'monitor' these two things – i.e. my parenting skills and my ability to communicate with Him - for a couple of weeks or so, noticeably twisting the knife yet further with such a vague time frame. Only then would He consider completing His paperwork for the buy out. I could not believe I had ever believed Him. I put a film on for my children and handed out smoothies and biscuits and then I lost it. I mean I lost my legs. I was floored. I was literally floored. I fell to the floor in the yard and hugged my knees and cried, yet again, for what felt like an eternity, as it always did. I could hear my children's laughter coming from inside the house which for some reason made me cry even more. Then my neighbour Simon came to see why I was not at the gathering and why I was not answering my phone. I got up off the floor and gathered up my children and told them we were going out.

Simon, along with my other neighbours and friends and my family, all hit a wall that afternoon, as I did. I could no longer play Him. I could no more believe that He would sign the final papers than I could believe He would stop eating four tubs of cottage cheese every day, relax His gym going routine or develop the ability to see anything from anyone else's point of view. Let me re-cap the ridiculous buy-out related, or rather buy-out *completely unrelated* threats, with some added information and musings in brackets after each one:

His buy out related threats

- Using our joint mortgage as leverage to secure a solo mortgage (WTF?)
- Taking half the contents of the family home or the value thereof (something He was not legally entitled to, but ended up taking, as I explain later)
- Mediation (when I was agreeing to everything, besides which, my research told me I would never be eligible for this, thanks to His abuse – perhaps the only time I found myself being thankful for His abuse)
- Cancelling a play date with our daughter (controlling His daughter's life, just when I thought He could not stoop any lower. Again, how stupid can I be?)
- Monitoring my parenting skills (remember I am a Bad Mother on at least three counts) and my communication skills (how *do* you negotiate with a terrorist?)

I finally had to do what I had always been scared of, what I had managed to avoid doing with moving Him out: I had to get legal on Him.

In preparation for this I flouted the grey-area-law (which quite frankly deserves to be flouted in my opinion, for being the *law* and a *grey area* – an oxymoron? Surely? This is, I believe, an area of the law that needs to be looked at, i.e. changed): I changed the locks. It was done in a heartbeat. It made me feel a curious blend of relief and fear. I knew that when He received the letter from my solicitor He could not come and bother me uninvited (and I would not be inviting anyone in who looked like they wanted to bother me). However, I was scared of what He would say and do if He ever found out that I had changed the locks on the house whilst He still co-owned it. Enter God (?)

The next day He came round to see the children and told me that He had lost His keys. I could not believe it. He would now never know what I had done. I tried hard not to beam at His tale of having been burgled. I saw my new friend Abbey that night. We had previously discussed our shared experience of wanting to believe in God but struggling to do so. We were not singing from the same hymn sheet, to tailor the expression. She declared quite simply, and beautifully (NB Abbey is not simple but she is most definitely beautiful) "That is God". I believe it has to have been. It was not as if I hadn't been prayed for that very morning. My friend Olivia had come to see how I was doing, having been updated on the whole it-is-now-not-happening-after-all front. She had asked if she could pray for me. I said yes. So we bowed our heads and Olivia talked to her friend, God, and I tried to keep my two year old son semi-quiet for a couple of minutes (and failed). That afternoon He got burgled. The only thing taken was His keys to the family home.

When I received the letter from my solicitor I could have scripted His sequence of responses, as I had with the enforced and surely most-futile-ever Relate session we attended post separation. Firstly, He was angry, all indignant at my daring to have been proactive, smart, just not completely stupid. He was adamant that He was going to get His own solicitor. I ever so slowly and clearly reminded Him that His dad is a barrister and can therefore read the letter and tell Him *for free* whether or not legal representation is required. I then, even more slowly and clearly reiterated what I had already explained, i.e. what the letter explains, i.e. that there are only two options facing Him: sign the TR1 form and get £30, 830 or refuse and in a week's time my solicitor will initiate legal proceedings which will result in Him getting less than £30, 830. Because the Transfer of Equity is the sale of the house from us to me and it will happen, He cannot stop it, it is the law.

Secondly, He became (more) stupid (than normal), leapt on my explanation about the Transfer of Equity being the sale of the house and declared that "Yes we should put the house on the market" (WTF?!) At this point I gave up trying to explain anything to Him. But about an hour later I received a text from Him declaring that He did not want to go down the legal route and would sign the TR1. I could not help but place a bet (with myself, in my head, because no one else was really playing this game with me) on how likely it was that His dad had ever so slowly and clearly explained to Him everything that the letter explained, i.e. everything that I had ever so slowly and clearly explained to Him about an hour earlier.

Two days later, He signed His TR1 - the final Transfer of Equity document. Two weeks later I received the following text from the NatWest solicitors Involegal:

Involegal is pleased to confirm completion of your NatWest remortgage

I have never deleted this text from my phone.

The re-mortgage and related Transfer of Equity were completed. On this day He received £30, 830 and my Best Nest became mine and mine alone.

The Transfer of Equity in Numbers

- £30, 830 given to Him
- 10 words
- 6 months
- 5 threats from Him
- 2 banks (including one *ridiculous* one)
- 1 solicitor's letter
- 1 (quasi-illegal or at least not at all moral) new lock

He still wanted £750 for half the value of the contents of the house. I said I could not afford to give it to Him, that I had spent quite a lot already on this particular day. He told me He would be withholding the Child Maintenance (£558.84 due the next day) until He received it. I have to provide some context here.

Firstly, the general context. At the time, He was earning c40k a year (in His Very Responsible, Stressful and Demanding Job) whilst I was earning c12k a year – an income so low that it gets topped up with Tax Credits by the government so that I can afford to work and care for two young children, and not become an absolutely feckless single mother of two living the high life on solely benefits. He has a father who came to visit the children and said, when the issue of the money I "owe" was raised yet again, that he could give Him "a lot of money" instead of His bothering me for it. He was living in a fully furnished flat at this point and was in the process of buying a house which He had told me was being sold to Him almost fully furnished.

Secondly, some very time specific context. The month when He refused to pay Child Maintenance He was having to pay the full rent on His two bedroom rented flat because His flat mate had moved out. It is hard not to conclude that this particular month He did not want to be feeling the pinch of paying double rent, and not paying the Child Maintenance *that He is legally obliged to pay* enabled Him to avoid that, to avoid going without anything Himself.

I must fast forward five months at this point, and explain that at this point, new year 2019, He did pay the missing Child Maintenance. In case you are wondering whether He had received some kind of blow-to-the head related epiphany and morphed into a decent human being and great father as a result, He had not. I simply found myself in the fortunate position of having something that He wanted, AKA a bargaining chip. The phrase 'there is no selfless good deed' could certainly have been written for Him.

As for the day I got the house, it was the same as on the day that I moved Him out, I was left with mixed feelings. On this occasion, they were a blend of relief, elation and euphoria alongside deep sadness for my children.

BODY

And now you've gone it feels as if the whole wide world is my stage
And now you've gone it's like I've been let out of my cage
I Could Say, Lily Allen

Annelle Dupuy DeSoto

My Emotional Support Worker told me to break some rules at home. She told me to let my children have their tea in front of the television sometimes. She told me to stay up late sometimes, watching a *whole* film. She told me to take up offers from friends and neighbours to babysit once in a while and go out for tea. She told me to break my relentless routine, basically, and allow a bit less structure in to my life occasionally. She basically told me to rebel. I think (for me) I did.

So far, apart from raising my voice to the previous mortgage lender, and enjoying the odd G&T, my recovery all sounds very Pollyanna doesn't it? I can certainly be quite the Pollyanna, but I believe there was always an edginess within me. Buried within me. Buried deeply within me. I did have my nose pierced when I was nineteen and when my nose rejected the piercing I instead got my ears pierced five more times, taking the total up to seven (go me!). To this day when I wear multiple earrings I feel in some way superior to women who wear only one neat pair. Utterly ridiculous of me, clearly. This nonsense shows me that I have been desperate for years to find my 'edge', clearly. I think it finally emerged and was essential to my recovery. Think Daryl Hannah's character in *Steel Magnolias* - although I already had the contact lenses, because He did not like me in glasses. (I was once told that I look like Daryl Hannah, funnily enough. I do not. I wish that I did).

My Behind Closed Doors Emotional Support Worker had said that I had changed, that day that she saw me when it was all over with the previous mortgage lender. And I *had* changed. The previous mortgage lender had helped to change me (as had what was still to come, which I will tell you about next). She told me that the next time she saw me she would bring the discharge paperwork. I did not like hearing his. But when I saw her a month later, and we worked through that paperwork, I knew that proceeding without my face to face sessions with her was the right thing for me to do.

Via separating from Him and moving Him out I was no longer controlled, I had reclaimed my time, I was back to managing my own time (very well). Via understanding domestic abuse, and experiencing great kindness and overwhelming love, I had reclaimed my mind by erasing all of (well, the vast majority of) the doubt that had been fogging it up, and filling it instead with kindness and love. But it turned out that there was one thing left that I had to reclaim: my body. Which, through two glorious experiences, I most certainly did.

F.L.A.G

"No form of skin modification is as layered with meaning

as tattooing, especially for women." (Mifflin 2013: 4)

I had heard so many positive things from people since I had left Him. Apparently I was "strong" and "courageous" and "brave" and all of the other words that mean similar things to these three. When my Godsister called me brave I joked that I ought to get a tattoo that said just that. She gasped and said she would hate to feel that she was responsible for me getting a tattoo. I reassured her that I was, of course, joking. I was 43 years old and had never wanted a tattoo. I had actually actively *not* wanted to ever have a tattoo. I was passionate about *not* having a tattoo. As someone who has always considered herself to not be a sheep in any way, and most definitely wanted to *not* be a sheep in any way, I could not possibly have one, because having one has, apparently, become more common than not having one, especially for women.

Two glorious books taught me that this is in fact true. In *Bodies of Subversion A Secret History of Women and Tattoos* Margaret Margaret Mifflin argues that "tattooing has finally jumped the boundaries of its subcultural confines." (Mifflin 2013: 135) In *Covered in Ink Tattoos, Women and The Politics of The Body* Beverley Yuen Thompson argues that estimates put the percentage of the adult population with tattoos at 20%. Both writers argue that for the first time in history, a woman is more likely to get a tattoo than a man.

It gets worse: In 1999 Matel celebrated Barbie's 40th birthday by giving her a tattoo. Oh great. Even Barbie has a tattoo, something which Mifflin argues is illustrative of tattooed women reaching "a tipping point of mainstream acceptance." (Mifflin 2013: 7) I most definitely had no choice but to draw the conclusion that *not* having a tattoo is now more different, original, subversive and edgy than having one. But this changed. I changed. Damn it. And at the same time, yay!

A curious thing happened to me, and it did *happen to me.* Vicky, one of my closest girlfriends had given me not only a Costa Coffee gift card laden with a small fortune, when I separated from Him, but also an intriguing badge with 'F.L.A.G' on it. The card said it was "A 'happy new life' present to remind you to stay strong and to look after yourself." She said she wanted me to still be able to treat myself and my children when single motherhood and the related reduced income might prohibit it. Hence the hefty Costa gift card. And she told me to look up F.L.A.G. I did. This is how I stumbled upon Clementine Ford's feminist manifesto *Fight Like A Girl*. It became fuel for my recovery. It was my mantra as I fought to get Him out of the family home and then to buy Him out of it. It was my affirmation. It was my modus operandi. And beyond being a mother and an advocate, my reason for recovering, for finding myself again, for being. If my story was an academic journal article, F.L.A.G would be the fun part of the title that comes after the colon. If my story was a movie, F.L.A.G would be in big font after the film title on the billboard posters, the strapline or tagline used to first pitch and then ultimately sell the movie (this explains why I quote Clementine Ford's book so very much in this book).

I didn't *decide* that I wanted a F.L.A.G. tattoo. Rather, gradually, I realised that I *had* to have it. I had to have F.L.A.G written on my body. Specifically, on my inner left arm, because I am left handed and generally left sided and because I wanted to see it and read it every day, to help me to never, ever forget what had happened to me and how I had got out of it. I truly did not decide this. It was a force external to me, telling me what I had to do. A burning desire which surprised me even more than all of my totally be-startled friends and family. Which does not seem possible to me (except for the fact that it was).

Once it had sunk in, I was excited, very excited. Actually, I was beyond excited. What is that exactly? Elated? Euphoric? Probably euphoric. But as it turned out, there was a waiting list for the tattooist who had been recommended to me by a dear friend, so I had to dial down the euphoria and try to remain only excited or at best/worst very excited, to get through the intervening weeks. The date for my tattoo was June 1st. It seemed so perfect a date. So memorable (as though I would ever, *could* ever, forget any date for this event, given my near hysteria (NB *not* HYSTERIA) at the mere thought of it).

As I waited for my date with my tattooist to come around, I asked her for references on women and tattoos. I poured over the two books she recommended. I read about tattooed circus ladies trampling conventional standards of feminine beauty and behaviour; women's interest in tattoos in the post-suffragist 1920s and a second wave of interest coinciding with the women's movement of the 1970s; and women in the 1980s getting tattoos to stand out whilst their conformist counterparts got cosmetic surgery to conform. Tattooed women did used to be edgy and subversive then.

According to Beverly Yuen Thompson those today who eschew the gender appropriate – i.e. small, cute and easily hidden – tattoos for larger scale tattoos on publicly visible skin, sleeves and depictions of images not considered feminine – all things 'scary': zombies, snakes and dragons – do flout normative beauty ideals and thus are edgy and subversive. However, "[s]imply having a tattoo is not gender transgressive. Tattoos are feminine so long as they are "small, cute and hidden," preferably located on a sexualized part of the body." (Beverly Yuen Thompson 2015: 44) My planned small, demure, easy to hide F.L.A.G tattoo was not going to make me edgy and subversive then. Again, damn it. But at least it was not going to be on a sexualized part of my body. And at least it was not going to be a complete cliché: a small heart or flower or butterfly or dolphin (NB women's bizarre fascination with dolphins leaves me both bemused and irrationally annoyed). And at least it was not going to be this:

"Using a computed tomography scan, researchers at the British Museum recently discovered that a female Egyptian mummy dating from 700 CE had the name "Michael" tattooed on her thigh." (Rosen, 2015)

Margaret Mifflin (2013) argues that women usually get tattoos for a reason, rather than just for the sake of getting tattooed as is the case with many men. I knew I was most certainly getting a tattoo for a reason. In another way, then, I was a cliché woman getting a tattoo. Damn it. But this did not bother me so much, because I believe that this is the smartest origin of a tattoo, and I want to be considered at least vaguely smart. I turned my attention to the sorts of reasons why women get tattoos and what they can represent to women. So much of what I read resonated with me. It is summarised below in a list (of course):

Reasons why women get tattoos

- An act of rebellion
- A re-affirming of a non-conformist spirit
- A gesture of self-expression
- An expression of one's personality
- An act of self-transformation
- A marker of a milestone or a personal transition or a special life event
- A badge of self-determination
- An emblem of empowerment or control
- An expression of personal or inner growth
- A reflection of a changing sense of self
- An illustration of taking control of one's life
- A celebration of work, life, love, heritage
- A representation of a strong spirit

Tick to all of the above. Again, damn it. There was more to my tattoo though. In an article for *The*

Hedgehog Review: Critical Reflections on Contemporary Culture, Christine Rosen argues that "[p]eople now embrace tattoos to honour someone who died, to commemorate an important life event, or to have *a permanent reminder of a personal mantra*." (Rosen 2015, emphasis added). Damn it. But at least this is not a totally ubiquitous reason for a woman to get a tattoo.

There was yet more to my tattoo though, sadly.

Prostitution 101

I never was the fantasy
Of what you want or wanted me to be
Playboy Mommy, Tori Amos

He never liked me to wear glasses. But it would be couched in such positive, complimentary terms, along the lines of 'They cover up your beautiful face'. I fell for this crap. His crap. For years. This does require a 'Damn it'. I had blonde highlights in my hair when He met me. Fast forward to the birth of our second child, I was extra busy, extra tired, 'me time' had dwindled to virtually nothing, I went back to my roots. He did not like this. This is when He campaigned for a long time for me to go blonde again. I struggled with this request - it was a request, not a demand, as I guess that would have been a step too far for Him, too retro, too vintage, too likely to blow His cover? I could not work out whether or not this was okay, living in 2000 whatever, as a feminist. Still, eventually, as I explained earlier, I went back to being made blonde. I like the way Epictetus describes what I did: Females are especially burdened by the attention they receive for their pleasing appearance. From the time they are young, they are flattered by males or evaluated only in terms of their outward appearance. Unfortunately, this can make a woman feel suited only to give men pleasure, and her true inner gifts may atrophy. She may feel compelled to put great effort and time into enhancing her outer beauty and distorting her natural self to please others. (Epictetus, The Art of Living)

What I more definitely consciously found to be worrying and hurtful and wrong was the way in which He made me feel that I was not sufficiently healthy. The body beautiful is what He lived for, so His suggestion that I was some kind of fast food gobbling couch potato who was 'letting herself go' was a huge insult coming from Him (to be fair, it would be from anybody). But this is how His constant policing of my eating made me feel. I remember vividly the first incident. It was at His dad's wedding. He asked me if I thought I should have two puddings (it was a very posh wedding and each 'pudding' was the size of a Ferrero Roche; they were very, very posh, expensive Ferrero Roche, basically). It was a loud comment. It was a public comment. I did not like it. This became a common occurrence. Not always loud and public, more often than not at home, behind closed doors, of course, as He honed His clever *modus operandi*, but His manner was the same: creepily smiley faux surprise. It was okay if I ate one treat food in a day, but if He became aware that I was doing it twice, He would refer to it in this manner. I had to account for myself. I had to account for this shockingly bad eating behaviour. I would give reasons: celebrating something, tired from a sleepless night, the food was a gift. These sorts of reasons never cut it with Him. He would refer to the fact that I could always exercise more (i.e. to work it off). Another opportunity to get me to exercise basically.

In *The Beauty Myth* (1990) Naomi Wolf argues that the emerging 'ideal' for women of extreme thinness was a socially mediated way to biologically suppress energy, defiance and resistance in young women who were otherwise the heiresses of feminism. With His policing of my diet and my exercising, it feels like He was attempting to do this to me. And why wouldn't He have been, when all He wanted to do was silence and control me?

Along with Wolf's theory, a very new practice resonates with me. I realise now that He was wordlessly, silently, body shaming me.

To criticize someone based on the shape, size, or appearance of their body. (Definition of body shaming in the Cambridge English Dictionary)

This delightful new social media friendly pastime tends to be very wordy, loud, explicit. But it was all about what was *not* said with Him. Another difference between regular body shaming and His policing of what I ate and my exercising was that His concern was that I did not *end up* too fat, too out of shape, too let go. That is, His body shaming of me was *preventative*. I feel very strongly that His brand of body shaming - silent, preventative body shaming – is every bit as cruel and damaging as the regular kind. It was also a near constant reminder that I was not living with unconditional love (or love at all, I realised, eventually, thank God, hence this book). Reading body shaming's synonyms and related words in the Cambridge English Dictionary brings home just how vile it is:

Aspersions; Attack; Bad-mouth; Be down on; Be gunning for; Be on somebody's back; Beat up on; Blast; Call somebody out; Censure; Condemn; Damn; Damn with faint praise; Deny; Denounce; Derogate; Dig; Disparage; Find fault with; Hate; Knock; Low blow; Malign; Maul; Nag; Needle; Nit pick; Pick holes in; Pick someone to pieces; Pot shot; Pound away at; Pour scorn on; Pull apart; Put down; Put the boot in; Rip into; Rubbish; Run down; Slag off; Slam; Slap down; Slate; Snipe; Swipe at; Tear apart; Think poorly of; Trash; and Turn on (not in the good way).

As I have explained, I had diligently, studiously and methodically worked my way through work sheets on domestic abuse, educating myself on all of the different forms and facets of domestic abuse, ticking off the ones which I had experienced as I worked. It took more than one read through various domestic abuse check lists (three, actually) for me to stop ignoring the sexual abuse pages, as I tried to work out why I had to reclaim my body. I ticked off issues that might, at first glance, seem to be less than serious issues, but what these issues boiled down to for me were two things. Firstly, He moaned profusely that I did not dress sexily, provocatively for Him, as other women do for their partners (apparently oh so happily and enthusiastically). Secondly, He was ever so subtly critical of my sexual performance (or complete lack of, apparently) and explicitly, vociferously critical of my refusal to dance for Him. He didn't so much want a Stepford Wife as a Stepford Pole Dancer. I will have to get quite feminist and political about this in a minute. Let's call that Reason Two Why I Won't Ever Dress Provocatively and Act Like a Pole Dancer. Reason One is not feminist nor political. It is purely practical.

Reason One Why I Won't Ever Dress Provocatively and Act Like a Pole Dancer

It is not possible to buy overtly, pole dancerishly (yes, a made up word but I think it needs to be a word) 'sexy' bras for someone as flat chested as I am. I am too tall and have very broad shoulders and so cannot simply shop in pre-teen underwear departments which would actually cater for my pre-teen size breasts, or cup size, to use the lingo of the bras world I am not a part of. But when I recently tried to buy actual bras, actual grown up women's bras, I was only able to find something that fitted me called 'bralets', something frighteningly similar to what can be found in pre-teen underwear departments. Except a bit bigger, as in wider, not more buxom. A pack of two cost me £6, so pre-teen underwear department prices then. Funnily enough, they are not overtly, pole dancerishly 'sexy'. They are practical, comfortable, plain – the kind of underwear that would be made for women if we ended up in a war with rationing etc. a la WW2, 'utility underwear' if you like.

Reason Two Why I Won't Ever Dress Provocatively and Act Like a Pole Dancer

In her book *The New Feminism* (1998) Walter argued that whilst the women's movement had quietened down, feminism ran through life. She argued that feminists could focus on achieving political, social and financial equality, rather than on women's private lives – sex, relationships, clothing. In her book *Living Dolls The Return of Sexism* (2010) she explains that she was not just wrong but *entirely* wrong.

Walter writes of slutty, sultry dolls aimed at young girls and argues that there is occurring the fusing of the doll and the real girl within the lives of girls and that it continues into adulthood. She links this disturbing development to the movement of the sex industry from the margins to the mainstream of our society, which has seen the emergence of city centre lap-dancing clubs and the related new fashion for pole-dancing, something which women are encouraged to take classes in because to do so is *liberating.* (WTF?)

There seems to me to be only one next logical step with this link between the sex industry and evening classes for women (two things which used to be poles apart – no pun intended - and thus most likely would never pop up in the same sentence): Prostitution 101. I do not think that this is a ridiculous idea. It is not so long ago that it would have been thought ridiculous that there might ever be any kind of women's evening class related to the sex industry. Learning to dance like a pole dancer is learning the skills of a kind of sex worker. How long before women are encouraged to learn the skills of another kind of sex worker: a prostitute, to give their male partners all the benefits of a prostitute without the attached price tag? I have to trot out the phrase 'having their cake and eating it too', as it seems so apt here, but it makes me feel sad for cake which, as you know, I adore.

Walter argues that liberation and empowerment have become equated with objectification. In the following extract, quoted at length because it covers so much history, so much feminism, she sums up this problem of the current link between femininity/feminine beauty/female sexuality and the sex industry:

"For more than 200 years, feminists have been criticising the way that artificial images of feminine beauty are held up as the ideal to which women should aspire. From Mary Wollstonecraft's *A Vindication of the Rights of Woman* in 1792, to Simone de Beauvoir's *The Second Sex* in 1949, to Germaine Greer's *The Female Eunuch* in 1970, to Naomi Wolf's *The Beauty Myth* in 1990, brilliant and angry women have demanded a change in these ideals. Yet far from fading away, they have become narrower and more powerful than ever. What's more, throughout much of our society, the image of female perfection to which women are encouraged to aspire has become more and more defined by sexual allure... The image of female sexuality has become more than ever defined by the terms of the sex industry.

Throughout our society, female sexuality now tends to be seen in a very narrow light, often defined by slender exhibitionists with large breasts gyrating around poles in their underwear." (Walter 2010: 3)

Later I write about objectification, about His objectification of me, at some length. Here I simply want to point out that objectification is gendered, that is, it is routine and inescapable for most women, yet it is not something that men have to deal with on a daily basis. It seems unsurprising, then, that it comes up in a book which explores gender - *Gender In World Perspective by* Connell and Pearse. They argue that "[a] whole industry, ranging from heavy pornography and prostitution to soft-core advertising, markets women's bodies as objects of consumption by men." (Connell and Pearse 2015: 8) In *Fight Like A Girl* Clementine Ford writes of men bonding over the degradation of women's bodies; of the omnipresent male gaze, of no woman 'earning' the right at any time to have scrutiny withheld and thus being dehumanized on a daily basis. She sums all of this up magnificently in what I believe is a devastatingly accurate rant:

"Girls are raised to believe that the most important thing we can be is pretty. We learn early on that this won't just garner us attention and rewards, but is in fact the rent we must pay in order to negotiate even the most illusory of powers. If we aren't offering something pleasant for men to look at while they're forced to listen to us, what's the point of us at all? The message isn't so much banged into us as it is kneaded into the fabric of our identities. To be granted an audience with the Gods, we must bring the appropriate tributes of beauty, complicity and deferential admiration. Those who turn up empty-handed will be punished. How many times have you heard or seen someone dismiss a woman's opinion by calling her ugly? By calling her a slut? Maybe even a dumb cunt?" (Ford 2018: 22)

Ford goes on to argue that allowing society to own women's bodies in this way is so long-standing and deep-rooted that it can pass by unnoticed today. This would explain young women's stories such as the following written about by Natasha Walter in *Living Dolls The Return of Sexism*. She writes of a young woman whom she interviewed – a well-educated young woman who wanted to become an actress – who found herself financially desperate and taking a job in a lap-dancing club. The young woman explained that she had got the impression from our culture that lap-dancing was *empowering for women*. However, she found herself *demeaned and worse dehumanised* (YOU THINK?!)

I steadfastly refused to ever cavort around in (the) sexy lingerie (that I would not have been able to purchase anyway) for Him because to do so, even to be *asked* to do so, felt demeaning. Walter argues that "[t]he messages and values of this revitalised sex industry have reached deep into the hearts of many young men and women." (Walter 2010: 4) They certainly reached deep into His heart. I am proud to this day that I never did demean myself. Not that I ever could have, actually. Never mind the bra problem, I cannot dance, I have two left feet, both of which are a size 9-10. In short, with my flat chest, broad shoulders and big feet would I not have resembled a man in drag – and probably have had to wear stripper shoes purchased from a shop for drag artists? (Maybe He is gay or at least bisexual or at the very least bi-curious?)

As I tried to work out why the idea of reclaiming my body was speaking to me so loudly, given that the sexual abuse issues I was aware of did not seem sufficiently alarming (I realise now that they are), I came across Renee Engeln's book *Beauty Sick How the Cultural Obsession with Appearance Hurts Girls and Women*. In it, Engeln puts forward the argument that our culture focuses on women's appearance over anything else they might do, say or be – which she argues is explained by objectification theory - and that this feeds 'beauty sickness'. She defines this condition as what happens when women's energy is diverted to what they see in the mirror and trying (desperately) to make it match to a wholly unattainable beauty ideal, so that other areas of their lives, or potential areas of their lives, suffer, along with their physical and mental health, and the quest for gender equality.

Engeln goes a step further with objectification theory. She argues that, over time, the awareness that other people are evaluating a woman's looks becomes internalised and the woman herself becomes the closest observer of her own body. This is self-objectification, also known as body monitoring and body surveillance. In the following extract she defines these two related concepts and explains why the second is so damaging to women:

"[T]he essence of objectification is thinking about women's bodies as things to be looked at. Self-objectification, in simplest terms, is what happens when you take that perspective on yourself – you start to see yourself as just a thing to be looked at. But self-objectification is actually a little more complicated, because it doesn't just involve thinking of your body in terms of how it looks, but also failing to think of your body in terms of what it does." (Engeln 2017: 286-7)

Engeln also argues that the more a woman's body becomes an object, the less she is aware of its *needs*. When I read Engeln's book I could not help but wonder how much His objectification of me had led to self-objectification, my not giving my body what it needs, i.e. the disordered eating of my ridiculous diet of porridge that I practised for a long time.

Vintage Tin

"A woman may need some time and distance before she can come to realise that she was not responsible for her partner's sexual mistreatment of her, before she can even name what he did." (Bancroft 2002: 173)

This was/is certainly true for me. As I tried to work out just why I so desperately felt that I needed to reclaim my body, from criticism and objectification and self-objectification, I remembered the following conversation:

I love my beautiful new vintage Jacob's Crackers tin. But I do not like Jacob's Crackers, never have, they are tasteless and dry. I could put other crackers in it? But I always have too many packets of different crackers on the go at any one time to fit them all in the tin, which is made for one packet of crackers only. Maybe people ate less crackers in The Olden Days? Maybe there was only Jacob's Crackers in The Olden Days and people only ever opened one packet of them at a time, hence they only needed a tin to fit a maximum of one packet of Jacob's Crackers? That must be it. Interesting. And clever me for working it out. Another food item? Actually, it might be made of dodgy old materials – lead tin with lead paint on it, welded together with arsenic laden vintage glue - so better not put anything edible in it, or it will be rendered inedible. How pointless would that be? My buttons? I have got a buttons jar, I like being able to see all of the buttons. Craft things? Yes! Pens. Perfect. It is a long and thin (Jacob's Crackers packet shaped) tin so it is perfect for pens. Brilliant. Sorted. Happy.

This was an internal conversation, i.e. a conversation that I had with myself. It took place (in my head) one 'date night' – which was a euphemism for sex - to get my mind off what was happening and thus enable me to get through it. I told two girlfriends about what I had done the following weekend. It made them laugh. I laughed. It was ridiculous. It was funny. It was darkly funny. But I fear that this humour was enabling me to go on masking the horror I had come to live with of feeling violated. Because deep down I did know that when I had sex with Him I was doing something that I did not want to do, hence I was being violated. In *Why Does He Do That? Inside The Minds of Angry and Controlling Men* Lundy Bancroft sums up why having sex with Him had become so horrific for me:

"[C]oercive, uncaring sex is similar to physical violence in its effects, and can be worse in many ways. And part of why it feels so degrading is that a woman can sense the fact that in her partner's mind she has ceased to exist as a human being." (Bancroft 2002: 177)

I returned one day, then, to the domestic abuse work sheets and re-read the notes on marital rape (which I am extending to rape within a cohabiting relationship):

If the victim does not have the choice to say 'no' without consequences it is still rape.

Consequences is a very vague term. I thought about the consequences for me and had to admit that I had thought about them whilst in the relationship. They had, for years, become the only reason I had sex with Him – think Julia Roberts' character at the start of *Sleeping With The Enemy*. I had sex with Him on as regular a basis as I could bear, because I feared that if I did not He would leave me (and the irony of this is not lost on me: being so scared for so long of losing someone I now know to be an abuser and have thus worked very hard myself to lose). There were lesser consequences too. He would make me feel guilty, telling me that He felt like I did not love Him anymore (His Damn Feelings Again), and I would experience His popular tactics of sulking and ignoring me (i.e. emotional and psychological abuse) and the equally common experience of being criticised for being a bad partner (He loved to criticise me, remember His Criticisms of Me and the four Bad Me's?) So I ticked a fifth box. I ticked the 'Rape' box.

Rape. A place I had already visited. I had been there and done that and I literally have the (self-harming induced) scars to prove it, worn like a sick badge of honour ever since. I was drug raped by a supposed boyfriend at university. I mean, I assume I was because, whilst I have no memory of the attack, I ended up a pregnant virgin: a cast iron oxymoron. It was hard not to formulate the argument that I am the common denominator, that I somehow attract or am attracted to the vilest men imaginable. But I decided that I would not go down this path. And I will never go down this path. I will never do it. That day I decided a lot of things that I will never do:

Things I decided I will never do

- I will never have sex when I do not want to
- I will never have sex with someone who has ever told me to "Fuck off"
- I will never let myself think that I am 'bad in bed' – because for me it is about feelings, not skills and performance and Trip Advisor-esque ratings
- I will never let myself think that I am not sexy and that I require lacy equipment to be so – because, for me, sexy does not equate to anything involving lace trimming – or that I need to cavort around like a lap dancer to be so – because, for me, sexy does not

equate to cavorting around like a lap dancer

I also decided what I will do (it is a much shorter list):

Things I decided I will do

- I will reclaim my body

This is what I did with my F.L.A.G tattoo. I reclaimed my body from being shrouded in a captive wardrobe. I reclaimed my body from being labelled not healthy enough, not fit enough, not sexy enough, not sexy *at all*. I reclaimed my body from being raped. I had no physical scars. But I wanted something on my body to remind me, to remind me in a *positive* way (unlike my self-harming scars) of what I had been through, recognised and got away from. Margaret Mifflin sums this up perfectly:

"In the never-ending project of women's transformation, tattoos are both an end and a beginning, a problem and a solution. Written on the skin – the very membrane that separates the self from the world – they're diary entries and public announcements, conversation pieces and countercultural totems, valentine's to lovers, memorials to the dead, *reminders to the self*." (Mifflin 2013: 147; italics added)

"Reclaiming your body". This is what the tattooist I chose wrote about her artistry on her website, and I discovered through my reading around women and tattoos that for many women they symbolize a reclaiming of the body. So I discovered once again that I am in no way different or special with my reason for wanting a tattoo. It is something that many, many women before me have done. But this never became a 'damn it' moment. I found it just too sad. But I still wanted to read and learn more about it.

Margaret Mifflin writes of women having tattoos to write over the sense of physical violation and rebuild their self-image following sexual abuse in childhood and to reclaim their bodies after rape and sexual abuse. Physical scars can be life-long reminders of abuse and tattoo artist Flavia Carvalho, who runs a studio in Curitiba, Brasil, decided to do something about it. Her project - A Pele da Flor - (The Skin of the Flower) is about giving hurt women tattoos free of charge to help women to cover scars left from knives and bullets. She's transforming these unpleasant mementos into tools of empowerment and beauty. "I started the project quite recently, and I had no idea it would receive this much media attention," Carvalho told The Huffington Post. "It began very spontaneously. As I said, my services are a hundred per cent voluntary, and the only 'cost' women need to invest is to [take the time to] choose a design for their tattoos!" (The Huffington Post)

In his book on coercive control Stark (2009) writes of perpetrators enforcing marks of ownership on women. Such marking includes bites, burns and tattoos. He argues that whilst there has been no research into this practice to draw on, the National Coalition Against Domestic Violence (NCADV) and the American Academy of Facial ,

Plastic, and Reconstructive Surgery have developed a jointly run free program for removing tattoos and other scars inflicted on battered women and their children by abusers, because it is so common.

Mifflin writes about a woman who had not an abuse scar but a mastectomy scar tattooed and the effect it had on her. It reminded me of my Behind Closed Doors Emotional Support Worker saying, at what turned out to be our penultimate face to face session, that I had changed, which I believe is in part down to my having booked my tattoo appointment (and having become deliriously happy about having done so):

"I have a picture of me taken before and after... and I can see the change in my eyes in those pictures. It's a feeling of having taken something essentially negative and turned it into something beautiful." (Mifflin 2013: 6)

Something beautiful, but painful. Or so I had assumed, and actually hoped. And quite gory:

"[P]ersonal tattoos often include a lesson learned through a particular life-changing event, the hope that the future will be enriched by this lesson – and its tattooed reminder. "A bloodied truce" is created during the moment of inscription, ensuring the pain of permanence in order to earn this lifelong memento." (Beverly Yuen Thompson 2015: 38)

Given why I was getting the tattoo, given what it symbolised for me, I was truly disappointed that I did not experience anything like "a bloodied truce" or "the pain of permanence". Getting my tattoo did not cause me any pain. I wanted a bit of pain, surely that was an important part of my tattoo? But I felt nothing. Nothing physical. Nothing negative. Nothing but happiness and joy and excitement and exhilaration. And there was no healing. Because there was never a wound. No blood. No scab. No wound. I waited for the apparently highly likely itchiness and scabbing over. I was waiting oh so diligently to not touch my tattoo, to leave it well alone, to let the wound heal. But it never happened. From the moment I took off the cling film, six hours after I had been inked, and washed my tattoo to wash away the remnants of the transfer, my tattoo looked as it does to this day: perfect; beautiful. I cannot help but wonder whether this was somehow symbolic, whether something, someone (the God I have always been unable to believe in? Olivia who I can and do believe in?) had decided that I had suffered enough, that I had been hurt and wounded enough already? A very wise girlfriend summed it up perfectly when she said my tattoo was easily gained but hard earned.

Mr O AKA Heroin

An attraction I just can't explain
But I knew I was never gonna be the same
I'd be lying if I said that I always chose what was good
Shelby 68, Kylie Minogue

In her book *Living with the Dominator A book about the Freedom Programme* (2008) Pat Craven not only describes and defines the Dominator but also his polar opposite: Mr Right. She defines him as "a blueprint for a reasonable friend or partner" (Craven 2008: 16). Mr Right has several facets: The Friend, The Liberator, The Confidence Booster, The Negotiator, The Truthteller, The Goodfather, The Partner and The Lover. I have always hated the term and concept of 'Mr Right' – indeed, it could be argued that my entire Ph.D. derives from this pet peeve – and I can state categorically that after separating from Him I did not fall into the arms of 'Mr Right', but I did fall into the arms - or rather the lap - of Mr Right Now.

A gregreat love affair played an enormous part in my recovery and healing process. It helped me so very much to heal after separating from the man I had loved with all of my heart for over a decade, the father of my two beautiful children, the man who I had come to know as a systematic and cruel abuser. Along with my F.L.A.G tattoo, it is the other experience which enabled me to reclaim my body.
After separating from Him, as I started out on the long and arduous journey of securing actual physical separation, I confided in a friend: Mr O. I emailed him. I told him, briefly, my story, my hell. He WhatsApped me back. He wrote that I could ring him anytime. But WhatsApping became our thing. And it became my lifeline. It brought me back to life. He brought me back to life. The part of me capable of feeling love and attraction and sexiness had long been dead and gone (I was a zombie, remember? There are no love scenes in zombie

films, are there?) Mr O became my biggest source of support. And then some.

Mr O read my messages full of pain and stress and fear and offered useful advice and kind words in response to them. He also cheered me up with (predominantly terrible) jokes (I loved them all). He sent me a beautiful extract from Simon and Garfunkel's *Bridge Over Troubled Water* when I messaged to say that I was feeling lonely. He messaged me "You are a special person. Believe it." After a day spent together he messaged me the beautiful *Perfect Day* lyric by Lou Reed. When I told him a service user at work had likened me to Hamlet's Ophelia he messaged me saying "Ophelia was a tragic beauty in Hamlet. Only the second part applies." He started to call me Dr O (and he does so to this day) and I woke one morning to the quote "Ophelia is a dangerous storm." (Leo Varadkar, 171017). He told me "Just keep battling. You will triumph." He messaged me "Long fingers, long toes, long legs and long on resilience."

Then, on 9th December 2017, I woke to one of the most beautiful experiences of my life. I woke to the message "**Apparently Helen means shining light**". If there is an exact opposite to being told to "Fuck off", then this surely has to be it. He had Googled my name. Out of the blue one day he had *Googled my name* and sent me a beautiful message to wake up to. I will never forget that morning. I will never forget that message. Needless to say, I had been falling in love with him (how could I not?) This sealed the deal (how could it not?)

Eventually, inevitably, hoping for closure, I wrote

him a letter explaining how I felt. But I never sent it to him. To this day, it lives in my memory box, a most treasured possession lying amongst many other such possessions, including drawings from my children; my late second dad's left handed silver cake fork; the liberty mirror my late great godmother gave me; the tiny pottery book I wore around my neck for many of my youthful years, filled with quotes and words of (back then believed to be) wisdom from friends; and Maurice and Alphonse, the tiny glow in the dark figurines from my university friend Rachel E – too long and probably boring a story for even me to go into.

I never did send him the letter because I ended up telling him, over lunch one day, quite simply that I had "grown far too fond of him". I needed closure. I had expected to hear, kindly and gently, that he did not think of me in that way. Then we could smile about my wholly inappropriate crush and carry on sweetly messaging and occasionally lunching. I had, of course, day dreamed about a different response, but it was just that: a dream, not real, it could never be real. But I had never day dreamed about what actually happened next, about hearing what he said to me that day. After a lot of sitting and talking and walking and talking, and talking and talking and talking and talking, he stood in front of me and said "I love you". The café that we had lunched in that day played Rihanna's *We Found Love* on the radio. With its joyfully accurate lyric "we found love in a hopeless place", I kind of love (and hate) the agonisingly ironic relevance.

I don't think I had ever been so (pleasantly)

surprised before (I had been very unpleasantly surprised on several occasions, hence my story i.e. this book). I don't think I had ever been so moved by those three words before. I think I had forgotten what hearing them can really feel like, because I had grown so used to hearing Him trot them out on a daily basis, each time waiting for me to dutifully say them back like a pre-programmed Stepford Wife. It is impossible to describe how surprised I was to hear them from Mr O, or of how hearing him say them to me made me feel.

A possible comparison is heroin - Trademark name. I enjoyed this very much once. Just once. When in labour with my daughter. In medical settings they use the chemical name of diamorphine, of course, maybe so as not to be seen to be promoting the delights of heroin; because it is delightful. I was in agony (hence the need for the heroin/diamorphine). I can remember so clearly being told that it would not take the pain away but that it would relax me. "Relax"? Not the word that I would have used. I remember so vividly thinking that I was still in agony but that it was totally fine, because everything was totally fine (and I distinctly remember thinking that I totally understood where heroin addicts were coming from). When Mr O stood in front of me and said "I love you" everything was totally fine. I was still in the early stages of terror and panic as my relationship, my family, my life imploded, but still, in that moment, in that beautiful moment, everything was totally fine. David Hamilton describes this oh so perfectly in the first of his books on kindness. He argues that

when we are in love
"oxytocin is flowing through our brain and body. And we see the best in people, even those who have hurt us in the past. We are more forgiving and accepting. We trust people more. The fear of betrayal doesn't register with us in the same way. For us, *the world is a beautiful place*." (Hamilton 2010: 65; emphasis added.)

What unfolded next was a love affair. It was beautiful. I was in love with him and all that he did and said told me that it was mutual. So we were in love with each other. And we made each other laugh. And we duelled with our brains and he love, love, loved it when I won, because he loved finding proof that I am clever (he thinks I am clever). He loved to tell me so and I loved to find arguments that proved him wrong (I don't want to be thought of as a complete idiot, but at the same time I really do not think I am all that clever; maybe this makes me delightfully complex or complicated? That would be good shoe-horned into the lonely hearts ad. I will surely need to write eventually, wouldn't it?) And it was incredibly passionate (aren't they always? Isn't this the point of a love affair?)

Naomi Wolf's Vagina

An ability that some people believe they have that seems to give them information without using the five senses of sight, hearing, touch, smell, or taste.
(Definition of sixth sense in the Cambridge English Dictionary)

I have a sixth sense. I truly believe in this sense.

Many times in my life a thought has pinged through my brain, startled me, surprised me, stopped me in my tracks. These thoughts have always panned out. After breaking up with a long-term partner in my twenties I had to tell a dear mutual friend. She instantly stated "I will not pick a side". She then went upstairs and spent the rest of the evening comforting the ex-partner who was still languishing in the house that I owned, licking his wounds. I never heard from her again. Another time, I bumped into a mum friend who introduced me to a new mum friend. I instantly thought 'I have been replaced'. What an odd thought to have, friends can have other friends. It is not a one-in-one-out situation. Except that it was, it seems. I never heard from this mum friend again.

I discovered that I have a seventh sense. One day He hugged me and I quickly drew back. He said that to an outsider it would look like I was being hugged by someone who was abusing me. I was taken aback, confused, baffled. I know now that this was my seventh sense. Because whilst I had no idea what He was talking about, my body did. My body knew that He was my abuser. My body knew this before my brain did. And this is why it was no longer working.

My body did not work anymore. Well, it worked as in it carried out work. In this sense it worked hard. It worked bloody hard, actually, seven days a week – as I have already explained and rammed home for good measure via the use of both a table and a diagram - for a long time with a 4am start, due to our robot baby son, which necessitated my having the bedtime of a six year old (I had a six year old for a while whilst having the bedtime of one, which was convenient). What I mean is it ceased to work in any grown up, sexual, sensual, womanly sense. This is why when I saw the counsellor and talked about "date nights" she said it made her skin crawl. I remember thinking that she really does not mince her words, which I loved about her, but when I returned to work with her the following year she explained to me that she was reflecting back what she saw emanating from me. This is why I had come to the conclusion that I was sexually dysfunctional, or to coin a misogynistic term that I do so hate: frigid.

Well, it wasn't the reason, really, or the complete reason. The complete, or overarching, reason that I had come to this conclusion was because I had come to believe that everything was always my fault in the relationship. I had come to a point where I doubted myself in every way possible and this was no exception. I decided, therefore, that if I had come to detest and dread sex with Him, there was something very wrong with me and so I needed to see a sex therapist. I got as far as asking a therapist friend to provide me with the relevant contact details. But, luckily for me, I was too busy with my children, simply too exhausted by my life basically, to ever act on the information. I say lucky, because it would have been an expensive way to hear from a professional that *it is normal to not want to have sex with someone who tells you to "Fuck off"*.

I know now that I was not in any way broken,

malfunctioning, ill or dysfunctional. A quote from Stephen Fry's character in the film *Peter's Friends* springs to mind: "I am not really in the vagina business." I was not really in the vagina business. I used to be. I used to enjoy sex with Him. I used to have orgasms. I enjoyed them, very much. Orgasms do tend to be enjoyable, don't they? But they ceased to exist. Sex ceased to be enjoyable. Probably because the orgasms ceased to exist. Enter Naomi Wolf's *Vagina* (no pun intended). In *Vagina A New Biography* (Wolf 2013) Naomi Wolf formulates a compelling argument concerning the link between the brain and the vagina (a word which Wolf uses for the entire female sex organ, including labia, clitoris, introitus and mouth of cervix).

The book began as a historical and cultural journey but soon became a very personal and necessary act of discovery for Wolf. She needed to learn the truth about the vagina following a medical crisis involving her experiencing a loss of sensation inside her body, an emotional numbness, a kind of depression, despair. She explains "I felt I was losing, somehow, what made me a woman, and that I could not face living in this condition for the rest of my life." (Wolf 2013: 13) When I first read this it felt instantly all too familiar. She went on to have an experience that suggested a possibly crucial relationship of the vagina to female consciousness itself.

I won't go into the biology of the pelvic nerve, the (as Wolf puts it) dreamy autonomic nervous system (ANS) and the sympathetic nervous system

(SNS), and her related argument concerning 'the Goddess Array', or all of the related neurobiological research into female sexual pleasure, because Wolf has done this already, obviously (and brilliantly, and ANYONE who enjoys sex or wants to enjoy sex involving a vagina MUST READ WOLF's VAGINA). I will just concisely restate her simple way of explaining the concept of a brain-vagina connection (and it is simple, or I would not be able to understand it). Citing the well known brain-uterus and brain-breast tissue connections she explains:

"If you look at the neurology and biochemistry of childbirth and lactation, you will see that it is not weird at all, really, to maintain that the vagina sends signals resulting in thoughts and emotions, because the uterus in labour and delivery –the breasts in lactation – send signals that result in thoughts and emotions, too." (Wolf 2013: 36)

How exactly, then, does Wolf explain why my body was not working with Him anymore? She argues that "[j]ust as being valued and relaxed can heighten female sexual response, 'bad stress' can dramatically interfere with all of women's sexual processes" (Wolf 2013: 34) I did not feel valued by Him in any way – not my work, not my personality, not my body, not my sexuality, nothing. And given the myriad ways He was abusing me there was a lot of 'bad stress' (I am slightly confused by the term 'bad stress' – what is 'good stress'? – but I still feel there was a lot of it in my relationship with Him).

There is more that resonated with me. Wolf

writes of the importance of female sexuality being treated with love and respect and the related silencing of the usual inner voices that say a woman is not good enough, not beautiful enough, not pleasing enough to others. Does an *external* voice (His), saying *all* of those things, *during* sex count? I think so, given that Wolf argues that how a man speaks to a woman even *beforehand* determines whether or not she can take an intimate touch.

Wolf's genius brain-vagina connection research, writing and theorising spoke to me and explained my confusing relationship, and indeed life, to me as much as everything I had read on domestic abuse – traumatic bond attachment, the cycle of abuse, objectification, gaslighting, all of it. Just as my domestic abuse reading and learning taught me that I was not a bad partner, mother or person in general, and thus was not in need of counselling, and that I was not going mad (and, indeed, had not already actually gone completely mad), and thus was not in need of medication, Wolf's genius book taught me that I was not sexually dysfunctional, and thus I was not in need of sex therapy *and never had been.*

I have written more than once in this book of how I ended up feeling like a zombie in my relationship with Him. Zombies are the walking dead. So zombies are dead. So they do not have souls. Very interesting, I thought, when I read the following:

"Female sexual pleasure, rightly understood, is not just about sexuality or just about pleasure. It serves, also, as a medium of female self-knowledge and hopefulness; female creativity and courage; female focus and initiative; female bliss and transcendence; and as a medium of a sensibility that feels very much like freedom. To understand the vagina properly is to realize that it is not only coextensive with the female brain, but is also, essentially, *part of the female soul*." (Wolf 2012: 4, emphasis added)

My body was not functioning, or was malfunctioning - I was right about that at least – and this was because I had ceased to feel loved, to believe that He loved me, or at least my vagina had before I had (as I explained earlier, my body was ahead of my brain; certainly my vagina was leading the way). This explains why contact with Him had become akin to being bothered by an oversized, insensitive salami (Note: if He ever reads this description He would be elated at being described as "oversized" given that growing such a sized penis seems to be His proudest achievement, not that He had anything to do with it, of course) and being mauled by someone wearing gardening gloves (I don't think He would be so fond of this description).

"Why a Goddess? Goddesses are powerful; those around them hold them in reverence. Goddesses do not need to doubt themselves, their value, or their allure – they can even be a bit self-absorbed... And Goddesses are entitled, without anxiety or guilt or self-reproach, to high levels of attention and pleasure." (Wolf 2012: 412-3)

Because of Mr O, through Mr O, gloriously with Mr O, I rediscovered my sexuality, my sexiness, my own body. I had a body again. A working woman's body. A sexual, sexy, working woman's body. And it worked so beautifully well with Mr O (read Wolf's explanation of 'The Goddess Array' if you need help understanding what I mean; if you have already read Wolf's book then you will be feeling very happy for me right now). Along with my tattoo, through my glorious love affair with Mr O, I reclaimed my body. I was no longer a zombie. I was "a Goddess", apparently. I was in lust as well as in love. AKA the holy grail or nirvana.

Love affairs or flings have to end though, don't they? The nature of the beast. I ended my glorious love affair with Mr O after a year. It was a sad decision but also a happy one, for he had given me so much. As well as making me feel like a woman again, he had given me the emotional support I needed to help me get through the most painful experience of my life; he had introduced me to music I would probably never have discovered otherwise; he had showed me what I want and need from a relationship; and, perhaps most importantly, through our love affair I discovered that I have the strength to hold out for one that gives me *all* of these things. We remain the closest of friends (how could we not?)

"Fuck off" v "Shining light"

Effects	"Fuck Off"	"Shining Light"
Facial muscles used	(to frown) 4 or 10	(to smile) 6 or 10
Space take up	Fall to the floor, hug knees, tuck head in	Stand tall (5 foot 10")
Energy use	Motionless; still; only energy used is for symptoms of crying: blowing nose and wiping tears away	Confidence boost = power through tasks, boring and fun ones, thus using a lot of energy, closest this single working mother of two gets to a work out
Appetite i.e. energy reserves created	Loss of appetite = do not eat (skip a meal) = low energy levels for the foreseeable	Healthy appetite intact = eat = normal energy levels for the foreseeable
Chemicals released	Fight / flight chemicals released: AKA The Three Major Stress Hormones: Adrenalin Cortisol Norepinephrine	Chemicals released when in love: Testosterone Oestrogen Dopamine Norepinephrine AKA Adrenalin Serotonin
Sociability	Chemicals released = low mood = withdraw from socialising = low mood persists because lonely and no one is lifting mood i.e. the most vicious of cycles	Chemical released = happy = up for socialising = mood raised up further via kind words and fun etc. i.e. a most positive cycle

WORDS

If I speak at one constant volume
At one constant pitch
At one constant rhythm right into your ear
You still won't hear
A Small Victory, Faith No More

The Voiceless Advocate

When I talked to anyone (and as I have already explained, everyone I could) about my relationship concerns – having given up getting Him to ever talk with me about them - I talked of being a skivvy - a curious role for someone with a Ph.D. to end up in, not wishing to toot my own horn. I also talked of having no voice, an even more bizarre situation: an advocate with no voice. This sick irony passed me by for a long, long time. The role of an advocate is to support people to have their voice heard on issues that are important to them, so that they can express their views and wishes and concerns and have them considered. Over and over again I said it to myself too, like a mantra: I have no voice. Whilst three days a week I would skip off, oh so happily, to my advocacy job, as the voiceless advocate, the advocate in desperate need of an advocate. How I missed this irony might have something to do with the fact my work was a haven, such a haven, and so I compartmentalised home (relationship hell) and work (advocacy bliss) to protect my much needed haven. This is an exaggerated form of Hochschild's 1997 Time Bind theory, that I addressed more fully in the earlier chapter entitled Time, which basically postulates that home becomes work and work becomes a rest from the work of home.

Relate

It was in the new year following the Christmas 2016 coffee and cakes incident that I asked if we could attend couples counselling together. He said no and told me that I am incapable of change. He also said that counselling is a load of rubbish. We had met on a counselling course and this felt like history being re-written (I did not know at this point that it needed to be). He was by now a therapist. Therapy is *amazing* by the way. The bees' knees. He makes people well and happy. With His magic formula He fixes broken, abused (yes, *abused*) people. He receives letters of thanks for the work He does in His Very Responsible, Stressful and Demanding Job.

With very little time to myself, counselling seemed impossible. So I did what I felt was the next best thing. I went on to the Relate website and educated myself (always keen to study, to learn, ever the geek) on how to do relationships well, how to be a better partner, the best partner I could be. I read about and recognised in my own behaviour some very negative ways to conduct oneself in a relationship. I did this reading at the end of each day, staying up beyond my usual ridiculously early bedtime to do it, sacrificing the sleep I very much needed with our robot baby son still waking daily at 4am. Below is what I wrote, my notes, my words about myself and my relationship. My up to date thoughts are added in brackets.

My bad relationship behaviours

- I can be passive aggressive. Flat. Unable to communicate as an adult that I am not happy, that I am hurt when I am hurting. (I guess I gave up trying to communicate with Him because He ignored me and/or told me to "Fuck off"?)
- I have a tendency to do too much for others and to neglect myself as a result. (What a hideous partner for Him to be stuck with).

Ways I can be a better partner

- Say how I feel without blaming Him, i.e. own my feelings, take responsibility for them. Every disagreement has two sides so take responsibility for my side. Listen to His side, His perspective. Tell Him I can see both sides. (But He never listened to mine, mostly I was not even allowed to verbalise it, I had no voice, I was ordered to leave the room with a stern, controlled voice and a long pointing arm.)
- Do not get angry. Do not use aggressive language. Control my emotions. Let go of anger. (I had no voice, He did not allow me a voice, so I most certainly was not allowed an angry one that has the audacity to shout at Him.)
- Do not freeze Him out. Be brave. Talk. Be forthright. Do not repress things as this makes things worse. Do not bottle things up. (Is it actually 'bottling things up' when you do not speak about things because you are

not allowed to?)

- Pick my battles. Do not fight over every little thing. Avoid petty conflicts. It makes a relationship a battleground. Over time these can erode a relationship. Learn to let go of the little things. Give Him some leeway. (It is hard to know how I feel now about Former Me suggesting giving Him 'some leeway'. What did He not have, take, believe to be His God given right?)
- The importance of forgiveness. Build forgiveness into the relationship. The first step toward forgiveness is understanding. You need to make a bold step in the right direction, to decide to put their transgression(s) behind you, so that you can move forward together. Let go of the moral high ground. (Two problems with this one. Firstly, I appear to have been suggesting I was a pain in the ass partner because I acknowledged to myself (and only myself, because I had no voice) that I behaved better than Him. Secondly, He never seemed to forgive me any of my 'transgressions' such as not wanting to pair His (all black) socks or buying the wrong (albeit apparently delicious) coffee.)
- According to psychologist John Gottman, the 'magic ratio' for predicting whether or not a relationship will last is five positives for every negative. I mentioned this to a divorcing friend and he laughed and said he and his soon to be ex-wife had struggled to

hit five positive interactions in a year. I laughed too. But I feel it does not bode well. (It certainly didn't, did it?)

- The importance of connection, that is, of being on the same team, achieved via spending time together. (I have already said that we were not on the same team; as for spending time together, this is hard to achieve when you go to bed around 8pm to get up with a robot baby son at 4am, every day, which He laughed at, whilst having as much free time as He wanted, to spend solely on Himself, at the gym, honing His body beautiful.)

One evening I had my notebook at the kitchen table and He read my notes over my shoulder. He laughed at me. And He criticised me. He said a normal person would not need to read on the Relate website how to conduct oneself well in a relationship. I cried. He was unmoved by my tears, yet again. I went to bed. Further heartbroken (which was, at that point, something I had not thought to be possible).

His Criticising Me

"We cannot achieve our full potential if we are constantly told we are stupid and useless." (Craven 2008: 54)

This Relate studying related criticism was just the

latest in a long line of criticisms from Him. Being criticised had become a big part of our relationship. After separating from Him I listed them (another not so beloved list). These are some of His words about my (flawed) self. Again, my up to date thoughts are added in brackets:

His criticisms of me

- I am not good at disciplining the children
- I shout at the children (seems to contradict the first criticism)
- I am not a supportive enough partner (maybe because I would not pair His all black socks?)
- I am not an affectionate enough partner (I found it hard to be affectionate to someone who tells me to "Fuck off")
- I am over sensitive (I don't like being told to "Fuck off")
- I was not attentive enough when He was off work with a poorly wrist (I was kind of very busy looking after two small children, working a part time paid job and running the family home, all whilst getting up at 4am every day with our robot baby son)
- I do nothing to work at the relationship (other than asking for approximately 9 months for Him to attend couples counselling, eventually giving up much needed sleep to read up on good relationship practices by myself, and eventually seeing a counsellor alone with

the sole purpose of trying to fix our confusingly broken relationship –NOTE: the counsellor pointed out the sad and basically doomed nature of this endeavour given that I was undertaking it *alone*)

- Since our son was born I loved him instead (Firstly, Freudian nonsense? Secondly, our son doesn't tell me to "Fuck off" which makes him a hell of a lot more lovable, alongside about a gazillion other reasons)
- (And one step beyond the above Freudian nonsense) I *never* loved Him, I only ever wanted children (when we got together I was 30 years old and did not know if I wanted children or not, a seemingly conveniently forgotten memory perhaps?)
- I am incapable of change (He had seen me go through many changes: academia to baking to advocacy; PAYE to self-employment and back again; solo living to cohabiting; childless to mother; happy to unhappy – to put this last one mildly)
- Finally, I cannot take criticism (bloody unlucky for me, given this list)

His (Damn) Feelings (Again)

In *Why Does He Do That? Inside The Minds of Angry and Controlling Men*, Lundy Bancroft argues an abusive man's emotional issues do not cause his abusiveness. Emotional upset and unmet needs have little to do with abusiveness. Feelings do not govern abusive or controlling behaviour, rather, such behaviour is governed by ingrained beliefs and values and core attitudes that drive his thinking (an argument clearly similar to Pat Craven's which I addressed in an earlier chapter). An abuser's value system is unhealthy, not their psychology. Core attitudes include that a partner has no right to object to how he treats them; that his word is final on anything that is important to him; that he is entitled to whatever he wants whenever he wants it; and that he is superior, so a partner is not his equal. All of these points could have been written by Bancroft about Him (so I am beginning to think the two of them must have met?) However, whilst the problem of abusiveness has little to do with how a man *feels* and everything to do with how he *thinks,* he will draw you into focusing on his feelings to keep you from focusing on how he thinks, i.e. the true cause of his abusiveness. When I read the following extract from Bancroft's book, again, it rang so very true for me:

"They have an exaggerated idea of how important their feelings are, and they talk about their feelings – and act them out – all the time, until their partners and children are exhausted from hearing about it all... They can fill up the whole house. When he feels bad, he thinks that life should stop for everyone else in the family until someone fixes his discomfort. His partner's crises, the children's sicknesses, meals, birthdays – nothing else matters as much as his feelings." (Bancroft 2002: 31)

Oh yes, His feelings were *constantly* brought to my attention: if I did not do a task IMMEDIATELY He did not feel that I was prioritising Him – this included an incident when I would not assist Him with writing a bereavement card NOW because it was time to set off on the school run; if I was too tired to stay up and spend time with Him, because I had been up since 4am with our robot baby son, He did not feel loved; when I would not dance sexily for Him – and I have explained already at length my two reasons for not doing so – He did not feel sexy (oh boo hoo). I could go on and on (because God knows He did). I lived with a seemingly endless commentary on how He felt, how He did not feel, how He wanted to feel and how badly I was failing at producing in Him the exact right feelings at the exact right moments (oh WTF was I doing for twelve and a half years?!). He probably uttered the words 'feel' and 'feelings' more than any others but, of course, I cannot recall once hearing Him use them in the context of enquiring as to how I was feeling or wished to be feeling or needed to be feeling.

The word 'birthdays' in the above extract reminded me of the heart breaking experience of our son's first birthday, which I addressed earlier. His behaviour on this occasion so perfectly captures His feelings smokescreen. On that terrible day, however, there was no barrage of words about His feelings, rather, He sat and fumed and sulked and was just so obviously unhappy, displeased and furious, because He had wanted to go to a different pizza place. On this occasion, then, He did not even have to verbalise His feelings smokescreen, it hung in the air like actual smoke. I truly do not know whether this was better or worse.

His Therapising Me

In *Why Does He Do That? Inside The Minds of Angry and Controlling Men*, Lundy Bancroft also writes of different styles of abuse used by abusive men when they are being abusive. One such style is Mr Sensitive. When his partner is hurt or upset, in lieu of showing genuine support for their feelings, he will use the language of feelings, emotions, fears and 'issues' and pepper his language with pop-psychology jargon. He turns each argument into a therapy session in which he can dissect his partner's flaws, explain the emotional issues that she needs to work through, and dismiss her perceptions of his abuse.

This sounds awful, doesn't it? Well, imagine if the abusive man did not just know a bit of pop-psychology to spout, but had a psychology degree, trained as a mental health nurse and then became a CBT therapist. Imagine the language, the terminology, the knowledge, the training, the *words* that he could spout. Well, He *has* a psychology degree, He *did* train as a mental health nurse and He *is* a therapist and He *did* – no *does* - like nothing more than to therapise, medicalise, pathologize me, including to other professionals – remember the Relate professional He insisted we see just after I left Him. And I have to mention 'evidence based practice' here. How many times have I heard Him spouting this phrase? His 'therapeutic' words also included two specific conditions, one which I believe to be fabricated – a 'perfection complex' – and one which I know to be a real and diagnosable condition – Generalised Anxiety Disorder. These were mentioned more often than not alongside more subtle and vague and quietly damning phrases such as "You are not well" and "You cannot cope" and (the slightly more emphatic and sinister I feel) "I think you would benefit from some professional help".

He had a special voice that He used to put on when He spoke all of these words, even when it was just the two of us, a tone, an intonation, something I cannot find the words to describe here but that I can hear in my head as I write as clearly as if it were happening to me right now. It chills me. Bancroft argues that:

"Mr Sensitive wraps himself up in one of the most persuasive covers a man can have. If you start to feel chronically mistreated by him, you are likely to assume that something is wrong with you, and if you complain about him to other people, they may think you must be spoiled." (Bancroft 2002: 88)

I have already written about just how much I came to be riddled with self-doubt, just how much I came to believe that there was something wrong with me, that what was wrong with me was *everything* basically. His cover was beyond persuasive. Through years of study in the field of mental health (which I had at times helped Him with, of course, because I love to study and I love to help people) He had accumulated qualifications and tools and words (and a lot of His beloved 'evidence based practice' remember) with which to construct a second cast iron smokescreen (i.e. alongside His Damn

Feelings), behind which He was able to conceal His complete lack of empathy or affection or belief that I was His equal or anything above a chattel or skivvy or sex object or just a (very) plain (and increasingly) old object.

Two Children and It

Five Children and It is a children's novel by English author E. Nesbit. It was originally published in 1902 in the Strand Magazine under the general title The Psammead, or the Gifts, with a segment appearing each month from April to December. The stories were then expanded into a novel which was published the same year. (Wikipedia)

I don't think I was viewed as a gift.

One word affected me like no other on my journey with Behind Closed Doors to understand domestic abuse and thus what had happened to me. Reality four from Lundy Bancroft's list of the Realities of Abuse spoke to me like no other form of abuse or facet of abuser that I had read about and written about and tabulated and listed as experienced: he disrespects his partner and considers himself superior and *objectifies* her. Objectification, also known as depersonalization, takes place over time, as the abuser sees his partner as less and less human and eventually sees her only as an object. In the following extract Bancroft explains exactly what objectification means in an abusive relationship:

"Objectification is a critical reason why an abuser tends

to get worse over time. As his conscience adapts to one level of cruelty – or violence – he builds to the next. By depersonalizing his partner, the abuser protects himself from the natural human emotions of guilt and empathy, so that he can sleep at night with a clear conscience. He distances himself so far from her humanity that her feelings no longer count, or simply cease to exist. These walls tend to grow over time, so that after a few years in a relationship my clients can reach a point where they feel no more guilt over degrading or threatening their partners than you or I would feel after angrily kicking a stone in the driveway." (Bancroft 2002: 63)

Oh if only He had angrily kicked me, in a driveway, or anywhere, just once. Reading about this reality – the superiority of the abuser which morphs into complete objectification of the victim – was my light bulb moment. At this point, all of my confusion dissipated. Everything became clear. Everything made perfect sense. Everything made perfect, grotesque sense.

As I have explained already, He did not start out abusing me, of course, it crept in. Initially the episodes of abuse were few and far between; months separated them. Eventually the episodes of feeling loved and happy were not few and far between, they were non-existent. There was a Sheryl Crow song playing on a loop in my head: (You Don't Bring Me) Anything But Down. Nothing had ever felt so apt, so true. But how could I feel like this when on a near as damn it daily basis He told me that He loved me? As I have already explained, my relationship - and whole life - had become a fog of confusion. My relationship did not make sense.

My life did not make sense. Nothing made sense. These are some of the questions running on a loop in my doubt and confusion addled brain.

If He loved me, how could He let me live exhausted whilst ensuring all of His needs were met (by me, which, along with the solitary child care, explained the exhaustion)?

If He loved me, why would He not talk about anything in the relationship that was making me unhappy and work on our relationship with me?

If He loved me, why was He unmoved when I cried? (On many occasions, He literally stepped over me crying in a heap on the floor, at the same time telling me where He was going and how He was looking forward to it).

If He loved me, why did He tell me to "Fuck off"?

The answer to all of these questions is one word: objectification.

A thing that you can see or touch but that is not usually a living animal, plant, or person (Definition of an object in the Cambridge English Dictionary)

"Sentient beings become persons only because they are recognized as such. When personhood is set in a matrix of unreciprocated authority, subjectivity atrophies." (Stark 2009: 192)

In His eyes I had ceased to be His equal, or even a fellow human, I was an object, the sole purpose of which was to serve Him, to meet His needs, to make Him happy, to make Him feel loved and the myriad other things He wanted to feel, whenever He wanted to feel them. When I looked at all that had so long confused me through the lens of objectification it no longer confused me. He did not need to love the object, because it was an object and objects do not have needs or feel tired. They do not need to talk about things that are upsetting or worrying them because they cannot be upset or worried about anything. Objects cannot cry, because they do not have feelings, so you can ignore the tears, they cannot be there, they cannot be real. And because an object does not have feelings you can say anything you like to it. 'I' was now 'it'. You can tell an it to "Fuck off", without feeling any guilt for doing so, can't you?

It was devastating to understand, finally and fully, that I had been abused, that I was still being abused, and that it had escalated to the point where I had been reduced to an object in His eyes, in the eyes of the man who I had believed loved me. Yet it was a relief to stop living in the fog of confusion, to make sense of my life, to truly understand it. So just one point from one domestic abuse check list had enabled me to understand everything that had been confusing me for years. I was even able to answer other questions which had long confused me: how could He be so cold, cruel and lacking in anything resembling empathy, and how could He be abusive to me, and yet work as a therapist? The answer to both questions, again, so simple: He must view His clients as His equals, fellow humans, with all that that entails. That is, He must *not* view them as objects as He does me. This must be the case, because He cannot be telling His clients to “Fuck off” can He?

Learning to talk again
Can't you see I've waited long enough?
Where do I begin?
Walk, Foo Fighters

Worries Diary

The following words are extracts from the Worries Diary I began keeping (and still keep to this day) at the suggestion of my Behind Closed Doors Emotional Support Worker. My Emotional Support Worker advised me to, each evening, write down the worries that were buzzing around in my head. She advised that the simple act of committing one’s worries to paper can stop them buzzing around in one’s head. These extracts capture the way in which the same worries repeatedly reared their heads. These fall into three key categories: general problems – both current and likely future ones; specific incidents of on-going domestic abuse; and overarching questions emanating from my very (damaged) core. To this day, I still write a Worries Diary. The start of my writing such a diary pre-dates the writing of this book, but only by a couple of months. Thus some of the story told in this book also unfolds in my Worries Diary, as the following extracts illustrate.

Extracts from Worries Diary

160318 Will I ever shake off the core belief that I am the reason I have been abused by Him? That I am the problem?

170318 Will He eventually want the children more than He currently does? If so, how will I cope with the loneliness?

180318 He was controlling over my having the neighbours here when He came to collect the children, will I ever stand up to Him?

210318 He was all smiles and 'concern' about me today. Reminded me of the whole Cycle of Abuse and scared me. It would be so much easier if I only saw and experienced His abuse. It was in front of His dad, so classic behaviour of being 'nice' to me in front of other people. His dad has never seen Him abuse me.

220318 Will I ever be undamaged?

250318 Will I ever sort out my credit rating and be able to buy Him out of the family home?

270318 Will I ever truly believe that it is not my fault?

280318 Did He ever love me, in the sense of the word as known and used by 'normal', non-abusive people? Can an abuser love?

290318 Will I ever get a solo mortgage?

300318 Will I ever stop feeling lonely in my head?

050418 I remain confused by His 'niceness' alongside cruelty. Am I still nice to Him because I believe it will eventually rub off on Him?

060418 Will I ever meet someone 'normal' and have a partner to share my life with? I was not built to be alone. It hurts.

080418 He kicked off today about taking half the contents of the family home. Will He really take it?

120418 He threw His weight around in front of my mum.

Will He ever stop doing so?

150418 He keeps trying to be tactile and affectionate. Will I be able to stop Him when I have the house?

160418 He wants even more money for the house and half the contents of it. It will never stop. I need to get legal advice but I am scared of the consequences if I do.

180418 He tried to make me move my regular hosting of the regular brunch with the neighbours again. Will He ever stop trying to control my life?

210418 He came around today in a T-shirt emblazoned with 'OBEY'. He has no insight? Or does He?

270418 He asked me again about my taking parenting classes. I continued the (white) lie. Will I ever dare to stand up to Him?

300418 He has still not set up a Standing Order for the Child Maintenance so I have to keep asking for it. Will He ever do this? Can I make Him do this?

010518 No solo mortgage with current lender. I need a new lender. I need a new deal. Will I ever get one in my situation? Now I am fighting Him and the ludicrous financial world.

060518 Am I having a 'mid-life crisis'? If so, when will it end?

140518 He wants the house valued again. What if it has gone up in value? How will I ever buy Him out then?

180518 He could not see the children today because He had a 'migraine'. I truly am a single mother. Will it always be this hard?

190518 He told me He is looking at a house to buy. Will He apply for shared custody? Will He get it? Scared. I don't want to lose my children.

230518 He interrogated me again about my taking parenting classes. Will I ever dare to tell Him the truth i.e. stand up to Him?

060618 He collected the laundry I had done for Him. Am I right to be so kind to Him still? To model kindness?

080618 He demanded half the contents of the house or He won't sign the Transfer of Equity. I cannot give it to Him. But I need Him to sign. He knows this. What can I do?

100618 He joked about 'gaslighting' me today and about abusing me over a packet of coffee.

110618 Properly scared again. Same as when close to His moving out day. He kicked off because He is so close to signing the Transfer of Equity. I need to speak to Behind Closed Doors. Terrified.

120618 So He gaslighted me again. Today told me papers arrived and He will sign them on Saturday.

230618 He won't sign the Transfer of Equity until I go to mediation. But how can you discuss and negotiate and agree with someone who seeks to control and hurt and scare you?

270618 He asked about parenting classes again.

040718 He has not paid the Child Maintenance still. How can I make Him? CMS?

100718 He brought around a Parenting Agreement for me to sign. I signed it. I had to. It cannot be legally binding? Can it?

140718 He was civil and fake-nice today. The Cycle of Abuse. I so recognise it now. Will it ever stop?

180718 I saw the police. I had to because I had reported Him. They told me I cannot stop them now. They will be talking to Him. Scared.

310718 Today I got the house. I cannot believe it. But He put in writing that He is not paying Child Maintenance until He has paid Himself back the value of half the contents of the family home. I spoke to the CMS. It will take ages to get to Him.

220818 I found the confidence to say He cannot come into my house anymore. What will He do?

310818 He rang and tried to pressure me into agreeing the children go to Him two nights a week. Very scared. He is talking of going for 50/50 custody if I do not 'agree'.

170918 His parents won't help me get the missing two months Child Maintenance. I thought they would. I feel alone. I am alone.

230918 I saw the police again. They will be talking to Him soon. Scared of His reaction.

011118 Bullying tactics from Him re. the children at Christmas. I have to be strong and stand up to Him. I have to remember what my cousin says, that I have the power here, because I never moved out, I never left the family home, I never left the children, I have never stopped looking after them.

221118 He moved into His new house today. I am worried He will start pushing for more sleepovers or shared care. I don't want to lose my children.

061218 Had a meltdown at work today over small mistakes. Sobbed and sobbed. Barely coping.

Introduction to The Ironyometer

When reading through David McCandless' two Beautiful diagrams books – *Information is Beautiful* and *Knowledge is Beautiful* - I came across the Good Relationships diagram in one of them (McCandless 2014: 184-5). I was not surprised by this stage to realise how many known good relationship practices had been missing from His relationship behaviour and thus our relationship. I decided to calculate them. What hit me, like the slap in the face I wished I had actually ever got from Him, was the irony that ran through so many of the points. The result of this exercise is this cathartic piece, which I have gleefully named The Ironyometer, in which I write rebuttals to the many hilariously ironic good relationship practices. Enjoy.

The Ironyometer

The Ironyometer Key is on page 266

Good Relationship Practices	**Irony Level**	**Totally necessary musings**
Shut the bathroom door	0	He did. Oh lucky, lucky me!
Outsource housework	0	He outsourced it to me – missing the point here?
Get a prenup	0	I did. A Deed of Trust. Hence I have my Best Nest.
Own your feelings	1	When did I *not* hear about His damn feelings? But I was an object and objects have no feelings
Balance dependence and independence	1	He got the balance just right: dependent on me for domestic work and child care and lived like single.
Enjoy a steady diet of good sex	1	He seemed to think it was good. I disassociated to get through it by the end.
Remember your partner is not you	1	Oh He knew this all too well: He is perfection personified whilst I am FLAWED TO MY CORE.
Before you argue, think 'is it worth it?'	1	I was not allowed to disagree with Him so there were no arguments.
Ask the questions	1	He was never afraid to

you are most afraid to ask		ask me anything: why won't you pair my socks and dance sexily for me?
Give little gifts	1	I was too into possessions, remember, so His lack of gifts was probably an attempt to cure me of this affliction.
Don't run away from conflict	1	He ordered me to leave the room when I annoyed Him.
Be fully present to bond	2	He was too busy and also too busy abusing me.
Boring is okay	3	Boring would have been BLISSFUL.
Never stop dating	3	Would you date someone who tells you to "Fuck off"?
Don't compare your relationship to others	3	He wanted a subservient but off the chart sexy lap dancing partner – which DO exist apparently.
Remember to laugh	3	At least I am laughing now.
Do not neglect your relationship post children	3	He neglected our relationship *pre* children.
Don't blame your partner	4	He blamed me for everything. If He could have blamed me for global warming He would have.
Find common goals	4	If only I had shared His vision of a controlled, subservient, off the chart

		sexy lap dancing partner.
Communicate empathically	5	He could not empathise with an object with no feelings.
Cook together	5	Hard to do when someone lives on cottage cheese and spinach.
Think of your partner first	5	His pecking order was 1: Him (no, I have not missed the end of sentence).
Be romantic	5	Doesn't romance end with "Fuck off"?
Ask your partner what they need more of	5	Unless He thought the answer to this was sex He was never going to ask this question.
Be polite	5	Again, doesn't this end with "Fuck off"?
Never stop working on your relationship	5	I didn't stop. Read the rest of this book. I did everything I could. And He laughed at me. And I cried.
Ask daily how you can make your partner happy	5	I think He asked Himself daily how He could make *Himself* happy, and then did it.
Eat and work out like you are single	OTFCI	He did. And now He is. Go figure.
Give to your partner what you want from them	OTFCI	Just read the rest of this book.
Do not try to fix your partner	OTFCI	See His list of criticisms of me and all the reasons I

		was a bad partner and mother and person and HYSTERICAL woman. What could He do?
Appreciate your partner's strengths and gifts	OTFCI	See above.
Share power	OTFCI	He wouldn't even share His cottage cheese.
Learn your partner's love language so they feel cherished	LSMIH	I very much doubt that "Fuck off" is considered part of anyone's love language.
Master the art of compromise; say sorry; make peace	LSMIH	Just read the rest of this book.

Ironyometer Key:

0 = not at all ironic
1 = mildly ironic
2 = ironic
3 = very ironic
4 = very, very ironic
5 = extremely ironic
OTFCI = Off The Fucking Chart Ironic
LSMIH = Laughing So Much It Hurts

Found Poetry

"Nothing hurts more than realising you've been complicit in your own silence. Nothing feels better than unleashing your voice." (Ford 2018: 27)

Found poetry is a type of poetry created by taking words, phrases, and sometimes whole passages from other sources and reframing them as poetry (a literary equivalent of a collage) by making changes in spacing and lines, or by adding or deleting text, thus imparting new meaning. The resulting poem can be defined as either treated: changed in a profound and systematic manner; or untreated: virtually unchanged from the order, syntax and meaning of the poem. (Wikipedia)

I decided to take some of His words and, through the medium of found poetry, use them to further help me to find my voice and tell my story.

His Criticisms Of Me

I am not good at disciplining the children
I shout at the children (seems to contradict the first criticism)
I am not a supportive enough partner (maybe because I would not pair His all black socks?)
I am not an affectionate enough partner (I found it hard to be affectionate to someone who tells me to "Fuck off")
I am over sensitive (I don't like being told to "Fuck off")
I was not attentive enough when He was off work with a poorly wrist (I was very busy looking after two small children, working a part time paid job and running the family home, all whilst getting up at 4am every day with our robot baby son)
I do nothing to work at the relationship (other than asking for approximately 9 months for Him to attend couples counselling, eventually giving up much needed sleep to read up on good relationship practices, and eventually seeing a counsellor alone with the sole purpose of trying to fix our confusingly broken relationship –NOTE: the counsellor pointed out the sad and basically doomed nature of this endeavour given that I was undertaking it *alone*)
Since our son was born I loved him instead (Firstly, Freudian nonsense? Secondly, our son doesn't tell me to "Fuck off" which makes him a lot more lovable).
(And one step beyond the above Freudian nonsense) I *never* loved Him, I only ever wanted children (when we got together I was thirty years old and did not know if I wanted children or not, a seemingly conveniently forgotten memory)
I am incapable of change (He had seen me go through many changes: new jobs, PAYE to self-employment, solo living to cohabiting, childless to mother)
Finally, I cannot take criticism (bloody unlucky for me, given this list)

The Rules I Had To Live By

Wake Him up every morning at the time stated on His post it note

Buy all of the foods He wanted every week, in the right quantities

Follow His method for teaching good behaviour to our two children, via giving Time Outs only for the bad behaviours that He gave them out for and giving them at exactly the right point of the tantrum or transgression in question

Do not ever ask Him a question when He is doing a task such as making His breakfast, because He finds this too stressful

Do not ever ask Him a question when He is getting ready to leave for work, because this would make Him late for work

Do not ever ask Him for help with the children when He comes in from work, because He finds this too stressful

Do not ever drink the last of the coffee in the pot and if I ever have the audacity to do so make a new pot of coffee in case He should want another cup

Back to Mr O

"When you honour a woman's sexuality and her very sex, you support the optimal functioning of the physical systems that support her intellectual creativity; when you threaten and insult her sexuality and her very sex, you do exactly the opposite." (Wolf 2013: 267)

In the chapter entitled Body I explained what I got from my glorious love affair with Mr O, how through it I reclaimed my body. I explained that I was in lust and in love AKA the holy grail or nirvana. Well, I would have been content with getting my hot clammy hands on the holy grail, funnily enough. I would have been fine with entering nirvana, unsurprisingly. But there is yet more.

It is no coincidence that it was a few months into my glorious, passionate, sublime affair with Mr O that I began writing, voraciously, every evening and at every possible other child and paid work free time. I ate (porridge usually) whilst writing, or else did not eat; and I slept too little. It is no coincidence according to Naomi Wolf, anyway. I have already extolled the genius of her book. But, again, there is more of her brand of genius which helps me to tell my story.

I have a Ph.D. I once read and consumed and wrote about and lived and breathed books, interesting, quite intellectual books. I no longer worked in academia but I missed the reading I used to do, the reading I used to *want* to do. And I missed the thinking. I had always had the (I do think) ghastly middle class dream of writing a book, whilst clearly having no book in me, nor even the inclination to devour anyone else's books that might have provided me with the faintest scrap of inspiration for my mythical, middle class opus. I told myself, and worse I actually *believed*, that I was ground down by child care, running the family home and holding down a job. Poor creatively stifled me. Poor Cinderfuckingrella (to quote Pretty Woman's vulgar but astute sidekick).

I now know this argument to be complete and utter rubbish. I am sure of this for two reasons. Firstly, I am writing this book as a single mother of two small children who is running the family home and holding down a job *and* dealing with the aftermath of an abusive relationship, which in large part takes the form of a continuing-to-be-abusive ex-partner looming literally and figuratively all too large in my life. Secondly, I have read the whole of Wolf's book and learnt about the astonishing, but at the same time also completely believable, link between women having great sex (tick) and experiencing an outpouring of creative and intellectual work (tick).

When I started writing this book it poured out of me. I was gobsmacked. That first night I wrote pages and pages and that was the pace and the tone set for the project: fast and fulfilling and fun. Then I read Wolf's book and I ceased to be gobsmacked. As I have already attempted with Wolf's vagina-brain connection theory, I will try to concisely sum up this next step in her theorising.

Throughout history, misogynist commentators have argued that brilliant women cannot be sexual and that very sexual women cannot be brilliant (isn't disproving the latter nonsense precisely why Madonna wrote *Sex*, which is perhaps one of the most vilified books ever written?) Wolf researched women writers, artists and revolutionaries from the eighteenth and nineteenth centuries and early into the twentieth century. She explored their work and their personal lives and related correspondence. She found a clear connection between sexual self-discovery, such as that found in a liberating and passionate affair, and creative and intellectual expansions in work – what she calls 'creative climaxes'. She cites so many brilliant women: Christina Rossestti; George Eliot; Edith Wharton; Emma Goldman; Georgia O'Keeffe; Mary Wollstonecraft; Charlotte Bronte; Elizabeth Barrett Browning; George Sand and Gertrude Stein. She concludes that:

"For many of these creative artists, apparent sexual awakening and creative surges had at certain key times in their lives seemed to fuse together, and seemed to elicit a phase of work that reached a higher level of insight and energy than had the just-previous work in their oeuvres. These arcs of accomplishment – these creative 'high points' – seemed as if they might help confirm further my growing conviction that women experience the vagina as integral to a core self, and that it can also serve as the trigger or entry point to an awakening of sensibility that can at fortunate moments fuse the creative and the sexual." (Wolf 2013: 53)

Wolf also talked to as many contemporary women as she could about her theory of a connection between the vagina and female sexuality and confidence, creativity and the ability to see connections between things. This included scholarly young women at university, creative actresses and many more. She found that "women, from many different backgrounds, confirmed... that they too had experienced a connection between their sexual well-being and their confidence levels and creative lives." (Wolf 2013: 61-2) She came to the concluding question that, through the release of dopamine and oxytocin and other opioids, really special sex might lead to female euphoria, self-love and creativity.

Once I had begun writing, I had to force myself to go to bed each night at a time that would give me enough sleep to get through all of the child care and paid work I had to do the next day with energy spare for writing when all that work was done. I am not saying that my book is an intellectual or even a creative work of greatness. But I did shift from sitting at my kitchen table alone every night when my children were in bed, writing bizarre lists of things to do and then ticking them off as I did them, until I could feasibly go to bed, to writing a book, writing this book (albeit whilst still sat at my kitchen table alone every night). To hammer home my point, to illustrate the difference between my evening outpourings before and after embarking on my love affair with Mr O, compare and contrast my writing of any section of this book with my writing of a list such as the following one (taken from an old notebook):

A Typical Evening's List Pre-Mr O and Writing

- Internet banking – has Child Maintenance gone in?
- Write a thank you card to Rachel M
- Cut up and box up cakes for Sam
- Ring Arnold
- Put dishwasher on
- Make a box of Sociable Salad and eat some of it
- Sort bags for work and swimming

Sadly, but unsurprisingly, Wolf's theory which explains why I was creatively and intellectually unlocked by my love affair with Mr O also helps to explain why I was able to be so abused by Him, for so long. She writes of the substances which hit women's systems before, during and after great sex and labels one of them, dopamine, "the ultimate feminist chemical in the female brain" (Wolf 2013: 69). She does so because of what it does to a woman: "it strengthens her sense of focus and motivation levels, and energizes her in setting goals. All those effects are involved with dopamine activation." (Wolf 2013: 69-70). When I read the following two quotes I found them beyond chilling:

"Serotonin literally subdues the female voice, and dopamine literally raises it." (Wolf 2013: 79)

I was the voiceless advocate, remember? I had no voice in the relationship, I talked for years of having no voice (paradoxically).

"If a woman has optimal levels of dopamine, she is difficult to direct against herself. She is hard to drive to self-destruction, to manipulate and *control*." (Wolf 2013: 77, emphasis added)

Another sick, clever cycle of abuse then:

Domestic Abuse > Bad Sex > Low (or non-existent) Dopamine > Low self-esteem/Low self-worth/Low self-confidence/Just plain low > More malleable > Easier To Abuse > (More) Domestic abuse > etc...

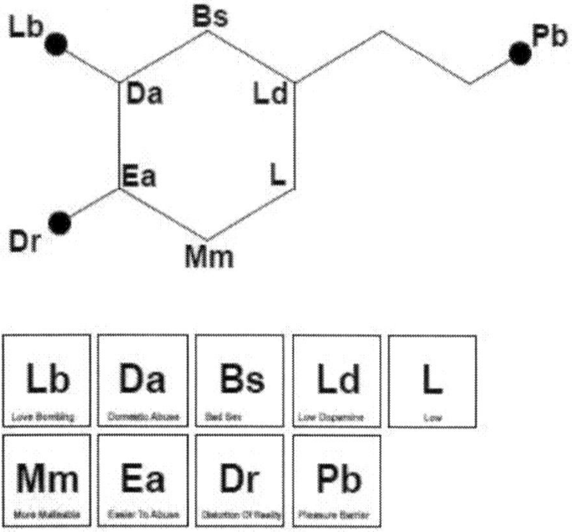

THE CHEMISTRY OF DOMESTIC ABUSE

With Him I was broken, controlled, stifled and wordless. My love affair with Mr O got my dopamine levels back up, back to where they should be, and I don't just mean via sex. I have already explained his beautiful 'shining light' message and cited other messages from him which boosted me and moved me and made me feel loved. As I have already explained, oh so happily, he transformed me sexually and also emotionally. It is so very clear to me, thanks to Naomi Wolf's work, that in doing so he unlocked other long dead parts of me – whatever intellect I have and my creativity. He would write of being in awe of my intellect and my writing. I woke one morning to the beautiful message "Helen, I said you were a shining light. Also means bright one, which fits with your enormous intellect Dr O." (I told you he thinks I am clever). But whilst Dr O has written this book, there would be no book without Mr O. And he runs through it, I read him on every page, I hear him in the quotes and in the songs, with some of them having been introduced to me by him.

He made me smile. He made me laugh. He made me love. He made me scream. He brought me back to life. So much so that I was able to write. A book. This book. He told me that I am a **Shining Light**. And I believe him. Why else would I have chosen those beautiful words for the title of this book?

LOVE

And I got angels on my side
I got angels flying high
And everything gonna be alright
'Cause I got angels on my side
Angels on My Side, Rick Astley

Impact

As I have already stated, many times, I am a geek, a born student, I love to study and to read and to understand, to educate myself on things that I do not understand and wish to understand. I had done this within the relationship a long time before I embarked on the Relate website based relationships studying before I separated from Him, (which He laughed at and criticised me for, remember?) This was something I had almost forgotten about, until I began writing my story.

It was three years earlier, in 2014, the year I had begun keeping a journal and then swiftly stopped because it was too distressing (addressed in the earlier chapter entitled Mind). I had become lower and lower and more and more lost until I became unrecognisable to myself. I was unhappy within the relationship and decided that *I* had to fix it. He does not have a diagnosis of Asperger's Syndrome (AS) but this was explored when He was a child. Given what the National Autistic Society writes about AS, I grabbed this possible explanation for His behaviours with both hands as a means to understand my confusing relationship, my confusing life. They write that for people with AS "understanding and relating to other people, and taking part in everyday family, school, work and social life, can be harder." (National Autistic Society website). I hoped that ultimately I could find some sort of support group for people like me, where I might find advice and tips and tools to help me to cope. I read up on the effects of being with someone with AS. I put together the following check list:

The effects of being with an Asperger's Syndrome partner

- Given up activities and interests to shoulder the majority of the responsibility for maintaining the household
- Feeling abandoned, isolated and lonely
- Low self-esteem
- Mental health problems: depression, anxiety and Affective Deprivation Disorder (AfDD)

I was living with everything on this check list but did not know what 'Affective Deprivation Disorder' (AfDD) is. So I read up on that as well (of course). As it turned out, I was also living with that. The following extract from an account from someone living with AfDD within their marriage spoke to me as though it were describing me, my relationship, my angst, my confusion, my hell, my life:

"After a while, one must ask: What is going on? Why am I in such pain? Why am I sick all the time? Why does he say that he is happy when I feel like a black hole has opened up in my chest? Let me introduce you to Affective Deprivation Disorder: Affective Deprivation

Disorder (AfDD) is a relational disorder resulting from the emotional deprivation sometimes experienced by the partner (or child) of persons with a low emotional/empathic quotient or alexithymia. Coined by researcher Maxine Aston, AfDD was first applied to partners of adults with Asperger's Syndrome, many of whom showed disturbing physical and psychological reactions to the lack of emotional reciprocity they were experiencing in their relationship." (MJ September 19 (2014) Affective Deprivation Disorder and Alexithymia in Marriage)

Let me repeat that phrase from the end of the above extract: disturbing physical and psychological reactions to the lack of emotional reciprocity. Let me repeat that first word: disturbing. It was true. I had become disturbing. I was disturbed. Never more so than when I flew into the rage (thankfully in His absence) when I discovered He had taken (without my consent) and lost (without replacing) my solitary phone charger, *for the third time in four weeks* (as I have already covered). The screaming and shouting and throwing things and the uncontrollable crying was me letting out years and years of rage stemming from not being listened to, from not having a voice, in my relationship, in my own home, in my life. I found another (sadly) useful check list:

The psychological symptoms of Affective Deprivation Disorder

- Low self-esteem
- Feelings of anger, depression and anxiety
- Feelings of guilt

- Feeling confused/bewildered
- Loss of self/depersonalisation

I knew I was living with everything on this list. As I continued my reading, another list followed:

The relationship problems associated with Affective Deprivation Disorder

- Reduced relationship quality
- Reduced relationship satisfaction
- High relational conflict
- Domestic abuse: emotional and/or physical

I knew I was living with everything on this list too, except for domestic abuse (which, at this point, I was still four – long - years away from comprehending).

As when I later saw the counsellor alone, this attempt to understand, work on and ultimately improve the relationship, through understanding Him better, was a solitary pursuit and therefore an utterly futile one. I never dared talk to Him about any of my reading. Just as I never dared to talk to Him about anything, for fear of being told off for 'stressing Him out' and being ordered out of the room – verbally and with His long arm outstretched pointing to the relevant doorway or staircase AKA the nearest portal to His solace. As I have already explained, I had no voice.

My unearthed notes from reading up on the effects of being with someone with Asperger

Syndrome showed me the hugely negative impact that the what-I-now-know-to-be domestic abuse was having on me approximately four years before I separated from Him having discovered He was abusing me. Fast forward four years and my Emotional Support Worker from Behind Closed Doors encouraged me to explore the impact His abuse had had on me, and was still having on me. I had worked hard to understand what exactly His coercive control had entailed for me (exhaustion, in a nutshell) and what all the other forms of domestic abuse He was guilty of meant for me (languishing in agonising self-doubt and confusion sums it up quite well). I thought long and hard about what living with exhaustion and doubt and confusion had meant for me, what they had *done* to me.

I was unable to relax. I could not watch TV. I could not pick up my knitting for more than about five minutes (but every cloud has a silver lining: loved ones got rescued from receiving my bad scarves for 'gifts'). I could not pick up the phone and talk to someone. Once the children were in bed I would sit at the kitchen table and write those ridiculous lists, explained in the chapter entitled Words, then complete the tasks and tick them off the lists. A colleague observed that I was jumpy and oversensitive at work. I had a job interview and the mere news of being offered the interview triggered a paralysing panic attack. I was anxious, restless, lost. I saw my GP about stress but was too scared to take medication for fear of Him finding out and saying I was an unfit mother for a fourth reason (remember I am already three different bad mothers rolled into one?) I felt less productive in my paid work – which is maybe why I was fabricating a sense of productivity during my evenings via the list writing. I felt cut off from the outside world, from the sociable socialising world. I felt dull and plain. Well I was dull and plain, living in my captive wardrobe (I will explain this soon) in my house, largely in my kitchen, with my notebook and pen for writing my bizarre lists. This did not worry me given that I had not only no sex drive but no sexuality, no sense of being a sexual creature, no sense of being a woman even (back to the zombie issue then).

As I have said, there was a lot to recover from.

The Recovery Diagram

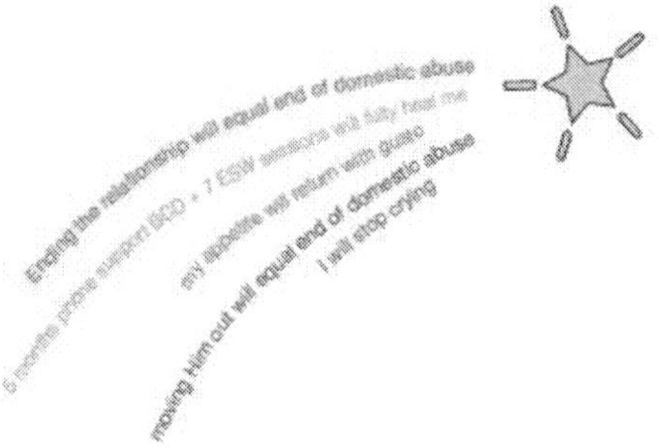

EXPECTATION

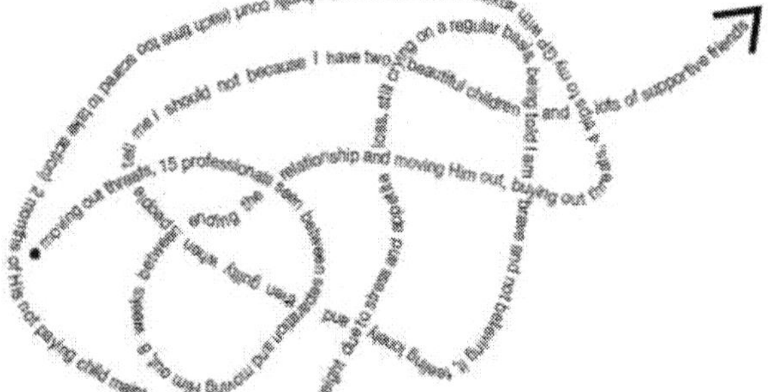

REALITY

My Solo Work on Recovery

There is a well-known and (I believe) over used and (in my opinion) also utterly stupid saying which I detest (just to be super clear): when life gives you lemons, make lemonade. When does life *give you* lemons? And who drinks *homemade* lemonade, made with *actual* lemons, outside of the era described in Enid Blyton's books? If given a lemon, ever, clearly the best thing to do with it is to make a gin and tonic and throw a slice of it in to that. More to the point, don't wait to be *given* a lemon, by 'life' (whatever the hell that means) or by an actual person (which is at least more possible), go out and buy one, and a bottle of gin and some tonic, and have a G&T. I find it takes the edge off a lonely evening following yet another day peppered with correspondence from and/or encounters with an abusive ex-partner, whose favourite post-separation pastime became hurling ever more bizarre threats at me (my absolute favourite, following His losing our son's shoes during a visit to His family, was His refusal to replace them or pay for new ones until the three pieces of post He had requested be delivered to my house had arrived. WTF? Like I can control Royal Mail. More to the point, why was He getting *His* post delivered to *my* house? Actually, forget that, HTF are His son's shoes and His post in any way connected?) Alongside having a G&T of an evening (sometimes two, to be honest) I did pursue proper, serious recovery work because, as I have explained above, there was a lot to recover from.

My friend Olivia sent me the following kind advice:

"Don't give up looking for those activities that help you slow down and be kind to yourself. One is much better company for oneself when one is being nice to oneself." (Olivia, 211218)

She also sent me the following list of what she finds to be soothing activities, which I dipped into from time to time:

Olivia's Soothing Activities

- Warm/cosy sock wearing
- Hot water bottle cuddles
- Blankets
- Munching of herbal remedies including valerian and hops (self-treatment feels kind)
- Research into self-care
- Soothing music
- Baths
- Sudoku
- Very light novels
- Aromatherapy (find your favourite smells)
- Walks in nature / nature photography (this was such a good one for me)
- Journaling, of course
- Painting
- Old photos (a special feel-good collection that excludes anything even slightly negative is good, maybe get help to put this together)
- Tea (obviously)
- Nice coffee / hot chocolate / whatever...

My Behind Closed Doors Related Work on Recovery

Whilst working on the Understanding Domestic Abuse And Thus Exactly What Happened To You Stage of the recovery programme (which is as lovely as it sounds, by the way) my Behind Closed Doors Emotional Support Worker had introduced me to the idea of writing a Worries Diary (as I explained earlier) which I diligently wrote nightly. She also suggested that I start keeping a Gratitude Diary (see below). When it came to the final stage of my work with my Behind Closed Doors Emotional Support Worker, the Recovery Stage, there was a myriad of other ideas that I was introduced to. I was told that it is okay to cry sometimes, to express the pain that I feel, and that I should make a ritual around this, for example with pyjamas and hot chocolate, make it therapy time. I was told to do some mirrors work, to spend some time each day looking in the mirror and mentally noting what I see (my Emotional Support Worker told me to *put my notebook and pen down,* being on to me and my studious, geek tendencies, and just do it). I was told to find a positive affirmation and stop with the negative self-talk.

I was also told to wear the nice clothes I said I never wear because I still live in my mum clothes – stretchy grey and black items, many formerly maternity wear, all plain and easy to wash – to keep the laundry work down, as I did when I was bogged down in doing all of His mountains of laundry on a daily basis – His work clothes and His various sports kits and all of His (all black) socks – on top of all of the kids' laundry. I was living in not so much a capsule wardrobe as a captive wardrobe. I read Mena Kandasamy's *When I Hit You* and her account of wearing – or rather of living in - a drab wardrobe made me feel uneasy:

"I wear a dull T-shirt and pyjama-bottoms because he approves of dowdiness. Or, I wrap myself in an old cotton sari to remind me of my mother. Some days, when I am especially eager to impress and to escape punishment, I slip into the shapeless monstrosity that is: *the nightie*. The effect of adhering to my husband's wishes gives me the appearance of a woman who has given up. But, I know that attired in this manner, I am all set to play the part of the good housewife. Nothing loud, nothing eye-catching, nothing beautiful. I should look like a woman whom no one wants to look at or, more accurately, whom no one even sees." (Kandasamy 2017:15-6)

I was not seen. And I did not see myself as anyone worth seeing. Kandasamy's words made me think hard about my wearing of a not so much capsule as captive drab wardrobe. I really had not thought about it before. But I should have done. My wardrobe reflected what I had become: utterly home based, completely domesticated, on a treadmill of domestic work and child care and paid work (significantly, I did wear other clothes for my paid work outside of the house, but another capsule and very easily washable wardrobe). And both wardrobes were dominated by the delightful combination of black and grey and black stuff that had faded to grey. Not loud. Not eye-catching. Not beautiful. I remembered what I had read about colour in my beautiful Orla Kiely book *Pattern*:

"Colour is an incredibly powerful element in design, as it is in life. A short cut to the emotions, it is almost visceral in the way it connects with our moods and feelings... Colour is happy, sexy and playful. It feeds the soul." (Kiely 2012: 88)

On the plus side, I was out of my dreadful drab clothes and in to my equally dreadful drab nightie by about 6pm most days.

This is not a plus at all, is it?

It all had to stop, didn't it?

I do have nice clothes. I seem to collect them. TK Maxx bargain finds. Even better pre-loved bargains from charity shops (as I have already explained, I love all things with a history). Occasional indulgent new-bought treats from fancy shops. Favourites are numerous. A polka dot, floral lined, Cath Kidston dress, found in a charity shop and bought largely because of its name on the label: Tea Dress, evocative of afternoon tea, a favourite pastime and concept of mine; a Dolce & Gabbana custard yellow, silk trimmed cardigan – TK Maxx uber bargain; a selection of vintage silk blouses – all clever pre-loved charity shop finds, doubly clever given that I am five foot ten and women tended to be smaller in the days of all things from the era now cleverly marketed as 'vintage'; a teal Betty Jackson coat and a Nicole Farhi coat with bracelet sleeves – both snapped up in charity shops; Shelley's Heeled knee boots that are a total homage to the 1970s, bought on the way home after a job interview, an interview which I truly believe I got because I was supposed to find these boots rather than get the job (which I did not get); and a collection of heeled Mary Jane's, my favourite kind of shoe, my favourite of which is exquisite in sparkly silver *and* comfortable to wear, so my dream shoe, yet still barely worn. I gather, treasure and adore them all. And I store them all. Like the wardrobe of a leading lady from a cancelled fictitious TV show. Think SJP's character of Carrie Bradshaw in *Sex And The City*. Then unthink it, a lot. Because I am not that fashionable, stylish or rich. Better still, try to think of another comparison entirely (I cannot).

I dug out a bright yellow top - silk Monsoon, bought in a charity shop – that had been squirreled away and never worn, like all of its drawer mates. This got me started dressing happily and sunnily and not dully.

I was told to work on goal setting with an action plan to make it realistic and achievable. I was already on this with my big goal of securing a solo mortgage and a Transfer of Equity, to achieve financial separation from Him. I was told to be alone with my children more, to stop masking any loneliness with having as many friends and neighbours as possible trooping through my house at every opportunity (tellingly, when an old school friend came to stay she commented that more people came through my house that weekend than probably did through Leeds train station). I was told to *do nothing* sometimes (I agreed instead to try and watch half an hour of television in the evenings whilst knitting my ugly scarves, because I am incapable of ever doing nothing). And I was told to start keeping the Worries Diary and the Gratitude Diary, which I did, and still do to this day.

For my penultimate homework from Behind Closed Doors I was told to listen to a specific uplifting show tune. This was the only Behind Closed Doors home work that I did not do. Not doing homework is a huge deal for me, because I love homework, as I have already explained many times . But not doing this homework was also a no brainer for me (as was the homework, as far as I am concerned). I do not do musical theatre. I had to draw the line at this homework. There was no way on this earth I was going to do this homework. I told my Emotional Support Worker (dead pan) that I would rather stay abused.

Finally, I was given a 'Five Ways To Wellbeing' work sheet by Behind Closed Doors. I did read through it (of course I did) but all five of the magical ways to being and feeling well I felt I had already got covered, as the following list explains:

Five ways to wellbeing

1: Be active: I have two small children. I rarely and barely sit down. Done.

2: Take notice: I was already practising staying-in-the-moment techniques such as keeping a Gratitude Diary as well as a Worries Diary to get worried and negative thoughts out of my head, to park them so I could stop worrying and stay in the present. Done.

3: Learn: I was learning through my Behind Closed Doors home works and studying through my paid job. I was already learning because this is what I do. The eternal student (the geek). Done.

4: Connect: I was, and remain, very strongly connected to a network of friends and neighbours. We look after each other's children. We brunch together most Saturdays. We feed each other at the drop of a hat. We have keys to each others' houses. Done.

5: Give: Acts of kindness have always been important to me - both performing and experiencing them. Performing them because I have a desperate need to be helpful and useful and to be considered kind (and not mean and selfish and greedy and materialistic) by others as a result. Experiencing them because I feel things so very deeply. Years ago I read an interview with Peter Morgan who wrote *The Queen*. I wrote down the following quote back then because it spoke to me so:

"I'm quick to be upset. My feelings are so close to the surface. There is not much gap between a thought and a feeling with me. It makes it difficult for some people, I feel too much, I think that's what it is.. I don't think I'm an unhappy person. It's just an intensity, not a depressive thing. It's just not having enough layers of skin. It's exhausting." (Peter Morgan)

Both performing and experiencing acts of kindness

became even more important to me after I separated from Him and felt that I was flailing about in the world. I did not need to action this. I look after friends' children whenever they need this help; help friends who do not drive with their weekly shopping; bake for people at the drop of a hat; and perform many other acts of kindness for neighbours, friends and family – and it is all reciprocal, of course. This box was more than ticked. And it needed to be. Kindness and love were essential to my recovery. Before I can explain this more fully though, a small tangent has to be explored (sadly).

The Myth of Neutrality

In *Why Does He Do That? Inside The Minds of Angry and Controlling Men*, Lundy Bancroft writes of the myth of neutrality, that is, that there is no such thing as taking a neutral stance on a case of domestic abuse. In the following extract Bancroft explains why:

"It is not possible to be truly balanced in one's view of an abuser and an abused woman… "neutrality" actually serves the interests of the perpetrator much more than those of the victim and so is not neutral. Although an abuser prefers to have you wholeheartedly on his side, he will settle contentedly for your decision to take a middle stance. To him, that means you see the couple's problems as partly her fault and partly his fault, which means it isn't abuse." (Bancroft 2002: 287)

I had what I thought was a very good friend. I had

got to know her through Him. This maybe should have been a warning sign, but she had said to me after a couple of years or so that she considered me more a friend than Him because I was in touch with her and He had drifted out of touch. I told her when I left Him. I told her why I had left Him. And for the best part of a year *before* I left Him, I had discussed with her the confusing, heart breaking and soul destroying state of my relationship with Him.

Then one day post separation I was really, really struggling with the problem of non-violent domestic abuse not being taken so seriously as violent domestic abuse, I don't know why this was dominating my thoughts on this day, but it was. I found myself blurting out to this friend "If He had hit me, would you stop speaking to Him then?" I think I was not just preoccupied with the wider issue of non-violent domestic abuse being down-graded in everyone's minds that day, I think I was also troubled and hurt by her overall lack of aghastness (not a word, but it should be) at my descriptions of how He had treated me, how we had been living, for years, *for over a decade*, and for some reason, on this day, I hit a wall with this, and I wanted to know that there was *something* that He could have done to me that would make her *explicitly* join Team Helen, 100%, once and for all, and not be officially (regardless of levels of keeping in touch) a friend to both of us, having actually originated with Him – which seems to mean something in Friendships Maths. Surely violence was the thing to do it? Apparently not.

Her response to my question / desperate plea: "I

don't know Helen, I am just not the kind of person who would ever say to someone 'I am not speaking to you anymore'." WTF? Way to miss the fucking point. I would not expect a friend to specifically call Him up and say "Hello, following this conversation, I will never speak to you again!" How weird would that be? WE ARE NOT SIX.

What I had been looking for, hoping for, *desperately pleading for* with my question, was confirmation that she was Team Helen, i.e. that she did *not* condone what He had done to me, *for over a decade* (did I mention that already?) I cannot find the words with which to explain how surprised, shocked, aghast, perplexed, dumbfounded, bemused and *hurt to my very core* I was at her bizarre response to my question. With her response, she took a middle stance. Thus in her eyes His treatment of me, classed as domestic abuse by a whole range of professionals, which includes the domestic abuse charity Behind Closed Doors AND THE POLICE, was acceptable and partly my own fault; she bestowed on Him her approval or at least forgiveness; she colluded with Him; she was His ally; she was on His team; she was *not* Team Helen. I don't think I will ever get over this, as long as I live (but I guess I did at least find the words then, with help from Lundy Bancroft's brilliant book).

Luckily for me, this was an isolated incident. All of my other friends understood it, got it, shared their surprise, of course – but I was beyond surprised when the counsellor told me I was being abused, so I understood this, 100% - but did not waver in their support for me. Their acts of kindness and words of love, so integral to my recovery, I will now detail, with great, great pleasure.

Acts of Kindness and Words of Love

"Sometimes with memories surging up from the depths of our (un)conscious-ness, we find ourselves at a loss as to what to do. We can be frozen in place, or stunned, or even trapped by these memories. On the other hand, sometimes, mercifully, our spirits are protected by the power of forgetting, at least for a time." (Poulos, 2008: 51)

There is a very well known, and well used, saying that time is a great healer. But a Christian friend of mine once said that it is not time that heals, it is love. I believe this to be true. I experienced many acts of great kindness and read and heard many words of enormous love. This played a huge part in my healing, in my recovery. I like the idea of practising mindfulness but have always struggled with actually practising it, for the most part (because of my pathological inability to do nothing). However, at this time in my life, experiencing and hearing what I did, I think I managed it. I was able to stay in the many very beautiful moments, letting go of the situation I was in, with all of its fear and stress and misery, to truly enjoy the deeds and the words. I forgot, at least for a time. To paraphrase Eckhart Tolle, I felt momentarily that the present moment was all I had.

There is another very well known, and well used,

saying, that it takes a village to raise a child. I discovered that it takes the same to raise a (downtrodden looking) middle aged woman up from the floor that she too often frequented. So meet my village (of angels).

The Godsisters

Between the point of realising that I had to separate from Him, and managing to do it, I spoke with my Godsister, Elizabeth. She had heard a great line on a radio 4 programme: **Hope is stronger than heartbreak**. They were the right words at the right time from the right person (Elizabeth is super clever, and I don't just mean academically, and someone I have always, and will always, look up to). I have never forgotten these words.

More kind and inspirational words came from Julia, my mother's Godsister (we sound like such a religious family but, for the record, we are not). To this day, Julia's beautiful card adorns a pin board by my bed:

"From one independent woman to another... you will have dark moments or days which will eventually turn into grey ones. Don't be afraid and take courage from your strength of character... Stay firm and be the person you truly are. You are a very intelligent woman and a good mother – you'll always do well in this world, and your children will."

Vicky

My very good friend Vicky, alongside other acts of kindness, rang around solicitors to pre-book free half hours of legal advice when I was struggling with a paid job and two children and the enormous task of getting Him to move out was swamping me (I should mention that Vicky also has a paid job and two children). It was Vicky who helped me to move Him out, in the lunch break of a busy working day. Vicky also announced she was coming to stay the night after we had moved Him out, so I was not alone. I would never have asked. As it turned out, I really needed it. And I have already explained that she treated me to a heavily laden Costa gift card when I left Him and introduced me to the Fight Like A Girl motto/mantra. And, of course, Vicky created the beautiful diagrams for this book.

The Super-Parents
My astonishingly supportive and completely non-judgemental and incredibly generous parents, very soon after I left Him, booked a summer holiday for us all. They never verbalised it, but I am sure they were worried that I would not be able to afford to take the children on holiday otherwise. This gift was a drop in the ocean compared to what they went on to do. I had never asked them for money. I had never needed to. And I didn't do so after I left Him. But I didn't have enough money to buy Him out of the family home, my beloved Best Nest. With their generosity I did.

The Super-Cousins
My cousin Harriet messaged me at work one day. She asked for my bank account details. She said she wanted to put some money in my account, because

Christmas was approaching, and I was unexpectedly a single mother with probably more limited finances than I had been used to managing on. She said the money was for anything: treats, bills, putting petrol in the car, anything. This is what moved me the most. My cousin Ben has a working knowledge of how to navigate and negotiate the whole issue of Child Arrangements post separation/divorce. He crucially advised me on the power I held as the primary (actually more like sole) caregiver of my children and then very kindly went beyond simply advising me on what to put in my letters to Him addressing our post-separation Child Arrangements and drafted letters for me.

The Neighbours

My neighbour Sarah sat with me in the house, on more than one occasion, between my separating from Him and moving Him out, when I was so uncomfortable with His brooding, menacing presence in the house, as He continued to play mind games and threaten me. She was calm, chatty, normal company as I sat, or stood, stressed, anxious, agitated, nervous and not at all normal company.

My neighbours Sarah (another one) and Johnny walked my daughter to school with theirs on many occasions when I needed to make last minute early morning dashes to see the various professionals I pillaged for advice and support as I was trying to get Him to move out. Another neighbour, Miranda picked my daughter up from school with her children, on two occasions, so that I could attend legal meetings in town. And, as I have already explained, my (very clever) neighbour Simon deciphered my credit report.

Emma and John

My friends Emma and John, on separate occasions, accompanied me to the family court and the Personal Support Unit there, both to help with child care and assist me with filling out and discussing the court orders I looked into, when moving Him out of the family home seemed like it was never, ever going to be possible. These acts of kindness helped me enormously and gave me enormous peace of mind. Emma also, to this day, keeps copies of all of my diaries and notes and legal documents at her house, which gives me continued enormous peace of mind.

The Old Friends

I came home from work one day to a beautiful bouquet of flowers on my front doorstep. The card said "Hope these brighten your day." They were from one of my oldest and dearest friends from primary school, another Sarah. She came to stay with me too. As did other out-of-town friends: Rachel E pitched up and made it her mission to be as helpful as she possibly could for the weekend, thus giving me the experience of not parenting alone and doing so with smart, funny, interesting and interested company (this was something I enjoyed immensely and sadly realised I had never before had). Rachel M came to stay with her children and gave my children the fun of sleepovers

(Rachel and I had the fun of the champagne she brought). Sam and Blathnaid visited with Blathnaid's three year old son, a perfect playmate for my son, and as Sam can do French plaits (Sam can do anything, by the way) my daughter was in seventh heaven too. Vanessa, another dear old school friend, visited with her daughter. I think my son fell in love with her that day (I am already a little bit in love with the beautiful Vanessa). All of these visitors lifted my spirits no end, giving me mini breaks from solo parenting and the solitude that defined my evenings.

Olivia and Her Friend God

Olivia is the friend who came and had lunch with me and my son after I had moved Him out. I needed that company. Having worked and worried and hurt so much in the run up to that morning I was all over the place. She is also the friend that prayed with me and my son. Olivia has a relationship with God, this is how she describes her strong and beautiful faith. As I have already explained, this is something I have wanted and tried desperately for years to attain, via Sunday School, Young People's Fellowship and finally the Christian Union at university. I wanted so badly to believe, to feel something, to get what others got. But it never happened. Olivia has always prayed for me, maybe in part because she knew I could not pray for myself. She asked God to help me get through whatever it was I was going through - the unhappiness, the turmoil, the confusion. As I have never been able to believe in God, I cannot say that he helped me. But I can say that I Believe in

Olivia and I know that she helps.

TC

Once I became a single mother I found myself enmeshed in the labrynthian Tax Credits system. Oh Joy. In short, this means receiving about 5 pages (that is 10 sides, A4 size) of indecipherable financial information - pertaining to what you earn, what you spend on child care and what you are therefore entitled to Tax Credits wise - roughly every eight weeks, whether or not you report any of their precious 'Changes to Circumstances'. If you *do* ever report any 'Changes to Circumstances' then, oh my God, you get the 5 pages (10 sides, A4 size) about every three weeks. Sometimes when you ring up about the latest dossier of unfathomable information that you have received a Tax Credits employee will actually tell you to *ignore it* and *wait for the next dossier*. WTF? Do they have a robot machine just periodically churning out pages and pages of gobbledygook *for no apparent reason*? And then actual human-beings-people-staff being paid to answer the phone when it rings *and tell people to ignore it all*? Again, WTF?

Enter my friend TC. A former career within the benefits system means that she is one of the (I would estimate) 15 people or so outside of the bizarre Tax Credits system who understands it (and why assume the human-being-people-staff within the system understand it when their jobs seems to involve answering the phone and telling people to ignore anything sent out rather than explaining it?) TC so kindly and patiently goes through my latest dossier whenever I ask her to. She translates the 5 pages (10 sides, A4 size), which always includes about eight sets of nonsensical figures, into what I always expected to start receiving from the Tax Credits system once I became a feckless single mother of two and thus had to dip my (giant) feet into it, i.e. one simple sentence that goes something like this:

> Until further notice, on the X day of each Month you will receive £XXX into the following bank account...

I cannot thank TC enough.

David

It was my friend David who looked after my son on moving day and he also sent me the following message which, to this day, I cannot believe anyone has written about me: "Without you I would be in a very dark place. You have no idea and I don't have the words. But I feel I can hold my head up because you are my friend". He made me feel useful to loved ones when all I felt for a long, long time was a problem-riddled, super needy friend, lurching from one crisis to the next, baking cakes in an attempt to redress the huge imbalance.

Sam

The words of my very wise and witty friend Sam are sprinkled throughout this book, but she still warrants her own section, along with all of the other special people who have been integral to my recovery. Her words of hilarious wisdom are what she brought to my recovery, along with many happy times which lifted my spirits. Oh, and she has a wealth of knowledge on domestic abuse law and women's rights, i.e. more words of wisdom.

Peter

My beyond special friend Peter is one of the most astonishing people I have ever met. I cannot do him justice if I try to describe him, and all of his qualities. So I won't even try. I will say just one thing: Peter is my yardstick. It is not intentional. It is instinctive. A knee-jerk reaction that I have when having to quickly evaluate a behaviour, a treatment, an encounter. I think of Peter and how he conducts himself and treats others. When I told Peter I had an Emotional Support Worker from Behind Closed Doors he enquired about the service: how many Emotional Support Workers are there? Are they paid workers or are they volunteers? How long was I on the waiting list for? I answered all of his questions. Shortly after I did, he wrote to me (our friendship is played out chiefly in letters and emails) to tell me that he and his wife had made a donation to Behind Closed Doors. Another day he sent me the following email:

"A friend of mine coined the term 'posigivity' – the belief that you have something positive to contribute to the world every day. I like the idea as it is easy to forget how much one contributes to others one meets – family, friends and strangers, at work and at home. I know you hardly have a minute to sit down and take a breath, but when you do, try to reflect on your posigivity, on how much you give to the world and to those you meet. I think you have a lot to offer."

'Posigivity' now adorns my fridge. Peter also started ringing me every week, after I left Him, to check in with me, to find out how I am doing, to let me hear the voice of one of my best friends, who, incidentally, lives in the USA. And there is yet more. Upon learning that He had not paid Child Maintenance over the summer, Peter sent me some money, which he insisted was a gift and not a loan. Like I have already said, Peter is beyond special, one of the most astonishing people I have ever met, and I cannot do him and all of his qualities justice here. So I haven't even tried. I can say though that I love him.

Matthew

I have to mention my late friend Matthew. He passed away seven months before I left Him. You might wonder, then, how on earth - or rather how not on this earth - he could have helped me to recover. Well he did. So many times I have thought about what Matthew would do and have strived to do the same. He was a Buddhist. He was beyond being a Buddhist. He was beyond being anything that we can define in terms of a religion or a set of beliefs. He was not of this time. He was not of this world. When I wrote a poem for someone, to tell them what they meant to me - not having written a poem since I was at primary school and was given the task of writing one about a hairdryer (why?) - I only did so because this is what Matthew would have done. He would not keep any beautiful feelings inside out of fear of rejection. I had been emotionally abandoned and rejected by Him, reduced to an object which does not need love. I was fragile. No, that implies I was easily breakable, but I was quite simply already broken. I was broken. Yet I decided not to fear rejection, or any kind of negative reaction to my poem, because of Matthew. I wrote the poem. I sent the poem. It felt good. I do not regret it.

These words from Lundy Bancroft capture what these acts of kindness and words of love from my friends and family have done for me:

"Despite the challenges, many, many friends and relatives of abused women stay by them. Their presence is critical, for it is the level of loyalty, respect, patience, and support that an abused women receives from her own friends and family that largely determines her ability to recover from abuse and stay free." (Bancroft 2002: 279)

Unexpected Acts Of Kindness and Words Of Love

It was not only people who I know and love whose acts of kindness helped me to recover. Jaime Thurston started 52 Lives, a charity which helps one life, anywhere in the world, every week. In her book *Kindness the little thing that matters most*, she argues that it is not the actual help so much as the fact that a complete stranger provided it i.e. cared, that changes people's lives. I experienced acts of kindness from complete strangers too and Thurston's point rings very true for me.

Sharon: The Child Minder Extraordinaire

I took my children to Costa one morning on the way to school, for a treat, with my son's stroller on its last legs. It died in Costa. I was not going to get my daughter to school on time with either a walking two year old or as a walking, very tired 43 year old carrying a wriggling two year old. I decided to try to push the dead stroller out of the café. This was completely futile (of course). A woman leapt up and said she had a spare stroller in her mini-van parked outside. She was a child minder currently without a toddler so not needing her stroller. She unpacked it and set it up for me and the two of us set about trying to convince my son to get into it (bribery worked in the end). She then grabbed the dead stroller and said she would drive it to the tip up the road. I was bowled over by this act of kindness from a stranger. We swapped phone numbers and I agreed to ring her when I had sorted out a new stroller later that day. I baked her some chocolate cup cakes to say a very big thank you and gave them to her when she came for her stroller. This incredibly kind woman put such a spring in my step that day. She put a spring in my life.

Abbey: The Serendipitous Star

So did another stranger a few months later. I was walking back from the beloved toddler 'gymnastics' with my son one morning and I saw a young woman trying to cut back her unruly yard with what looked to be blunt shears. I have two pairs of not blunt shears and found myself offering to lend them to this woman who I had never spoken to before. She accepted my offer. Later that morning she returned them to me and thanked me, explaining that she had got the job done. She returned to my house again that afternoon. She said she was going to the supermarket and asked if there was anything that I needed and there was: dishwasher salt and rinse aid. She said no problem and returned later that afternoon with my shopping and a bar of very fancy chocolate. She said she thought I had looked a bit stressed earlier and wanted me to have a treat when I had some time to myself. I was slightly alarmed to hear of how I had come across earlier - a cliché stressed, harassed single mother of two (well, given that I urgently needed things for my dishwasher, a very middle class stressed, harassed single mother of two). But it was such a kind thing she did for me that day. It turned out to be the first of many as we became friends. She is incredible. A kind, clever, vibrant, beautiful silver lining.

Concerning all acts of initiative (and creation), there is one elementary truth, the ignorance of which kills countless ideas and splendid plans: that the moment one definitely commits oneself, then Providence moves too. All sorts of things occur to help one that would never otherwise have occurred. A whole stream of events issues from the decision, raising in one's favour all manner of unforeseen incidents and meetings and material assistance, which no man could have dreamt would have come his way. (William Hutchison Murray)

I was so very excited about writing this book and my goal of publishing it that it is hard to believe that I could ever have become even more excited about it. But I did. This is because of Abbey. Without Abbey, there would be none of the beautiful diagrams in this book. One night, we chatted over a gin and tonic and the contents of my treats tin. We nibbled on a bar of very dark chocolate, a favourite treat of mine. As we ate and talked I noticed a diagram on the packet. It was a radar diagram depicting the taste profile of the chocolate. By this point, everything I saw and heard made me think in some way of this book, because it is about everything in my life, so everything that resonated with me, everything that moved me, I began to see through the lens of my book. I decided I wanted to work on a radar diagram of my abusive relationship (see the finished diagram at the end the earlier chapter entitled Mind). I said as much to Abbey. She was very quickly Googling on her phone and showing me images from a book entitled *Information is Beautiful* by David McCandless (2009). I was mesmerised as I poured over images of the most beautiful diagrams depicting data of all kinds. I ordered copies of the book and its follow-up.

The next day I saw Vicky. Architect Vicky. Drawer of exquisite architectural diagrams Vicky. I felt sure she too would be in awe of the book. She was. She told me that she owned a copy. I was not surprised. Then she told me that she is friends with someone who worked on the book. I was quite surprised. Then she told me that she could help me turn my domestic abuse data into beautiful and educational/helpful diagrams. I was *not* surprised, given her skills and her kindness. But I was at the same time completely blown away. Such providence.

I had never experienced such an astonishing chain of events in my life before: from garden shears to the discovery of a whole new concept for my book, via a new and beautiful friendship, and encompassing an old and equally beautiful friendship. Without Abbey, there would be no diagrams in this book. And I believe it is some of the educational/helpful diagrams which, more than anything I could ever write – no matter how detailed i.e. wordy I am – describe, explain and capture my experience of domestic abuse. Thus I believe it is some of the educational/helpful diagrams which, more than anything I could ever write, could help other people who are on the path that I found myself on.

Gratitude Diary

The following extracts are taken from the Gratitude Diary I began keeping at the suggestion of my Behind Closed Doors Emotional Support Worker (and, as I have already stated, still keep to this day). I chose these extracts as they illustrate the range of things which I feel deep gratitude for – the support of neighbours, friends and family; feeding these loved ones; problem solving (more often than not via the help of these loved ones); my work, which I adore and feel so very privileged to be able to do; helping others – including strangers; being able to treat myself; and writing. What these extracts also illustrate is that it is my loved ones – the angels on my side - which I am clearly the most grateful for (I wonder, is this good enough proof that I *am* the people person who He so hatefully decreed I was not?)

Extracts from Gratitude Diary

170318 Family and neighbours day. Fed a lot of people.

180318 A snow day full of neighbours. I invited all for brunch/lunch. Busy 8am to 3pm. Blissful.

200318 Positive feedback from Behind Closed Doors regarding how I handled a situation with my daughter.

210318 My friend Olivia planned a fabulous day for the two of us.

230318 My friend David said that 'posigivity' is me all over and that I turned his day around today.

260318 Lovely day with my parents. So kind and generous and supportive.

290318 I coped with a day of work when I was anxious about it again.

010418 Peter has donated money to Behind Closed Doors.

020418 Hosted the annual family Easter get together, involving baking cakes for everyone.

050418 I had a panic attack at nursery when I heard via text that I had got a job interview. Nursery staff stayed with me. Friends going to help me with interview preparation.

060418 Behind Closed Doors said I am doing very well working through the recovery programme.

090418 Simon helped me with my credit report problem.

190418 A good morning on the hospital ward. I felt good at my job. I felt useful.

279418 I found shoes I like in my big, big size today and could afford to treat myself, so I did.

010518 I booked my F.L.A.G. tattoo today and paid the deposit. Very excited.

060518 Amazing day at the community garden then back to mine for a BBQ. So many lovely people.

120518 Fun brunch with neighbours then a water fight for/with all of the children.

130518 I helped a marathon runner today. I feel blessed that she asked me.

170518 Got to know a nice neighbour today, Abbey, she brought me chocolate, an act of kindness, it moved me.

190518 A second amazing writing session on My Story.

240518 Solo mortgage agreed by new lender. I cannot quite believe it.

270518 Received homemade chocolate treats from David.

010618 I got my F.L.A.G. tattoo today with David.

060618 Really positive feedback from my tutor on my studies.

110618 Good writing despite terrible fear after incident with Him.

120618 I received a gift from Mr O today, a mug emblazoned with I CAN'T KEEP CALM I'M WRITING. Love it.

160618 Simon helped me with my Transfer of Equity paperwork because I was so stressed.

260618 Help from friends – David and Olivia – with the children so I could see a solicitor child free.

300618 My Behind Closed Doors fundraiser went well and I wrote a piece I love for the book entitled "Fuck off".

060718 A service user at work wants to swap advocates so we can simply be friends.

080818 When I did not turn up at the community garden BBQ Simon came and got me up off the floor, where I was because He refused to sign the Transfer of Equity, yet again.

090718 Friends were here with me all day on this horrid day – Ewa, Simon, Julia, one by one, they made me not be alone.

120718 Vicky came and helped me sort out my notes and other documents for my next solicitor meeting and my police meeting. She wants to go to the police meeting with me. Big love.

130718 I managed to restructure My Story. So very excited.

150718 A beautiful day with Vanessa from Derby. I think my son fell in love with her.

180718 He signed the Transfer of Equity papers.

240718 An incredible first meeting with Vicky to work on the diagrams for the book. Brilliant. Buzzing. Euphoric.

270718 Attempted found poetry. Really pleased with the results.

280718 David brought his dad around for tea, he wanted

him to try Sociable Salad. He loved it.

030818 A service user at work gave me a beautiful flower and herb bouquet.

110818 A fabulous evening with Karen. Watched Bad Moms. Genius. A great quote from Karen for the book.

140818 Emma came today to help with the children so that I could ring the CMS. Big help. Big love.

220818 I saw the service user at work whose advice got me writing on May 18th. I thanked her. It was so lovely.

230818 I got more hours at work. I may not need His damn Child Maintenance so badly now?

110918 Blissful day with my son.

250918 Peter sent me some money today, he had been worrying about the lack of Child Maintenance over the summer. I said I will pay him back for sure if/when I publish my book...

011018 Mr O came to see me because he felt I needed a hug.

041018 *Try Praying* book came through the door today from Olivia – she surely does not remember it is a year *today* since I left Him? Spooky. Beyond spooky. So God then?

111018 The After School Club manager gave me a bag of lovely things for my son. I made her some chocolate tiffin to say thank you, to take in tomorrow.

301018 Olivia had the children so I could meet with Super Roger. He was incredibly helpful as always. The family finances are and will be okay.

311018 Special day with my daughter.

081118 A service user gave me a beautiful box of cakes

for me and the kids today. How lucky am I to have my job?

171118 Shining Light tattoo. Beautiful.

211118 The unending support and friendship of Peter.

241118 Met with K, a sort of 'spiritual guru'. I think it will be useful. And then a great diagrams meeting with Vicky, we work so very well together, and so happily.

261118 I was able to help out three friends today. Grateful for friends who turn to me, who trust me, who feel they can ask me, and so ask me.

021218 Wrapped all of my Christmas gifts.

061218 Nafeesa comforted me so sweetly at work when I had a meltdown.

111218 Good support from the Personal Support Unit at the Family Court today, from a nice lady called Anne. I have a plan regarding Christmas and worst case scenario.

131218 Astonishingly nice message from someone called Tim who bought my old filing cabinet.

161218 Great advice from Olivia's husband Bill regarding agents and publishers. Very useful. Got a plan now.

181218 I cried my heart out at my daughter's school Christmas show, at a song: Love Song. Friend of a friend, Amy, offered me a hug. It helped.

251218 A lovely Christmas Day with my children and friends and neighbours.

Theorising Kindness and Love

Erin Pizzey set up the first battered wives refuge in the UK. In her book *Scream Quietly Or The*

Neighbours Will Hear she writes of the mental health conditions diagnosed - and barbarically treated - in some of the women who she saw going through her refuge. The following extracts outline two treatments:

"[T]he psychiatrist bored with her crying, decides sometimes that the most useful move would be to perform a leucotomy and remove the anxiety. We see the results of this operation when the women come in and recount their horrifying life histories with utter indifference. The operation does indeed remove all their anxieties and usually their children have been taken away and put into care because the mother has lost all sense of responsibility. The husbands continue to beat them but now they put up with it with cheerful indifference. A surgical triumph?" (Pizzey 1974: 104)

"It is more common to see mothers who have had ECT, or 'shock treatment' as it is commonly called. Nobody really knows how or why it works but it does relieve depression. Unfortunately it also erases memory and has other side-effects if used too often. Again, many of our mothers go into the mental hospital and are given a course of ECT. It helps for the moment, but they go home and are repeatedly battered until in the end you find a confused, witless forty-year-old sitting in front of you, trying to remember when and where she was last jolted out of her rapidly deteriorating mind." (Pizzey 1974: 104-5)

Whilst such horrific treatments of women made mentally unwell by domestic abuse are, thankfully, a thing of the past (with leucotomies no longer performed and ECT vastly moved on from the above description), the connection between the experience of domestic abuse and mental ill health is not. The link between domestic abuse and depressive symptomatology is well known and well documented. For example, In *Why Does He Do That? Inside The Minds of Angry and Controlling Men* Lundy Bancroft argues that:

"I speak with some mothers who have developed psychiatric symptoms from being abused, such as nightmares, severe anxiety, or depression. Research studies have found that these conditions and related ones, including post traumatic stress disorder, are not uncommon in women who have been abused by their partners." (Bancroft 2002: 251)

This is, quite frankly, obvious: why would being abused by a supposed loved one *not* make a person depressed? I have never had a formal diagnosis of depression but, as I have written about throughout this book, I was left anxious and low due to my abusive relationship. I would certainly describe myself in the relationship as, if not clinically depressed, then on a pathway to it.

A piece of research on women, domestic abuse and depression has been carried out which explored what such a pathway may be. A disconnectedness is commonly associated with experiences of domestic abuse. And a similar process – a loss of belongingness, defined as an unpleasant mental state that is experienced when the innate need for relationship and connectedness is not met - is something positively associated with depression.

The research therefore explored a loss of belongingness as a potential mechanism connecting domestic abuse and depression.

In their research paper entitled 'Understanding How Domestic Abuse is Associated With Greater Depressive Symptoms in a Community Sample of Female Primary Care Patients: Does Loss of Belongingness Matter?' the researchers explain that they found a positive association between domestic abuse and depressive symptoms and a negative association between belongingness and both domestic abuse and depressive symptoms. They found that the inclusion of belongingness fully accounted for the positive association between domestic abuse and depressive symptoms in women. That is, women who are abused by their partners are likely to experience greater depressive symptoms if their basic need to belong is rejected or thwarted by their partner.

They continue by pointing out that a person's sense of belongingness is not usually based on one relationship alone. It will rather be predicated on a range of valued relationships. They therefore considered another question: whether the presence of real or perceived external sources of support and interpersonal connections with others might mitigate the development of depressive symptoms in abused women. They concluded from their findings that yes it did. Furthermore, they cited other studies with similar findings.

So there is research based theory behind what was so central to my recovery ("Yay!" says my inner geek). All of the acts of kindness and words of love that moved me and helped me, and are helping me to heal, having given me a sense of connectedness to others, a sense of belongingness. I felt, and I feel still, that I belong to several groups of friends – local and long distance; a geographically scattered but supportive family; a network of parents; a group of incredibly supportive co-workers; and my chosen family, to coin the sociological terms of Carol Smart and Lynn Jamieson, whose work I learnt about whilst studying sociology and social policy at university – my brunching and co-parenting group of neighbours. I see my incredible brunching chosen family as perhaps the single most important embodiment of this sense of belongingness that is so integral to my on-going recovery.

Parallels

What is that well known saying: there but for the grace of God go I. As I have written, I have always struggled to believe in God, despite wanting to my whole life. So sod that saying. How about how bloody privileged, blessed and lucky I am (and every other synonym you can think of but I cannot) that I lived with domestic abuse for over a decade but have come out of it ostensibly intact. By 'intact' I do not just mean alive, I mean also still ensconced in the family home, my Best Nest, with my two beautiful children, holding down a job which I love and which enables me to pay for said family home, and not living with a formal diagnosis of a mental health condition. How can this be? How can one person be so lucky? Before I attempt to answer these questions, another question needs answering:

how do I know just how lucky I am?

I work as an Independent Mental Health Advocate. I work with women in the community and women residing on an acute psychiatric ward, including both informal AKA voluntary patients (if there is a more cruel Catch 22 situation, please fill me in on it) and patients detained under The Mental Health Act 1983. As I have already explained, I have never received a formal diagnosis of a mental health condition, I have 'only' been signed off work for two weeks due to the stress of His post-separation unrelenting house-related domestic abuse. However, the stories I hear from some of the women I work with have so many parallels with my story. Their stories encompass domestic abuse; in some cases the specific forms that I live with – emotional and psychological abuse and coercive control; and in some cases some really specific micro-similarities, as the following list illustrates:

Micro-similarities between my domestic abuse experience and those of other women

- An abusive ex-partner who works in a very well respected and well paid job within the field of health
- An abusive ex-partner refusing to sign the papers for a Transfer of Equity
- Domestic abuse following an earlier experience of rape
- Domestic abuse leading to a creative outpouring because the pain has to be channelled into something worthwhile

Their stories also include the following devastating experiences:

More serious consequences of domestic abuse experienced by other women

- Losing the family home and becoming homeless as a result
- Losing their job and becoming completely at the mercy of the benefits system as a result
- Losing their benefits and having to fight tooth and nail to get them back
- Losing their children *to an abusive ex-partner*

How, then, with so much overlap in experiences, can I be so lucky to have avoided any of these terrible things that have befallen the kind, generous, loving, talented, creative, hard-working, vibrant, and beautiful women that I work with? I have hinted at the answer already when I write of the many acts of kindness and words of love, especially from my brunching chosen family, that have given me the sense of belongingness necessary to divert an abused woman from the path towards poor mental health. But this does not fully explain my avoidance of what has happened to the women I have met whose stories are so hauntingly familiar to me. I have to go back to my sociologist roots again to fully explain this, with two words: social capital.

In the 1990s Jennifer Aniston was in a shampoo advert in which she famously uttered the line "Here comes the science part", before introducing someone else to explain why the magical, mystical elixir being marketed as shampoo will not only wash the dirt and grease out of your hair but turn it into something more akin to the spun gold-like hair she appears to sport - which, incidentally, is what such shampoo manufacturers are basically doing for themselves, I believe, when they market such substances in such a way to desperate women wanting to look like Jennifer Aniston just via switching shampoos, they are spinning gold for themselves, whilst women wander about with totally normal, average, non-Jenifer-Aniston-on-the-advert like hair. So, rant over, here comes the social science part. Social capital is defined as follows:

The term generally refers to (a) resources, and the value of these resources, both tangible (public spaces, private property) and intangible ("actors", "human capital", people), (b) the relationships among these resources, and (c) the impact that these relationships have on the resources involved in each relationship, and on larger groups. It is generally seen as a form of capital that produces public goods for a common good. (Wikipedia)

It is the acts of kindness that I thus need to focus and elaborate on here, to explain why they not only, along with the words of love, helped me emotionally, but also helped me practically, life-changingly so (sorry, another made up word, which I believe needs to be an actual word), meaning that I am surviving over a decade of domestic abuse pretty much intact. The issue here is *who* has performed these acts of kindness, or more specifically, *what they had to bring to the table in terms of resources: finances, time, skills, knowledge and experience.*

Let's not forget, first of all, the (social) capital I started out with: a chunk of my inheritance from when I was twenty one, to put towards the project of keeping i.e. buying the family home, my Best Nest. This was not enough. But it did not need to be. Because my parents, seemingly without a second thought, or a first thought actually, made up the difference. As I have explained, my friend Vicky and my cousin Harriet also passed on some of their financial resources to enable me to treat myself and the children.

Vicky and another friend, David, were able to help me out on moving day due to not only their great kindness but also their great jobs which enable them to work from home and in Vicky's case have some flexibility over the hours she chooses to work. This flexibility also enabled Vicky to ring around a bunch of solicitors for me and book slots of free legal advice during the long process of getting Him to move out of the family home. My cousin Ben shared with me his knowledge on parenting and child care arrangements post-separation gleaned in part from his social work background. My friend Sam shared her enormously useful knowledge of domestic abuse and the law to advise me on my rights and the related actions I should take throughout my journey, gleaned from her community and voluntary work background. A colleague with a background in law also advised me on my 'credible witness' status to reassure me (and I was, I am, totally reassured) that if He ever took me to court over child care arrangements, my diaries, notes and whole story basically would be believable and thus believed and so chances are I won't lose my children (as three of the women that I work with have).

To reiterate what I wrote earlier then, how bloody privileged, blessed and lucky I am (and every other synonym you can think of but I cannot) that I lived with domestic abuse for over a decade but have come out of it ostensibly intact. I believe I have done so due to words of love and acts of kindness carried out by loved ones brimming with not only kindness (obviously) but resources - finances, time, skills, knowledge and experience – i.e. social capital. Do you think they all did it because, to paraphrase Jennifer Aniston again, I am worth it? Their words and deeds make me think I might be.

My Acts Of Kindness Towards Him

"Always try to be a little kinder than is necessary." (J.M.Barrie)

"Send out light and love. To all. Even those who have hurt you." (Munson 2010: 273)

"If it is not right do not do it; if it is not true do not say it." (Marcus Aurelius)

"We must be the change we wish to see." (Gandhi)

"Three things in human life are important. The first is to be kind. The second is to be kind. The third is to be kind." (Henry James)

"Peace cannot be kept by force; it can only be achieved by understanding." (Albert Einstein)

When trying to decide which beloved quote to preface this section with I could not pick one. I wondered why. Is it because I am so desperately trying to hammer home the point that *I am not a complete idiot*? Probably. Especially by shoe-horning in Einstein, how can *anyone* fail to agree with what I am going to write next if I quote probably the most well-known *genius* who seems to agree with my *modus operandi*? This is not enough, though. I have to go on and explain myself further.
How I conduct myself has always been important to me. This is linked to how I was raised. I was taught at Sunday school to 'treat other people as you would wish to be treated yourself', a la Jesus. Furthermore, I grew up hearing sayings (truisms, I believe) from my parents, such as 'two wrongs do not make a right'. I now regularly find myself trying to indoctrinate my children with all of this, in exactly the same way as I and my sister were (thankfully) as children.

Then there is Matthew. Alongside the above Sunday School and parents related core belief, I have a burning desire to do what Matthew would do, if he were still here, i.e. the right thing. So, to the disbelief of many of my friends, I continued to conduct myself with as much kindness and respect as I could with Him. However monstrous He was behaving towards me. However cruel He was being to me. However much He continued to abuse me. However much I was hurting.

I told Him whenever He came to the house to see the children He could help Himself if I had a pot of coffee on the go (remember coffee is very important to Him?) The same went for any home baked treats. Given that setting up a new home can be expensive, to save Him some money I gave Him things that I was not using that He needed for His new flat. This included the beautiful vintage 'patent pending' salad spinner I had found and bought, because He used it more than I ever did (with me having switched to the grated courgette based 'Sociable Salad' explained in the chapter entitled Food). I also gave Him a pin board decorated with photographs of our children and some of their art work. And when His washing machine broke I said He could bring His laundry around and I would do it for Him. Not at all shockingly, He took me up on this offer.

I believe that, bizarre though it may seem to others, my decision to conduct myself in this way helped me towards healing as much as the acts of kindness and words of love which I experienced. This was how I had always strived to conduct myself whilst in a relationship with Him, partly because, as I said, I believe it is the right thing to do and also partly because, back then, before I knew what He is, I was desperately trying to get Him to be nice(r) to me in return, i.e. via modelled behaviour. This was not me being ludicrous. There is academic theory behind it: the work of David Hamilton.

In his book *Why Kindness Is Good For You*, he writes of the effects of kindness and argues that "[one] effect of kindness is that it is contagious. Being around kind people can make us kinder" (Hamilton 2010: 14). In his second book on kindness, *The Five Side Effects of Kindness*, he elaborates on this theory of kindness being contagious by introducing not one but *three* concepts with which to explain it: the ripple or domino effect, elevation and the three-degree rule:

"Just as a pebble dropped in a pond creates ripples that lift lily pads on the other side, so acts of kindness lift the spirits of people who witness it and they carry that kindness forward, lifting the spirits of others." (Hamilton 2017: 134)

"Elevation lifts us and produces an immediate desire to emulate the kindness we witness. It inspires us to carry the spirit of kindness forward." (Hamilton 2017: 135)

"In real life, the 'three-degree rule' means that each time we are kind, we inspire someone else to be kind (one degree), who inspires someone else (two degrees), who inspires someone else (three degrees). And of course in real life we inspire more than one person at a time, and each of these also inspires further people... On average, if your kind act inspires four people, and each of them does something kind that inspires four more people, who each inspire four more, then just from your single act of kindness you will have indirectly helped 64 people (4 x 4 x 4). And most of them you will never meet in your lifetime." (Hamilton 2017: 147)

I am afraid that it does not matter how many well

defined and argued concepts apparently lie behind this kindness-is-contagious theory, it appears not to apply to my acts of kindness towards Him. Unless I am misunderstanding the term 'contagious', I must assume that He has a cast iron immune system. But then this seems strange given how often He was bed-ridden with a cold – yes *bed-ridden*, with a *cold* – and given the time when the whole family had a sickness 'bug', which I recovered from in about 4 hours – well, I was as sick as is humanly possible to be in the night, then went back to sleep, and 4 hours later our robot baby son woke me up at 4am and so it was business as usual – whilst He was, again, bed-ridden for 48 hours, that is for TWO DAYS (to co-opt the totally PC language of transgender, He is a cis, but at this point I am completely unable to stop myself from co-opting the following totally non-PC term to describe Him: a cis*sy*). Despite His being seemingly impervious to the apparently contagious disease of kindness, as I started to understand Him, it seemed ever more right to be kind, in an attempt to achieve peace. Michelle Obama has coined the expression that when they go low, you go high. Using this phraseology, I was high as a kite, I was completely stoned, I was totally off my head (oh that I actually had been, it would have made my journey a lot more enjoyable).

I must return to my first reason for my acts of kindness towards Him, my quite simply believing that it is the right thing to do (not a surprising belief of mine given that I am quite simply quite simple). I am reminded of yet another well known, and well used, saying: there is no selfless good deed. Indeed, Epictetus extolled the virtues of forgiveness for the purpose of self-help:

When people do not act as you would wish them to, exercise the muscles of your good nature by shrugging your shoulders and saying to yourself "Oh well." Then let the incident go... Forgive others for their misdeeds over and over again. This gesture fosters inner ease. (In *The Art of Living*, Epictetus)

Part of me wonders whether Epictetus would ever have written this had he had the misfortune to meet Him. But another part of me thinks Epictetus must have met Him (I am aware that this is not possible) because the above was totally written *for* Him, given its "over and over again" point. I must (more sensibly) return to the scientific kindness theorising of David Hamilton here. His work definitely fits with the whole 'no selfless good deed' issue. In his first book on kindness he writes of many, many benefits to our selves of performing acts of kindness. In his second book on the subject, he boils this down to a concise list, which includes his whole contagious argument. As I love lists (as you know) here it is:

The Five Side Effects Of Kindness

1. Kindness makes us happier
2. Kindness is good for the heart
3. Kindness slows ageing
4. Kindness improves our relationships
5. Kindness is contagious

In a nutshell then, David Hamilton argues that kindness makes us feel mentally and physically good. In his first kindness book he even refers to a laundry experiment which, needless to say, startled me beyond belief with its relevance to my acts of kindness towards Him:

"In another study, people labelled as hostile and who had chest pain were asked, as part of the study, to clean each other's laundry. This simple act led to much less chest pain. It's funny how dong someone's washing can do the same as a heart drug. Thoughts of kindness replace thoughts of hostility and oxytocin flows through the heart." (Hamilton 2010: 122-23)

That acts of kindness serve to benefit oneself is something that I have always felt to be the case and, again, I am glad to know that there is both philosophy and academic (that is, inner geek pleasing) work to back it up. So always trying to be as kind as possible to Him, including post-separation, was about me being kind to *myself*. This theory makes me come across as a little less ridiculous, I hope, as surely this self-kindness was more needed than ever post-separation?

When you are faithfully occupied with performing the acts of a wise and decent person, seeking to conform your intentions and acts to the divine will, you do not feel victimized by the words or deeds of others. At worst, those words and deeds will seem amusing or pitiable. (Epictetus, The Art of Living)

I have to return to the laundry doing here, to introduce The T-shirt Incident. AKA the second most surreal experience of my life (after the first coffee incident). He arrived at my house one day, a few months after I had moved Him out, wearing a T-shirt emblazoned with the word OBEY. I asked if I could take His picture. He asked me why. I said no reason. He said no. He was wearing this T-shirt when He brought the first load of laundry around for me to do, totally unnecessarily, I thought, given that I had *offered* to do His laundry, that is, He had not needed to ask me let alone to *order* me to do it with the aid of a menacing but also kind of comedic and definitely bizarre logoed T-shirt. Maybe He wanted to be absolutely sure it got done?

I am thinking of getting Him a T-shirt that says MY WAY OR THE HIGHWAY. Or maybe I should go the full hog and get one that reads DOMINATOR. No. Scrap that. I will find Him one that simply says GOD. Alternatively - a girlfriend pointed out - or as well as - another girlfriend pointed out – I should get myself one that says ‘NO’. Or ‘Fuck Off’. Or ‘NO: FUCK OFF’. It is hard to decide. I like all three.

The Fantasy Rebuttal T-Shirts Diagram

FUTURE

I want my love, my joy, my laugh, my smile, my needs
Not in the star signs
Or the palm that she reads
I want my sun-drenched, wind-swept Ingrid Bergman*
kiss
Not in the next life
I want it in this
I want it in this
Good as Gold (Stupid as Mud), The Beautiful South
*Please substitute for Dave Grohl

Focusing On The Positives

It is possible to develop positive lift. To go forward and resolve the horizon to configure a new beginning. (Prophetic found poetry post card sent to me by my friend Peter just before I saw a counsellor in Sept 2017)

Unsent Letter to Mr O from January 2018

Dear Mr O,

I am going to tell you a story, my story, to get it out more than anything, as it is consuming me. I remember vividly the day that I met you. You turned my head. It felt as though the world stopped for a moment. I think it must have. It was instantaneous attraction; physical and sexual attraction. I was left reeling from it.

Then I got to know you and found nothing not to like, not to adore, about you – your sense of humour, your values, what you stand for, what you won't stand for, your supposed 'grumpiness', which I think I love most of all. Being in (what I thought was) a relationship I of course tried to bury my feelings for you. I wanted a baby and focused on that. I of course had a baby, which made me very happy, and I enjoyed so much the times I saw you whilst on maternity leave. Then I returned to work and simultaneously my relationship began to disappear, despite my every effort to stop that happening. I had stopped feeding my baby at night in preparation for returning to work and assumed my partner would come back to me, but He never did. I lived confused and heartbroken (and eventually learnt I was living abused). My feelings for you remained buried because that part of me capable of such feelings had all but died. I was a mother, an advocate and a zombie. I was happy with my children; I was happy in my work; I was numb otherwise.

Eventually I got help (counselling) and through that I got knowledge and from that I got the strength to pick up my heart and separate from the man I had loved with all of it, before He trashed it. (I have never told you this, I don't think, but the first thing He said when I said yes, I want to separate, was "Can I see other people?" Five words which broke my heart all over again if, a heart can be broken twice by the same person).

Soon after separating from Him I saw you and I wanted to tell you my story, because you are such a great listener and I respect your opinion so very much. But I was too distressed to talk, so later that day I told you my story via email. I turned to you for emotional support and you have become my biggest source of it. The part of me capable of feeling love and attraction was so dead I had no idea that communicating with you so much would un-bury my feelings for you. But it has.

As I once told you, you have brought me back to life. Aside from my children, you make me the happiest; you make me smile. You have been so kind to me, sending me a beautiful song lyric when I said I was lonely and out of the blue Googling my name. Waking up to the "shining light" message is one of the nicest experiences of my life. Your Googling my name is one of the most amazing things that anyone has ever done for me. You have done things to make me smile as I was going through the most agonising and traumatic experience of my life - getting away from a man who brought me nothing but down. And I am completely in love with you.

I wanted to tell you how I feel. I wanted to be honest. And keeping it inside has become too difficult. I hope it makes you smile to know that you have a very big fan. I hope it pleases your competitive streak too, given that I don't have a very big fan anymore. I don't think I ever did.

I believe I am capable of great love and I thought I had lost that capability. Loving you has proved to me that I have not. This is a positive to take from this situation of unrequited love. And I am going to focus on the positives. Surely this is what a shining light would do?
hx

I read something once, I cannot remember where,

but I believe it: Action almost never leads to regret in the long term. I believe this. Because I can never regret my relationship with Him. As I did when I assumed my love for Mr O was unrequited, I focus on the positives: I have my two beautiful children. I have my story, my book. I have learnt. I am changed. I am if not recovered then recovering. I know this for sure.

At my last session with my Emotional Support Worker from Behind Closed Doors I asked excitedly about a task I thought we were supposed to work on that day: my Self-esteem Charter. I was looking forward to the work sheets, the reading, the home work. My Emotional Support Worker said that there is no work sheet for getting a Fight Like A Girl tattoo, nor for writing a book about your experience of domestic abuse, with the aim of publishing it to help your children and to help others. She had observed me changed (the 'light bulb moment') a month earlier. Now she observed me in possession of greater self-confidence, self-worth and self-esteem. In sum: a greater sense of self. So she observed me ostensibly recovered; and we completed the exit paperwork. My Behind Closed Doors Emotional Support Worker was right to discharge me from the service that day.

Self-esteem Charter

"An abused woman's self-esteem will have been steadily worn down. She may not believe she will manage on her own, or that she has any other options. She may have been brainwashed into thinking she's worthless. She will feel ashamed of what has happened and perhaps convinced it is her fault." (Lisa Firth (ed.) Domestic and Relationship Abuse, *Issues*, Volume 224 (2012) Cambridge: Independence; p3)

I am managing on my own (well, let's face it, with Him I always had to anyway). I know I am not worthless. I am not ashamed. This was not my fault. As for my self-esteem, let's just call that a work in progress. A big part of this work is the writing of my very own Self-esteem Charter. Yes, my inner/outer geek decided to write an actual self-esteem charter, despite my Behind Closed Doors Emotional Support Worker explaining it was not at all necessary given my totally bad ass tattoo and new found writing voice (you know I love homework, even if I have to set it myself it seems).

I must preface my self-esteem charter with some home truths. I know I would not make the easiest of partner – I can be insecure and needy and I am fastidiously (obsessively?) tidy. I am not the best mother – I can lack patience and be too quick to incentivise (i.e. bribe) with treats when I am exhausted. And, to get a bit biblical, I am guilty of sex (and motherhood) out of wedlock. But I also know that I am not the intrinsically flawed character – fourfold no less - that He led me to believe that I was. I have drawn up my very own self-esteem charter in part to remind myself of this.

My self-esteem Charter

- I am a good mother
- I make an amazing partner

- I am endlessly affectionate
- I am capable of great love
- I am capable of change
- I am a sensitive person and I don't like being told to "Fuck off" and I am wise not to
- I can take constructive criticism - and I welcome it
- I do not have a 'perfection complex' – I am sure of this *because there is no such thing*
- I work hard every single day
- I am beautiful
- I am generous
- I am sexy
- I am not bad in bed
- I am a good person
- I am not a skivvy
- I am of sound mind (and I am very grateful for this good mental health)
- I am not a victim
- I am lucky
- I Fight Like A Girl
- I was born to resist
- I focus on the positives
- I am a shining light

Goals

"I have always followed my instincts. I firmly believe that being true to yourself is a guarantee that quality and integrity will shine through. What motivates me is the possibility that my work can give pleasure and be uplifting." (Kiely 2012: 11)

And helpful.

As I have already said in this book, I do believe that there is no selfless good deed. I cannot deny that I want this book to sell and make me some money, enough money to have no financial need for His Child Maintenance payments for my two children. I would, of course, always pursue such payments for my children, to squirrel away for their futures, but to be able to provide for them fully on my own in the here and now is another goal. Whilst I am on the subject of goals, I also want to learn to dance. I want to take ballet lessons. I left ballet at the age of about four because I was too self-conscious to be seen in a leotard and I was not old enough to be allowed to wear a ballet skirt over my ballet leotard, such is the fascist regime that is the world of children's ballet. I am fully aware that I am FAR TOO BIG AND TOO TALL AND THUS TOO HEAVY to be a ballerina, whose (sole?) purpose is to be flung about and twirled around by a ballet dancer. I am not deluded. I want to do ballet *on my own*. I do most other things on my own. I do not see why I cannot add ballet dancing to the list. But I am getting side tracked here.

"One late night, sitting by the cold iron woodstove alone, frantic with questions, and feeling hopeless, I began literally bargaining with the universe, as one does in times of great crisis. I actually prayed, proposing a deal – if God (or whoever was listening; I would go with anyone who was willing to take the call) would somehow heal me, somehow restore what I had lost, and if I learned anything worth knowing in the process, I would write about it if there was the least chance that what I had learned could possibly help anyone else." (Wolf 2012: 17)

Two things in this quote from Wolf jumped off the page when I read them. As I have explained before in this book, despite years and years of trying to believe in God, I have never been able to. But like Wolf – and also Liz Gilbert in *Eat, Pray Love* (2006), another book I love and probably actually worship; another writer I adore and who I probably actually want to befriend, in a creepy stalker super fan fashion – I 'prayed' to someone or something or other, several times, when I hit my version of rock bottom, several times (I had thought rock bottom was a place you only ever landed on once, I was wrong, I am sorry to be writing this, although I do also feel it is useful information to be passing on). Also like Wolf, I specifically 'prayed' that I would do everything I could to help other souls avoid going through what I was going through if she/he/it/they would just make it stop, make the confusion and the fear and the anguish and the hurting all just stop. What the hell I meant back then I do not know. I was desperate. I was demented. I was broken. I now know what I mean when I say I want to help others avoid going through what I went through: I want people to read this book and to recognise what emotional and psychological abuse and coercive control are *before they have lived with them for over a decade*. This is my goal with this book.

Feedback from friends and acquaintances who

have read extracts from this book, along my journey of writing it, suggest to me that I may achieve this goal. As the following quotes illustrate, some people explained that they themselves found the book helpful - in which case I have achieved my goal, because if just *one* person finds this book helpful and lives with domestic abuse for a shorter length of time than I did then I have achieved my goal. Others suggested a wider usefulness, which gives me real hope for helping more people:

"As someone who has suffered abuse myself I really think this book will help heal so, so many people. It resonates with such power and determination." (DG)

"I now feel like I need to look at things in my life. I still hold onto that horrible event that happened last year but I push it away. But I haven't forgiven him. Everything has been great between us because we always talk about things, thoughts and feelings are transparent and out in the open, but I have a small niggling doubt. I'm being totally honest as you have laid everything out, this book is going to be amazing and change people's lives." (SF)

"This book in its whole cannot fail to bring unfathomable amounts of posigivity and light into the world." (AS)

"This is a book that needed to be written." (FD)

One friend suggested that this book could, or even *should*, be a self-help book. But that is not what this book is. It is a memoir, it is my story, it is my story of my abusive relationship. But it is a story which I hope desperately that other people will read, and if they are living with the sorts of domestic abuse that I was and have not yet realised it then I hope it helps them to do so. To this end, I have put together a list of questions, based around the themes of my story – which are the themes of my abuse - which summarise it and which I hope serve as a useful check list for signs of the subtle, insidious, largely invisible forms of domestic abuse that I experienced.

Hopefully Helpful Questions

MIND:

Are you living in a state of confusion? Do you constantly doubt yourself – your actions, your motives, your self-worth and just about everything? Whilst all the time walking on eggshells?

TIME:

Is your time your own? Do you find yourself constantly doing things that you do not actually want to be doing - that leave you worn out? Do you get to do the things that you want to do? Do you get enough you time? Do you get *any* you time? Are you living exhausted?

FOOD:

Do you buy food but it is never your choice what you buy? Do you ever get to eat what you want to

eat, when you want to eat it? Do you enjoy eating at all? Do you eat too little? Do you eat too much? Do you eat unhappily?
MATHS:

Did your partner go from your biggest fan to your biggest critic?

NEST:

Do you clean and maintain your home and yet beyond those chores have no control over it? Is it designed and run to meet the preferences and needs of someone else – who does *not* clean and maintain it?

BODY:

Do you find yourself doing things with your body that you do not want to be doing?

WORDS:

Do you feel that you have to think really, really hard before you speak? Are your words sometimes used against you? Do your words fall on deaf ears? Do you sometimes think that there is no point speaking at all? Have you actually already virtually given up speaking, beyond phatic communication?

LOVE:

Do you feel disconnected from the people that you

know love you? Do you feel pretty sure that the *one* person who is supposed to love you - and probably tells you so *a lot* - actually does not? Do you find yourself saying 'I love you' back when you know you do not mean it, because it is easier/less scary than not saying it?

Future Lonely Hearts Ad

I watched my daughter performing in her school Christmas show, entitled *Gold to Bethlehem*. She was an angel (she learnt the meaning of a new word – irony – after I cackled with laughter when she told me what she had been cast as). She wore an ABBAesque white and silver floor length gown, a halo of silver tinsel on her head and the proudest smile I have ever seen. She looked so beautiful (I am not at all biased). She was the most beautiful of all the angels (OK, I am a bit biased). She was quite simply the most beautiful little-girl-angel ever to adorn this earth (alright, I am totally very far too biased). When she sang the following song, in the beautiful dress, with her tinsel halo and beaming proud smile, I lost it. I lost it completely:

It's no matter where you look, if you look, you'll find love
It may be hidden well or unused or neglected
But if you search quite hard, with your eyes open wide
There's no need for anyone to feel lost or rejected
Love Song, anon.

I fled to the school's foyer to sob uncontrollably as discreetly as possible (i.e. not at all, which was a good thing really, as a friend of a friend, Amy, spotted me and offered me a much needed – and even more snotty – hug). After I had almost fully composed myself, and thanked lovely Amy, I began thinking about that final session with my Behind Closed Doors Emotional Support Worker. We had talked about moving forwards and whether I would, or could, ever imagine myself in another relationship. At first I said no. I explained that my children and I are a family and that the family home is our Best Nest and ours alone. We are a unit. We are complete. Then I softened (a bit) and said that any future partner would have to fit in or fuck off.

My Behind Closed Doors Emotional Support Worker had already told me that loneliness is in the head. I have thought about what she said a lot (to this day, those words still play over and over in my head some evenings). I felt guilty for having said it. She was right in that I do have many, many amazing friends and the best family a middle aged single mother of two could wish for. My brunching neighbour- friends constitute a second family, a 'chosen family', to coin the sociological term again that I remember reading and writing about years ago before I knew what it meant to have one, and to need one. Yet I still find myself gazing upon happy looking two parent families, wherever I go, and dwelling on the fact that I do not have one and, worse, that probably I never will have one and, worse still, that I never did. And, yes, I get lonely.

My children and I are my family and we reside in the family home, my Best Nest, and I am adamant that no one else ever will. However, at the same time, I crave a best friend-lover hybrid, not to overcrowd and mess up my beautiful Best Nest, but to offset this often felt loneliness, just every now and then. What did my Godsister say? “Hope is stronger than heartbreak.” I am not scared (much). I am hopeful (a bit). Wish me luck (lots). Please. Because Kylie’s lyrics play in my head and pray on my mind because they ring so painfully true for me: “If I get hurt again, I’d need a lifetime to repair” (*A Lifetime to Repair*, Kylie Minogue).

I recently bought a preloved Orla Kiely handbag which a friend described as “Simple and classy”. My immediate response to this was “Same as me then”. However, I do not think two words are enough for this ad. so I will add a few more details.
Woman looking for companionship and passion. Age: 43. Height: tall. Size: 8-10 (feet). Former Profession: Academic. Current Profession: *Independent Mental Health Advocate. Future Profession: Writer. Cutting edge hobbies: Baking, knitting and crochet. Baggage: two children and an abusive ex-partner. Fights Like A Girl (not literally). Applicants must not take themselves, me or this ad. too seriously.

*Possible substitute fake current profession: on an episode of the popular American TV show *Sex And The City*, the lawyer character, Miranda, struggled to get a date out of a Speed Dating event. Concerned that her qualifications laden job was the problem she marketed herself as an Air Stewardess (to use the American job title) and secured a date.

Fantasy Afternoon Tea Party Guest List

(Listed in the order in which they appear in this book)

- Mary Oliver
- Epictetus
- Albert Camus
- Roald Dahl
- Shakespeare
- Vivian Ward
- Stephen Fry
- My Grandad
- Frank Zappa
- Frieda Kahlo
- Plato
- Haruki Murakami
- Peter Morgan
- Eckhart Tolle
- William Hutchison Murray
- J.M.Barrie
- Gandhi
- Henry James
- Albert Einstein
- Marcus Aurelius
- Annelle Dupuy DeSoto
- Flavia Carvalho
- Naomi Wolf
- Madonna
- Willis Polk
- Kit De Luca

Now I'm gonna get myself happy
Freedom! '90, George Michael

WORD COUNT

The following extract is from an article entitled *10 Years on, the effects of gaslighting are still here with me:*

"My imbalanced hormones became another reason as to why our relationship was so volatile. For context, other reasons included: that I was too career-focused; that we argued because *I knew "too many words";* because I earned too little money as a journalist; because I cried too much; because I looked ugly when I cried; because I dressed like a slag; because I didn't appreciate that I would be "nothing" without him (because he "had money" and I did not)." (https://www.the-pool.com/news-views/opinion/2018/27/the-residual-long-term-effects-of-gaslighting, emphasis added)

Shining Light word count: c88 000 words

Do you think I too know too many words?

"There is a light shining out of you." (Sam Baines, 220518)

SOUNDTRACK

Sad / Down / Low

- Everything's Ruined, Faith No More
- Fair, Remy Zero
- Zombie, The Cranberries
- Nothing Lasts Forever, Echo And The Bunnymen
- **Enjoy The Silence, Depeche Mode**
- Only Love Can Hurt Like This, Paloma Faith
- Midlife Crisis, Faith No More
- Receive, Alanis Morissette
- Team, Lourde
- If you tolerate this then your children will be next, Manic Street Preachers
- So Cruel, U2
- Not Fair, Lily Allen
- **Doll Parts, Hole**
- Baby Don't Cry, INXS
- **Praying For Time, George Michael**
- Anything But Down, Sheryl Crow
- Barbies, Pink
- **Stop Crying Your Heart Out, Oasis**
- **Playboy Mommy, Tori Amos**
- Only A Woman's Heart, Eleanor McEvoy and Mary Black
- **Mathematics, Little Boots**
- **A Small Victory, Faith No More**
- Little Baby Nothing, Manic Street Preachers
- **Holiday, Madonna**
- **A Lifetime To Repair, Kylie Minogue**

Transitioning

- Cigarettes And Alcohol, Oasis
- What Now? Rihanna
- Where Is My Mind? Pixies
- **Best Of You, Foo Fighters**
- Ninety Miles An Hour, Bob Dylan
- **Walk, Foo Fighters**
- Us Ones In Between, Sunset Rubdown
- Bridge Over Troubled Water, Simon and Garfunkel
- **Like A Prayer, Madonna**
- Beautiful Trauma, Pink
- What If God Was One Of Us? Joan Osbourne
- Out Is Through, Alanis Morissette
- Shut Up And Let Me Go, The Ting Tings
- Resolve, Foo Fighter
- Willow, Joan Armatrading
- Barely Hanging On, A Ha
- Whatever Gets You Through The Night, John Lennon

Happy / Up / High

- If it Makes You Happy, Sheryl Crow
- On The Mend, Foo Fighters
- We Found Love, Rihanna
- Sexual Healing, Marvin Gaye
- **Freedom! '90, George Michael**
- Love The House You're In, Moonface
- Har Gobinday, Belinda Carlisle
- Rooms On Fire, Stevie Nicks
- **I Could Say, Lily Allen**

- I Can See Clearly Now, Johnny Nash
- I Feel Good, James Brown
- (Blue) By Myself, Aretha Franklin
- **Shelby 68, Kylie Minogue**
- Bend Me Shape Me, Amen Corner
- Girl On Fire, Alicia Keys
- **Good as Gold (Stupid as Mud), The Beautiful South**
- Since U Been Gone, Kelly Clarkson
- Sweet Lover, Aretha Franklin
- **Angels On My Side, Rick Astley**
- All These Things That I've Done, The Killers
- Perfect Day, Lou Reed
- (If Paradise Is) Half As Nice, Amen Corner
- All You Need Is Love, The Beatles

READING LIST

Asperger's Syndrome and Affective Deprivation Disorder

Mendes E (XXXX) *Marriage with Asperger's Syndrome: 14 Practical Strategies*

MJ September 19 2014 *Affective Deprivation Disorder and Alexithymia in Marriage*

Domestic Abuse

Bancroft L (2002) *Why does he do that? Inside the minds of angry and controlling men*, New York: Berkley books

Burman, M. & J. Johnstone (2015) 'High hopes? The gender equality duty and its impact on responses to gender-based violence', in *Policy & Politics,* 43, 45-60

Chang Edward C, Kahle Emma R and Hirsch Jameson K (2015) 'Understanding How Domestic Abuse Is Associated With Greater Depressive Symptoms in a Community Sample of Female Primary Care Patients: Does Loss of Belongingness Matter?' in *Violence Against Women*, 21(6) 700-711

Craven P (2008) *Living with the Dominator A book about the Freedom Programme,* Knighton: Freedom Publishing

Firth L (ed.) (2012) 'Domestic and Relationship

Abuse' in *Issues*, Volume 224 Cambridge: Independence

Fletcher M A (2016) *We to Me: An Autoethnographic Discovery of Self – In and Out of Domestic Abuse,* Thesis submitted to the Graduate Faculty of North Carolina State University

Graham-Kevan N and Archer J (2003) 'Intimate terrorism and common couple violence. A test of Johnson's predictions in four British samples', *Journal of Interpersonal Violence*, 18, 1247-1270

HM Government (2019) *Transforming the Response to Domestic Abuse: Consultation Response and Draft Bill*

Kandasamy M (2017) *When I Hit You,* London: Atlantic Books

McCarry M & Lombard N (2016) 'Same old story? children and young people's continued normalisation of men's violence against women', in *Feminist Review,* 112, 128-143

Myhill A (2015) 'Measuring Coercive Control. What We Can Learn From National Population Surveys?' in *Violence Against Women*, Volume: 21 issue: 3, page(s): 355-375

Oliver R, Alexander B, Roe S and Wlasny M (2019) *The economic and social costs of domestic abuse*, Home Office

Pizzey E (1974) *Scream Quietly Or The Neighbours Will Hear*, Middlesex: Penguin Books Ltd.

Stark E (2007) *Coercive control How men entrap*

women in personal life, Oxford: Oxford University Press

Sweetnam S (2013) 'Where Do You Think Domestic Abuse Hurts Most?' in *Violence Against Women*, Volume 19, issue 1, pp.133-138

Food

Ghillie J (2016) *Grains Are Good 120 Delicious Ways To Cook With Ancient Grains,* London: Kyle Books

Lawson N (2001) *Nigella Bites*, London: Chatto & Windus

Pratt S and Matthews K (2004) *SuperFoods Fourteen foods that will change your life,* London: Bantum Books

Thompson J R (for The Huffington Post) 'Psychologists Explain The Benefits of Baking For Other People'

Gender Roles AKA Women and Time AKA Women and The Lack of Time

Connell R and Pearse R (2015) (Third edition) *Gender In World Perspective,* Cambridge: Polity

Hochschild A R (1989, 2012) *The Second Shift: Working Parents And The Revolution At Home*, New York: Avon

Hochschild A R (1997) *The Time Bind: When Work Becomes Home and Home Becomes Work*, New

York: Henry Holt and Company

Scott J & Clery E (2013) 'Gender roles An incomplete revolution?' in *British Social Attitudes 30,* Park A, Bryson C, Clery E, Curtice J & Phillips M (eds.)115 - NatCen.

HYSTERIA

Meek H (2009) 'Of Wandering Wombs and Wrongs of Women: 'Evolving Conceptions of Hysteria in the Age of Reason', *ESC*, 35.2-3 (June/September), xx-yy

Shorter E (1997) *A History of Psychiatry From The Era of The Asylum to The Age of Prozac*, Chichester: John Wiley and Sons Inc.

Showalter E (1985) *The Female Malady Women, Madness and English Culture 1930-1980*, London: Virago Press

Tasca C, Rapetti M, Carta M G and Fadda B (2012) 'Women And Hysteria In The History Of Mental Health' in *Clinical Practical Epidemiol Mental Health*, 8: 110-119

Kindness

Hamilton D R (2010) *Why Kindness is Good For You*, London: Hay House

Hamilton D R (2017) *The Five Side Effects of Kindness*, London: Hay House

Thurston J (2017) *Kindness The Little Thing That*

Motherhood

Faircloth C (2013) *Militant Lactivism? Attachment Parenting and Intensive Motherhood in the UK and France*, Oxford: Berghahn Books

Faircloth C (2015) 'Negotiating intimacy, equality and sexuality in the transition to parenthood' in *Sociological Research Online,* 20, 3.

Objectification

Engeln R (2017) *Beauty Sick How the Cultural Obsession with Appearance Hurts Girls and Women*, New York: HarperCollins

Walter N (2010) *Living Dolls The Return of Sexism*, London: Virago Press

Wolf N (1990) *The Beauty Myth,* London: Vintage

Women and Tattoos

Mifflin M (2013) *Bodies of Subversion A Secret History of Women and Tattoos,* Brooklyn, NY: powerhouse Books

Rosen C (2015) 'The Flesh Made Word: Tattoos, Transgression, and the Modified Body', in *The Hedgehog Review: Critical Reflections on Contemporary Culture*, vol. 17, no. 2

Yuen Thompson B (2015) *Covered in Ink. Tattoos, Women and The Politics of The Body*, New York and London: New York University Press

Miscellaneous

Eastman P D (1968) *The Best Nest*, New York: Random House

Elena F and Francesca C (2016) *Good Night Stories For rebel Girls 100 Tales of Extraordinary Women*, London: Particular Books (Penguin Random House)

Fisher M (2005) *Beating Anger: The eight-point plan for coping with rage*, London: Rider

Ford C (2018) *Fight Like A Girl*, London: Oneworld Publications

Gaiman (2018) *Art Matters Because Your Imagination Can Change The World*, London: Headline

Gilbert E (2006) *Eat. Pray. Love. One Woman's Search for Everything,* London: Bloomsbury

Greer G (1970) *The Female Eunuch*, London: MacGibbon & Kee Ltd

Greer G (1999) *The Whole Woman*, London: Doubleday

Hodgkinson Tom (2006) *How To Be Free*, Hamish Hamilton, London: The Penguin Group

Housden R (2001) *Ten Poems To Change Your Life*

Kiely O (2010, 2012) *Pattern*, London: Conran

Octopus Ltd.

Lebell S (1995) *Epictetus The Art of Living The Classical Manual on Virtue, Happiness, and Effectiveness, A New Interpretation by Sharon Lebell*, New York: HarperCollins Publishers

Munson L (2010) *This is not the story you think it is,* London: Piaktus

Poulos C N (2008) 'Narrative conscience and the autoethnographic adventure' in *Qualitative*

Inquiry, 14(1), 46-66

Wallman J (2013, 2015) *Stuffocation: Living More With Less*, UK: Penguin Random House

Walter N (1998) *The new feminism*, London: Little, Brown and Company

Wolf N (2012, 2013) *Vagina A New Biography*, London: Virago

Keep In Touch with

HELEN WILLMOT

Connect on Twitter

@DrHelenWillmot

Follow on Instagram

@DrHelenWillmot

Find on LinkedIn

DrHelenWillmot

Printed in Great Britain
by Amazon

38436048R00215